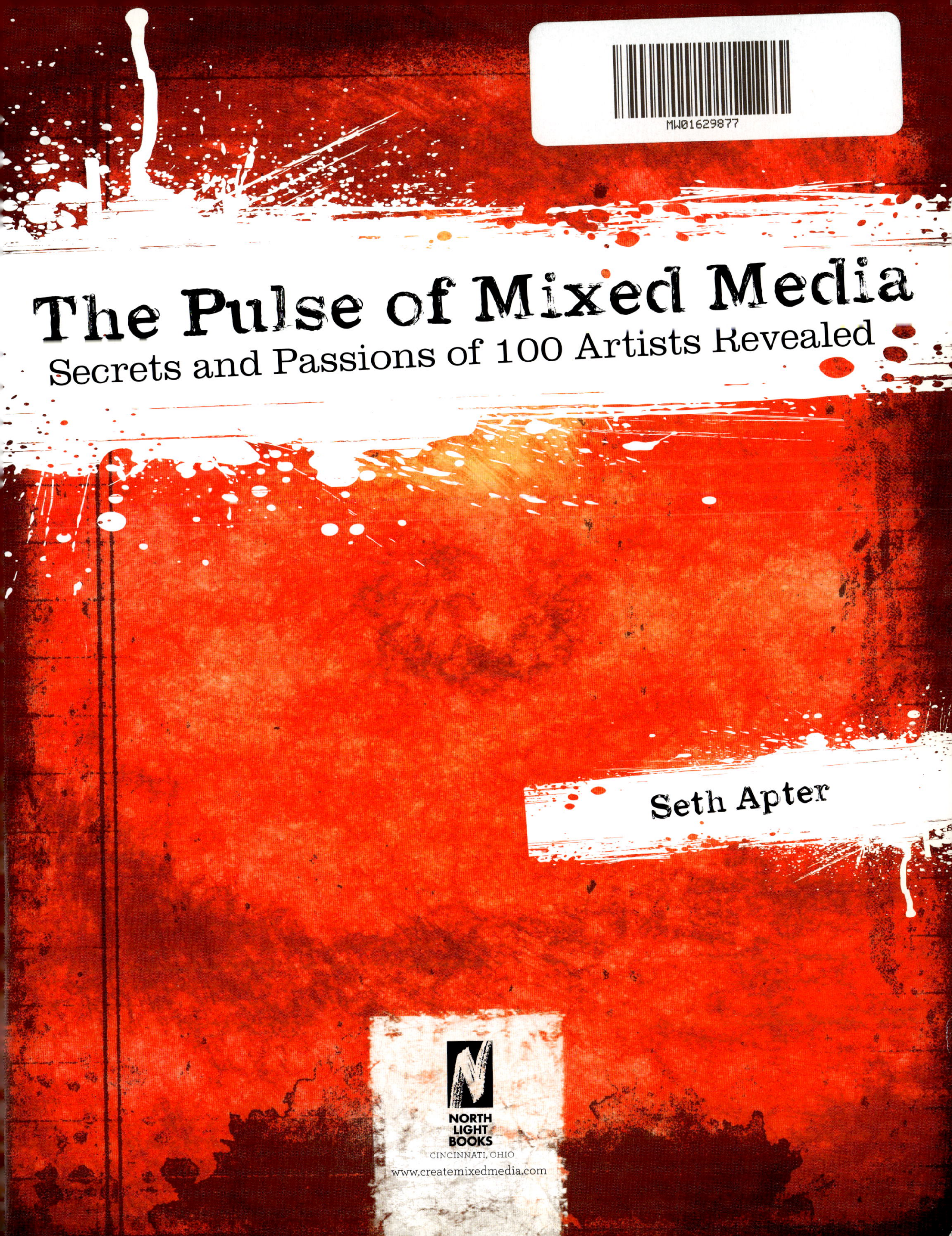

MW01629877
The Pulse of Mixed Media
Secrets and Passions of 100 Artists Revealed
Seth Apter
NORTH LIGHT BOOKS
CINCINNATI, OHIO
www.createmixedmedia.com

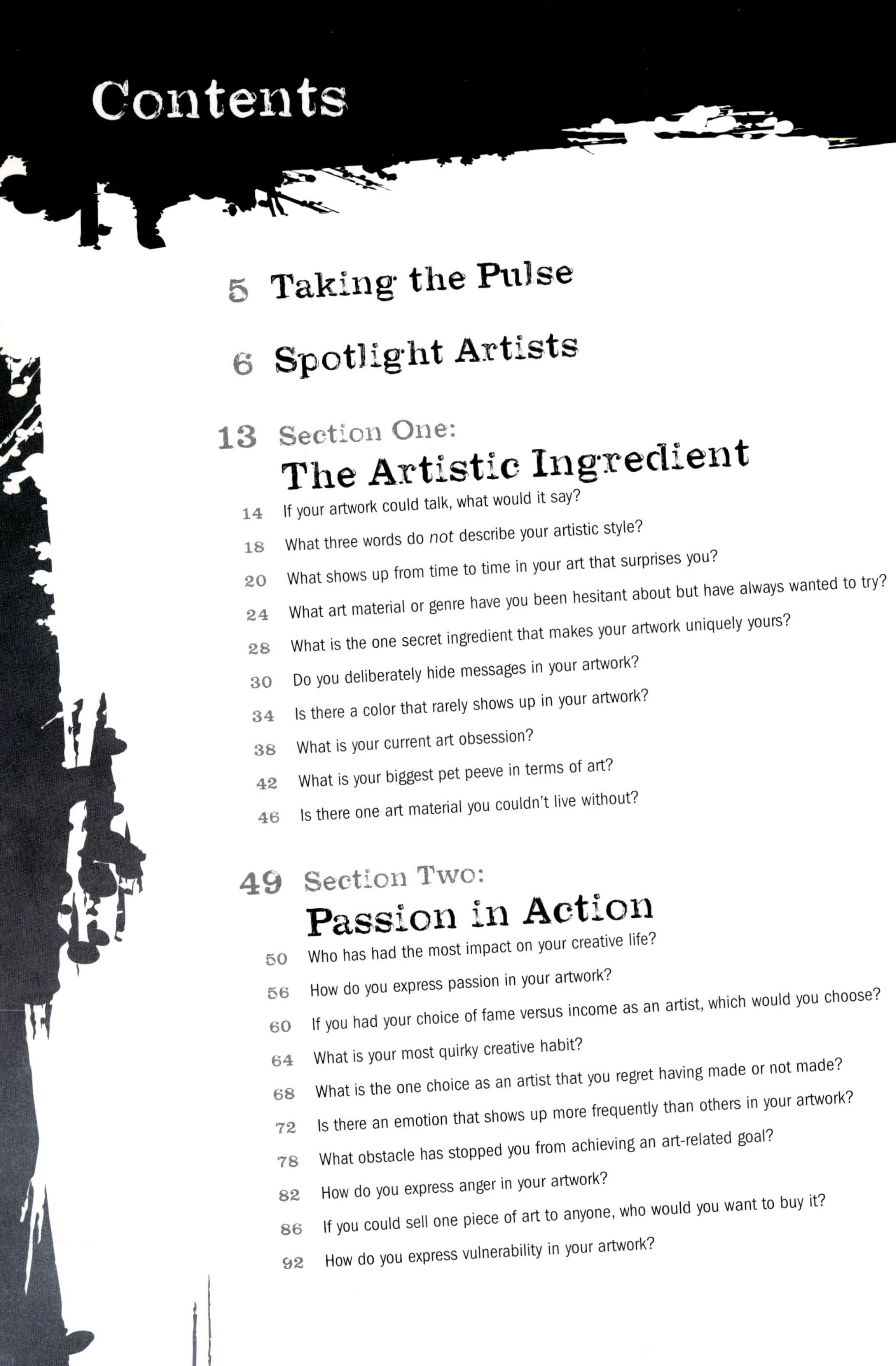

Contents

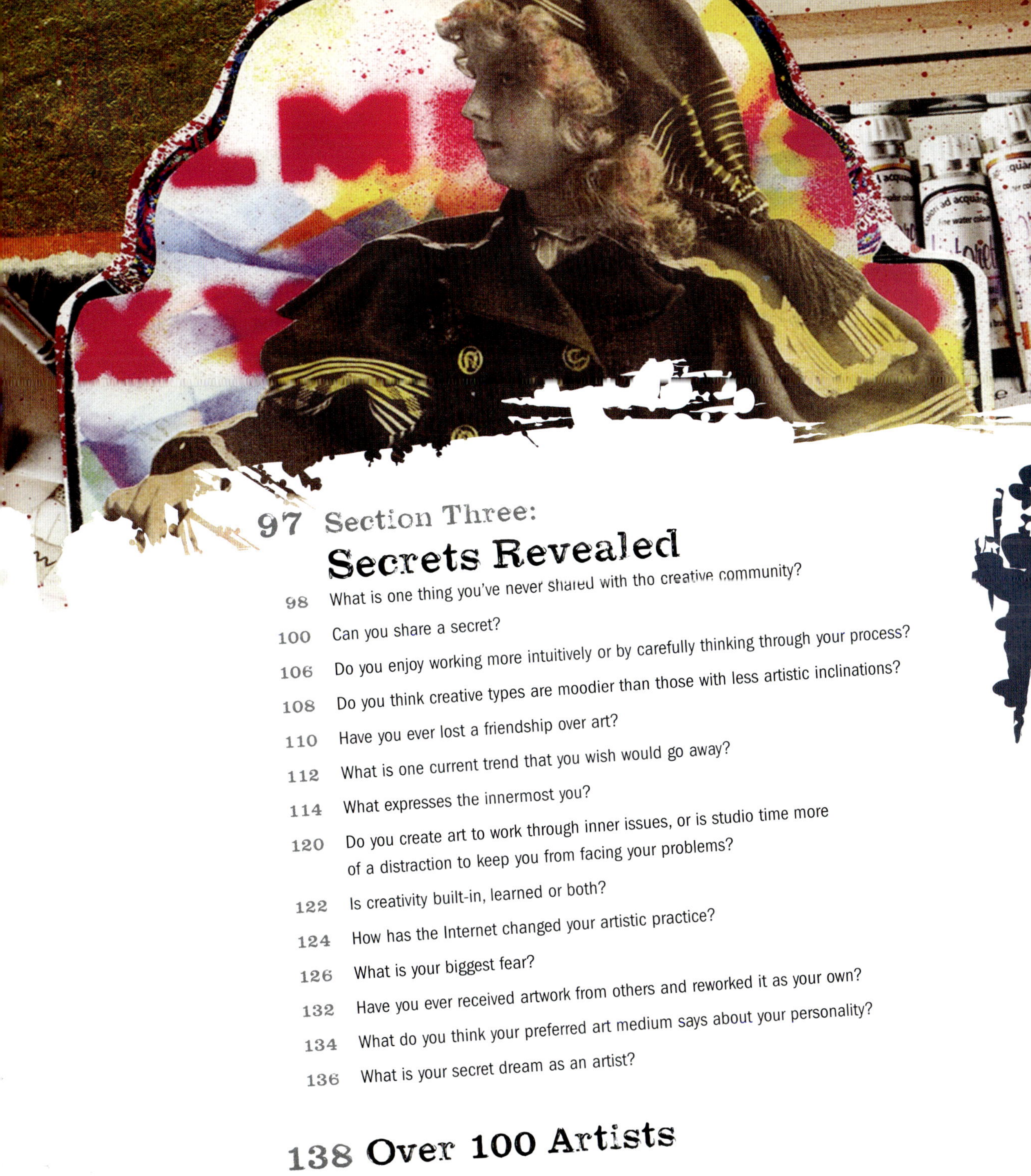

97 Section Three: Secrets Revealed

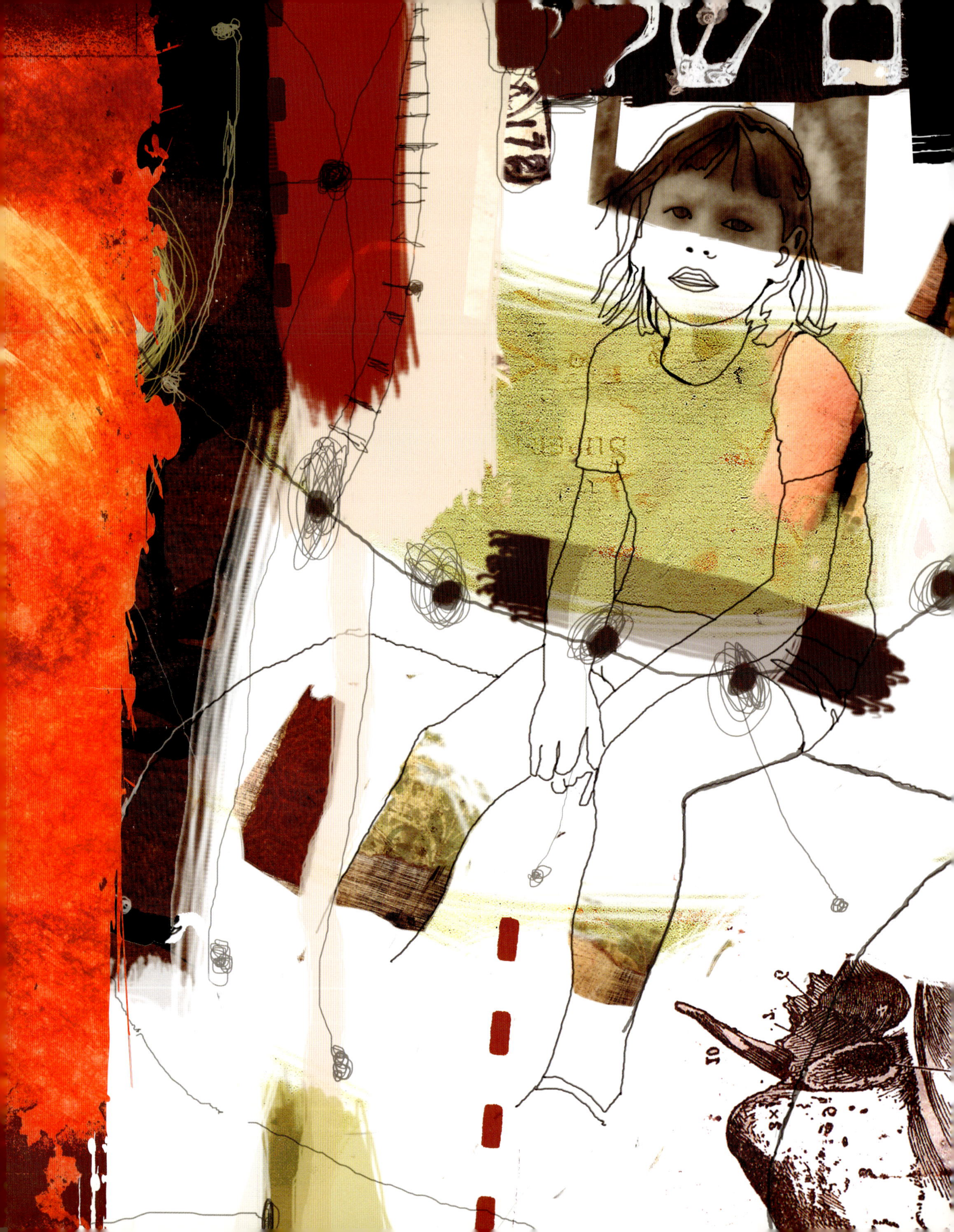

Taking the Pulse

If you gave one hundred artists the same set of art supplies and asked them to create, you would end up with one hundred unique works of art. This is because the magic ingredient in every artwork is the artist. All artists bring their own history, personality, creativity and personal perspective to the pieces they create. They bring their joy and their pain, their successes and their failures, and all the quirks that make them who they are. Knowing the story behind the artist elevates a viewer's appreciation of the art and brings their understanding of the work to a completely new level.

With this idea in mind, in 2008 I started an online artist survey called The Pulse. The goal of the project was to provide a window into the creative hearts and minds of the artist community. Much like an archeological dig, I wanted to go below the surface and uncover the inner workings of the artist. There have been four online editions of The Pulse to date, and it has grown from 35 participants to nearly 150. This book has grown out of the online version and expands on the original premise in many ways.

This book is not your typical how-to guide. Instead, you will be taken on a journey deep within the soul of the artist. Imagine that you have been invited to have an intimate discussion with all of your favorite artists: a one-on-one show-and-tell. You can ask them anything, no holds barred. You can learn their secrets, feel their passion, and experience their vulnerability. You can hear firsthand the personal stories behind their artwork. This is what you will find on the pages of this book.

In the first two sections, you will be introduced to thirty-one spotlight artists, some of whom you will already be familiar with and others who will be new to you. Threaded throughout the pages are their answers to a series of personal questions. Some of these questions focus on their art; for example, the art material they could not live without, their art-related pet peeves and the colors they avoid. Other questions focus on the artist; for example, their art-related regrets, the obstacles they have faced and the one person in their life with the most creative impact.

But what is an art book without art? You will also find new artwork created by the spotlight artists in response to a series of twelve prompts. See how they use their artwork to express anger, passion and vulnerability. Find out about the artists' obsessions, secret ingredients and hidden messages, all of which find their way into their completed piece. Discover how they see themselves in their self-portraits. And for every image, each artist shares in-depth the personal meaning behind their creation.

In the third section of the book, you will meet 103 additional artists who are representative of the larger art community. Each of these contributors has also generously shared their most intimate thoughts and feelings. You will find their answers to a different series of eleven questions and will learn about their secret dreams, their friendships lost as a result of art, and the one trend they wish would go away. You will learn about the inspiration behind new artwork created in response to prompts about their secrets, fears and innermost self.

Join me and all the artists on an adventure that will make you a true art insider. After reading this book, you may never look at art or the artist the same way again. It's time to take *The Pulse of Mixed Media*.

Spotlight Artists

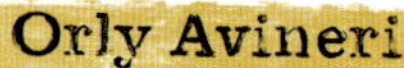

Orly Avineri

www.oneartistjournal.wordpress.com

I am a gatherer. While on my tracks I find sky-kissing mountains and deep valleys, barren deserts and lush rainforests, wandering nomads and firm settlers. My tracks take me places. At times I get lost. Enchantingly, as soon as I gather my findings, lay my images and words on a physical or virtual canvas, I get found.

Nina Bagley

www.ornamental.typepad.com

Nina Bagley has been a professional jewelry designer since 1987, a mixed-media artist for as long as she can remember (thinking here of a little clay mushroom "ensemble" that was created in perhaps the third grade, for starters), and has been teaching mixed-media/jewelry workshops worldwide since 2000. Her artwork is featured in many books and magazines, and has been carried in multiple boutiques and museum shops across the world.

Vivian Bonder

www.vivianbonder.wordpress.com

I create from a space of silence and solitude . . . A space where at times emotional turbulence and noise are ruling . . . Where intense happiness and suffering meet face to face . . . A space where I am balanced within myself, between extremes and feeling grateful to be alive.

John Borrero

www.johnborrero.com

You may have seen me walking ahead of you on the street, looking around to see who is watching, and bending down to retrieve metal from the curb. You may have passed me at the book store, investing in mythology and folklore, smiling with a childlike enthusiasm as ancient stories speak to me. Maybe you've noticed me at the antique shops, buying photos of faces of people forgotten to lovingly give my creations their grace and humanity.

Pam Carriker

www.pamcarriker.com

It is both my personal goal, and my artistic goal, to have my life and art reflect my true self. Some days my "true self" has paint on her elbow for more than one day at a time, and can't find the TV remote under the pile of socks that have lost their mates, but there are days when her skinny jeans fit and all is right with the world. I strive to convey the importance of the things in my life that matter most to me through my art.

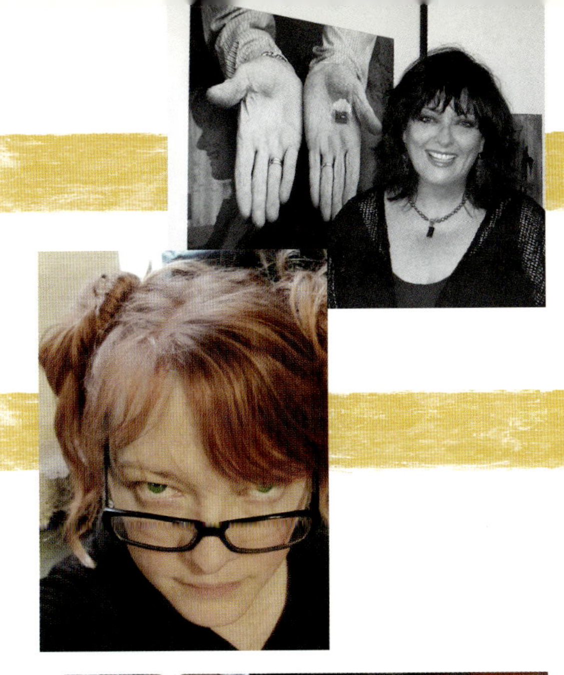

Angela Cartwright

www.acartwrightstudio.com

I am an unruly artist. I feel naked without a camera in my hand. When you are a photographer I think it trains you to see life differently. I can't imagine a world without art.

Alicia Caudle

www.alteredbits.com

I paint. I collage. I assemble. I sew. I'm a "mad eco-scientist" of sorts in that I devise natural, earth-friendly recipes for dyes, stains and inks to use in my art (largely due to annoying allergies to chemicals), and I like to make light-up and mechanical art from scrap electronics bits. This is my husband's fault as he teaches me things such as which value of resistor is needed to power an LED light.

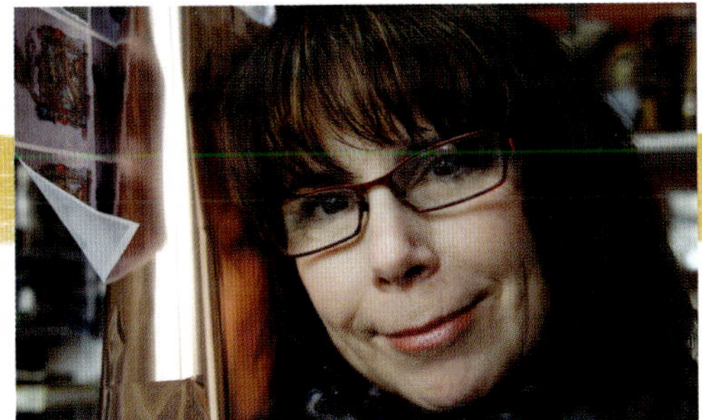

Karen Cole

www.karencole.blogspot.com

My artistic process is a bit like a journey without a map. I look at every piece as an experiment, an exploration and also a collaboration between my artistic journey and the mixed media. I am going to continue this wandering forever. Just hand me a crayon in the nursing home, please. I will help you reach your destination.

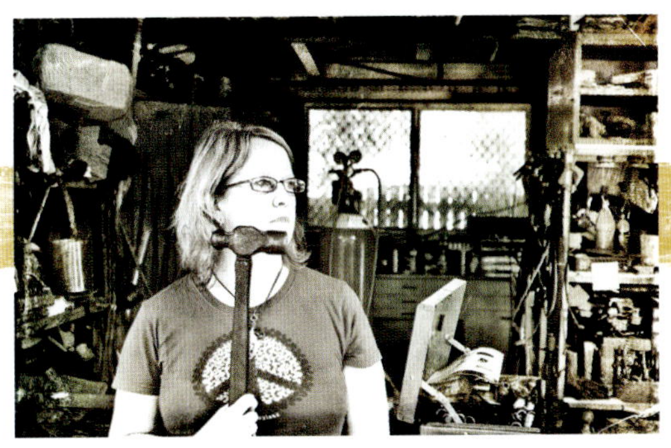

Jen Crossley

www.amarkintime.blogspot.com

Hey I'm Jen Crossley from the Land of Oz (Australia). A woman of many talents, and a master of none—I'm all smoke and mirrors. Dazzle them with big words and techniques I say, and most importantly have fun with what you do. Love what you do and it will show in your art and your life.

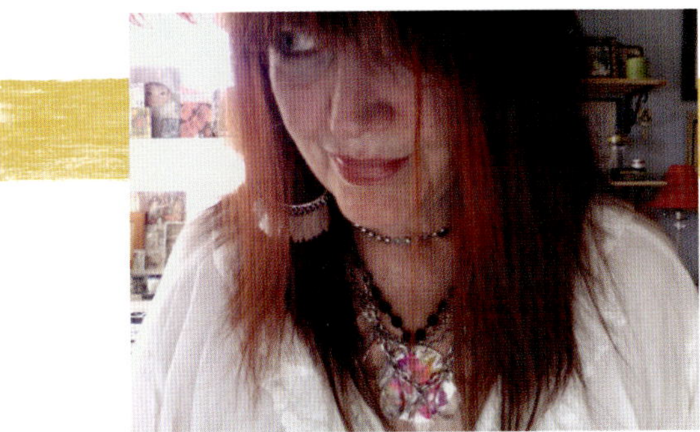

Sarah Fishburn

www.sarahfishburn.com

Once upon a time there was a red-haired girl who loved to read and write, and felt that art should be for everyone. She made this and that (and called it all ragtags), in a little house where the prairie ends and the mountains begin and the skies are the bluest of blues. And she thanked her lucky star, for every single day.

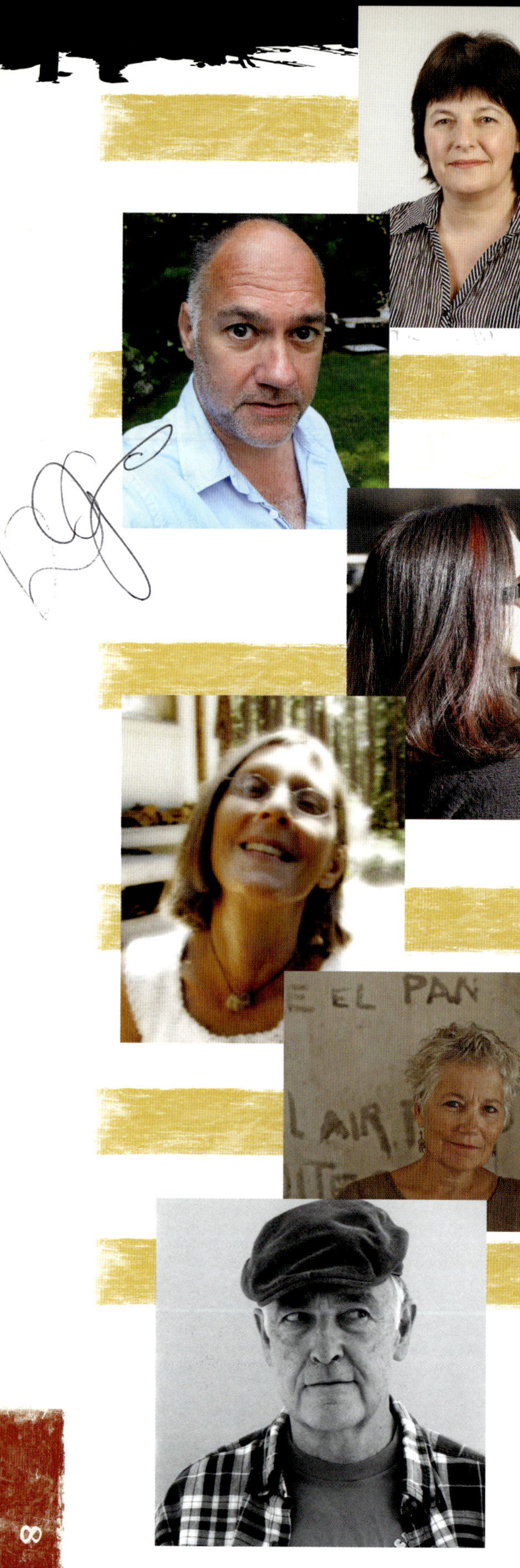

Robyn Gordon

www.artpropelled.blogspot.com

Since commandeering my mom's unused chisels way back in childhood, it seems that I have been carving forever. A hobby that was once used to fight boredom on lamplit evenings on the farm has now become a form of meditation. There is nothing better than spending the first few hours of every day carving in the courtyard with a troop of wild monkeys for company.

Danny Gregory

www.dannygregory.com

My art is an opportunity to reflect on the everyday, from the clutter on my desk to my neighbor's fruit stand, from what I ate for lunch to my unfolded laundry. I find beauty and significance in the things I do. I work exclusively in books, so the progression of my days unfolds with each page. I love the look of juxtaposed images and calligraphy, so my journals are diaries as well as sketchbooks.

Lisa Hoffman

www.lisahoffman.typepad.com

After living in close proximity to very competent people from all walks of life, my goal as an artist is to do everything that I can to make people raise their right hand and swear to never take themselves or anyone else too seriously . . . And no, I'm NOT kidding.

Lynne Hoppe

www.lynnehoppe.blogspot.com

I paint what's inside of me without a thought of "what it might mean." I like to see what one color looks like next to another; how the presence of a line here or a shadow there changes everything. I like to experiment.

Patricia Larsen

www.patricialarsen.com

I drawrite. I paint. I find. I lose. I draw. I paint. I glue and stick things in2 empty spaces.

Don Madden

www.donmadden.blogspot.com

I'm running out of time. I should have been an artist all my life. Actually, I always have been an artist but it was just hidden under my corporate three-piece suits. Now I have ideas of pieces I want to make, of art I want to create, of techniques I want to try, and, based on my age, I need to be working at a much faster pace. Don't ask me to chat or to share my feelings or talk about my art—I'm busy and don't have time for all that. And no hugging!

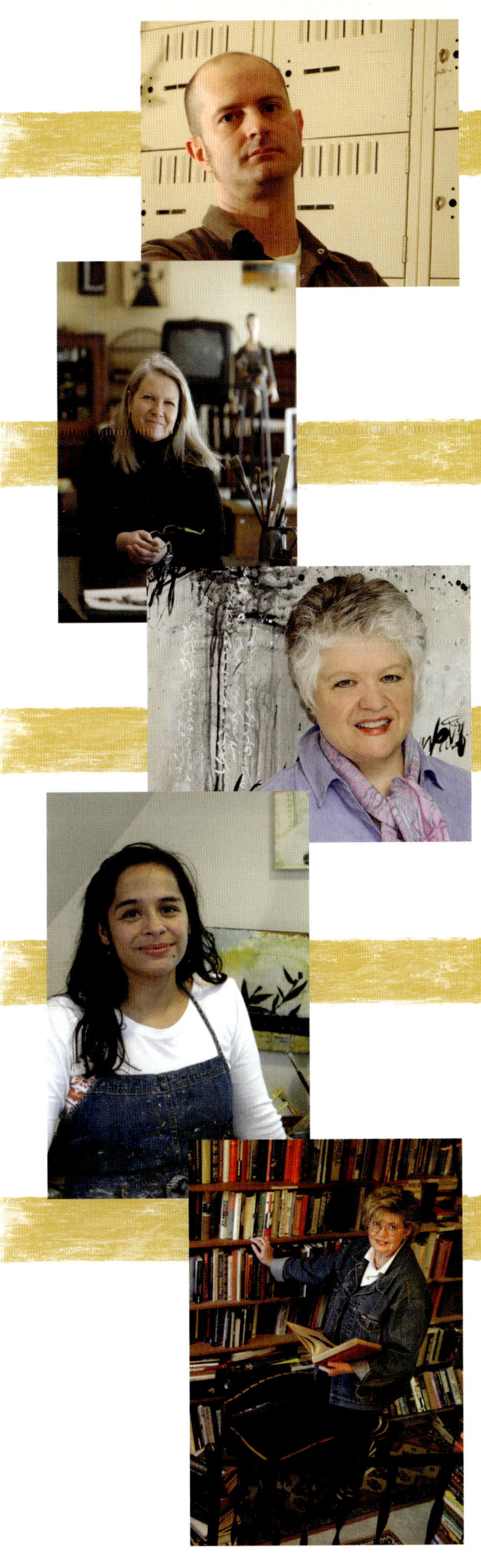

Robert Maloney

www.robert-maloney.com

My work focuses on the elements of modern life that often go unnoticed. That hand-painted sign on the side of an old building; the pipes that poke in and out of just about every structure we see; the boarded up windows of an abandoned factory; the billboard that advertises a discontinued product; the scaffolding grid work of an old bridge. What history do these structures hold? What lies inside of these vessels? These are the things that go through my mind in a normal day.

Leslie Marsh

www.snipsandsnailsandpuppydogtails.blogspot.com

There are boxes and bags of family photographs sitting on a shelf in my house. Some of them simply make me smile, while others make me curious about the stories. This becomes art when I take the hidden, the forgotten, the sometimes damaged, and bind them into books people may be compelled to pick up. My shoebox inspirations become bound expressions of life. I'm a photographer too, and I've got my own shoebox.

Leslie Avon Miller

www.texturesshapescolor.blogspot.com

Begin. Fling paint, make marks, rip and tear. Use sticks, palette knife, brush and tools. Rags, papers, spray, move paint around. Explore, experiment, discover. Build layers of dark and light. Scratch, scrub, sand to reveal. Contemplate, integrate, design, adjust. Express, connect, communicate, be content. Begin again.

Bridgette Guerzon Mills

www.guerzonmills.com

I am a creator of things, a maker of images, a weaver of words. I seek peace and stillness in the worlds that I create. Memories and experiences are sewn together, bound with thread, painted and layered with fire and wax. My work is a vision of where I have been, who I am now, and a vision of what I am becoming. The rest will be written as the story unfolds.

Lynne Perrella

www.lkperrella.com

Within the open unguarded moments of childhood we discover what we truly resonate to. As long as I can remember I have enjoyed working with paper, glue, paint and found objects. My goal is to maintain the same excitement and uncluttered instincts about making art that I felt in childhood.

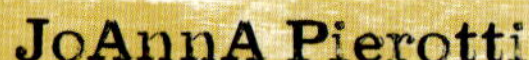

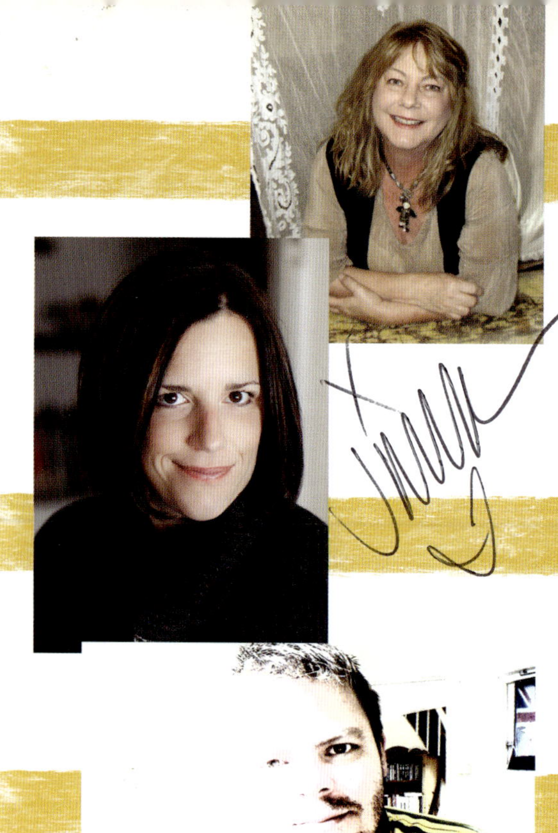

JoAnnA Pierotti

www.mosshill.blogs.com

Some very early mornings you will find JoAnnA jumping out of bed, slapping on a tinge of makeup and forgetting to comb her hair. She heads to a dusty field where the local flea market is held. She'll move through the crowd and then suddenly stop in her tracks, eyes opened wide, as she finds the box of treasure with her name on it. She heads back to her studio where she hoards her vintage finds and creates from her heart, unique found object assemblages.

Julie Prichard

www.julieprichard.com

I gravitate toward analogous colors, darkened hues, and monochromatic palettes rather than a bright cartoony plethora of paints, which I find too distracting. I always create with my eyes and inner self. My hands are only a tool, a trowel—think Captain Hook—and I never smile at a Crocodile.

Gary Reef

www.garyreef.com

I am a bower bird, I collect, I recycle, I try to turn the ordinary into extraordinary and discarded things into treasure. Burning, dropping, splashing, carelessness, cutting, scratching, layering, experimenting would be some words to describe my process. I care less for image and outcome; my work isn't about that. I live for the moment, the now and if something good comes as a result then I am pleasantly surprised.

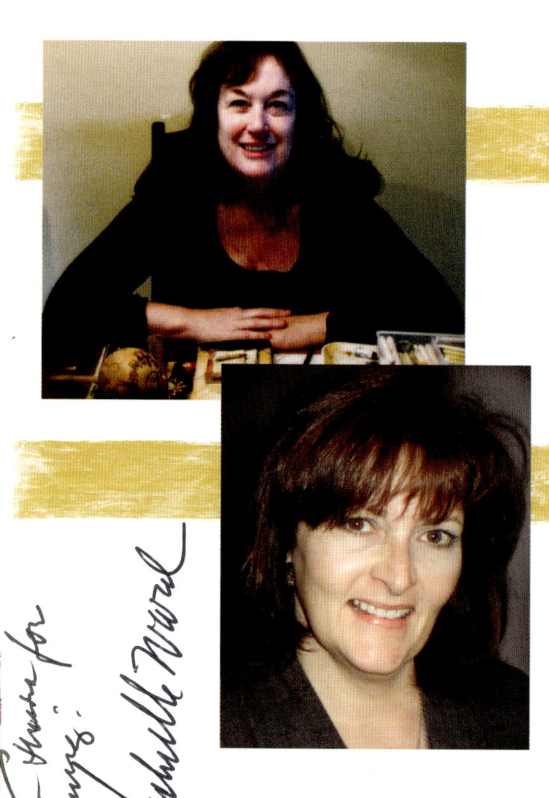

Roxanne Evans Stout

www.rivergardenstudio.typepad.com

Through my art I would like to convey the feeling of connecting, timelessness and re-creation. When I look at nature, or walk down a street in an old town, everything makes itself noticed to me—from a decaying leaf, a white moth on a metal wall, the expression on a person's face, to the colors in the air and all around me. As an artist I am constantly learning and growing. Art is my passion, my love, my soul.

Michelle Ward

www.michelleward.typepad.com

All my jammies are speckled with paint. I am fortunate to have a home studio that is my daily destination. It is filled with abundant supplies and books and rarely will you find a clear space on my table. While I love being surrounded by my favorite things, I frequently find myself happiest with just a surface to paint on, a few brushes, and some handmade tools. It's not about your workspace, or your materials, it's about plugging in, getting messy and seeing what emerges.

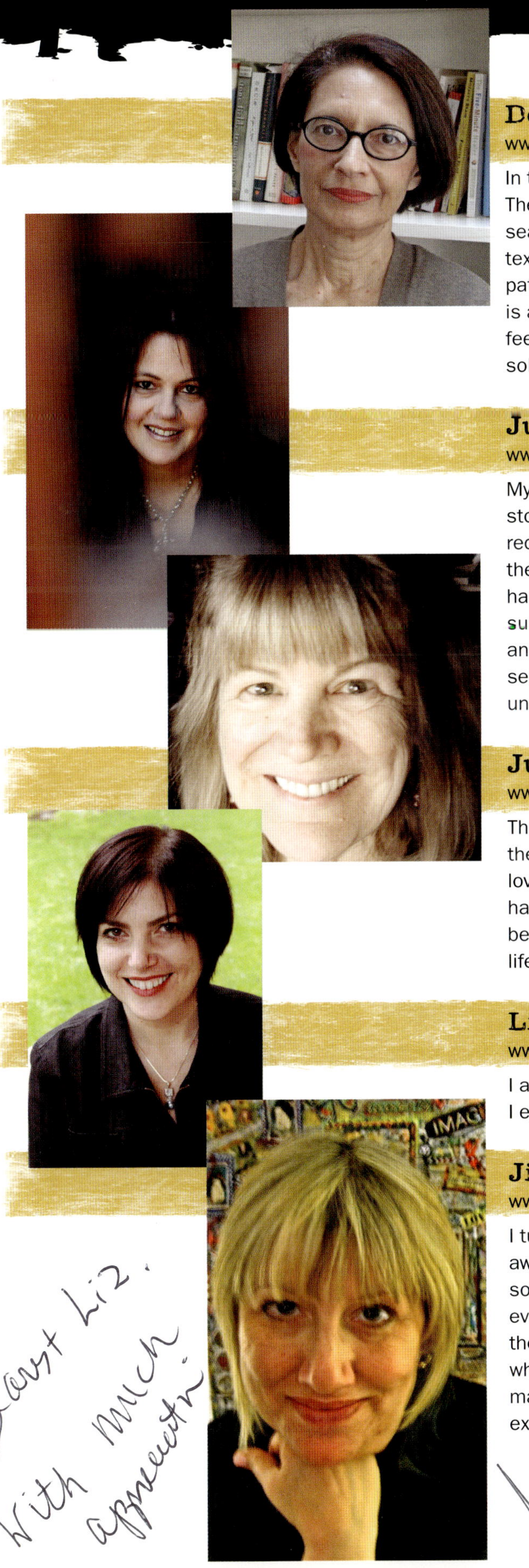

Donna Watson

www.donnawatsonart.blogspot.com

In the moment. I sift through black river rocks from Japan. The light and shadows draw me to the edge. The changing seasons are in black, white, gray with a touch of color. The textures and layers are weathered and rusty with a subdued patina. I look for dots, marks and circles on surfaces. There is a quiet strength in the riverbed as I seek memories and feelings. Bound by nature and the passage of time, I find solitude. Balance.

Judy Wilkenfeld

www.redvelvetcreations.blogspot.com

My mixed-media art works, Visual Anthologies™ tell the story of a life or lives, past or present. I use layering and the recontexturalization of the materials to build the history of the subject matter. My pieces portray the good and the bad, happy or sad elements of life and sometimes, the complex subject matters of the persecution of races, religions and minority groups that are tackled with the utmost of sensitivity. To communicate the message of tolerance and understanding is imperative in my pieces.

Judy Wise

www.judywise.blogspot.com

There is a thread through all my work. A search and a love of the search. Without the passion for the search and a love of the materials (wax, paint, paper, clay, nature)—life has no meaning. I am looking for my stubborn idea of beauty and often enough I find it. That is enough for a lifetime of devotion.

Linda Woods

www.colormetrue.com

I am an artist, author, and a rule breaker. I eat cookies for breakfast.

Jill Zaheer

www.jazworks.blogspot.com

I turn and the clock flashes 11:11 (the date my mom passed away), rainbows shine with the blink of an eye, I think of someone and they appear—these are all synchronistic events that play a major role in my creativity. I incorporate these occurrences into my works. My art is the expression of who I am—reflected in my work through color, vibrancy, varied materials, layers, textures and ultimately, the optimism and excitement I have in life which can be seen in my smile.

Dearest Liz, With much appreciation for your excitement about our art! Please keep in touch - Very best, Jill

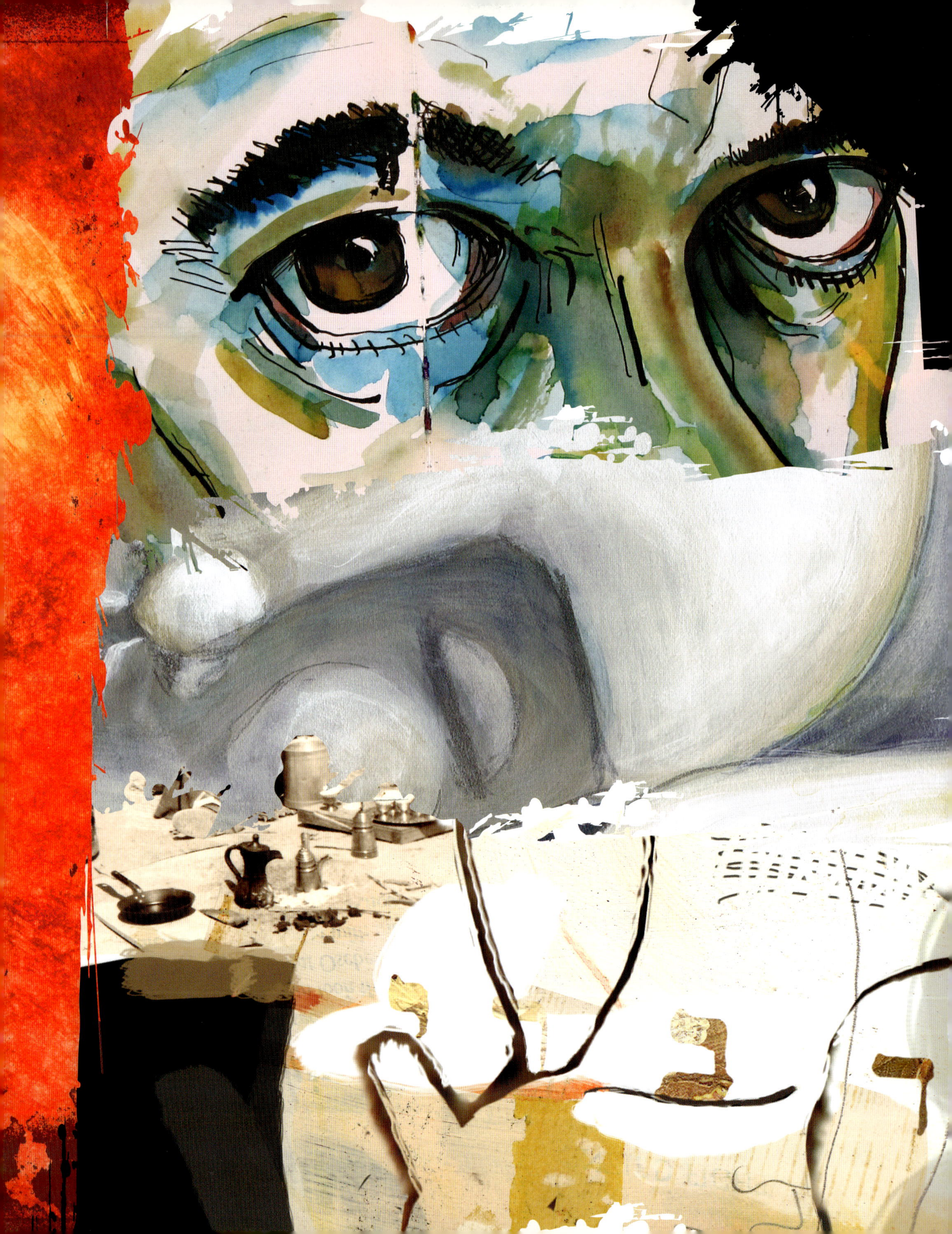

section one

The Artistic Ingredient

Art is more than the sum of its parts. So much more goes into a painting than just the paint on the canvas, and so much of what makes an artwork compelling is below the surface. The key ingredient is the artist. You can find the voice of the artist in every brushstroke. You can hear the story that they are telling in the colors they chose. Buried deep within the layers is the emotion within them and the secrets that they have to share.

Thirty-one spotlight artists are included in Section One. Each person has generously shared their thoughts about their artistic style, their creative beliefs and the personal ingredients that they use to create their artwork. You will find Questions and Answers, artwork created in response to a series of prompts, and intimate self-portraits created by the participants. Responses from a larger group of artists to a series of survey questions are also sprinkled throughout this section.

Think of this book as your guide to a journey to the creative hearts and minds of the artistic community. The Artistic Ingredient is the first stop of your travels and provides a key that unlocks the door to the inner workings of many of your favorite artists and some who may be new to you but whom you will come to love. The responses to the questions asked of each artist will provide you with a window into their unique and creative process. Turn the page to begin your journey.

If your artwork could talk, what would it say?

Almost by definition, an artwork is the voice of the artist, and the responses to this question suggest they all have a lot to say. Some artworks speak to every viewer and some just to the artist. Many pieces invite the viewer to look more closely. Some remind us to be still, breathe and live fully. All of them tell their own story.

"I really hope that I touch, move and inspire you."

—Patricia Larsen

"Thank you for letting me tell my story and express my vision." Then it would say, "Are you finished yet?"

—Jill Zaheer

"Whoa-oa-oa! I feel good. I knew that I would, now!"

—Lynne Hoppe

My assemblages may say something like, "Look a little closer; things are not always as they seem" in a capricious but clear tone. My handmade books would speak in a completely different voice. They would likely say, in very hushed whispers, "I know your secrets."

—Alicia Caudle

"Be still. Be quiet, tranquil and balanced where places in your heart and mind are found, and where the moment is present, and then past memories come."

—Donna Watson

"Be still . . . shhh . . . listen . . . now allow yourself to feel."

—Vivian Bonder

Because I use mostly vintage objects in my work, each piece would tell me first where it originated from. Then it would disclose who the original owner was. As I unite the elements and accomplish a finished work, it would then tell me what it means to be an old soul.

—JoAnnA Pierotti

"Your mascara's smudged . . . again."

—Lisa Hoffman

"Jen, don't give up your day job." Only kidding. It might actually say, "Keep it simple, stupid."

—Jen Crossley

"Why aren't you doing this more often?"

—Karen Cole

"You people on Earth are pathetic. When are you going to stop whining? Don't make me come down there. When are you going to get it right?"

—Don Madden

"Help! Get me away from this madman before he changes his mind!"

—Gary Reef

My art would say that I am not a robot. I am alive and aware and seeing everything around me. It would tell you I am paying attention. I think my art does talk, though. I often use words in my art.

—Linda Woods

"Look closer, touch me, feel my textures . . . see the world through my eyes. My art would speak of connections between nature and our souls, the written word and image, the past and the future. And of memories real and imagined."

—Roxanne Evans Stout

It would smile. Maybe it would say, "Let's play."

—Judy Wise

"Breathe, go inside to your center and experience being harmony. It's all okay."

—Leslie Avon Miller

How many art projects/pieces do you prefer to work on at a time?

Three or more . . . bring 'em on: **55%**

I like to switch between two: **26%**

One and only one: **19%**

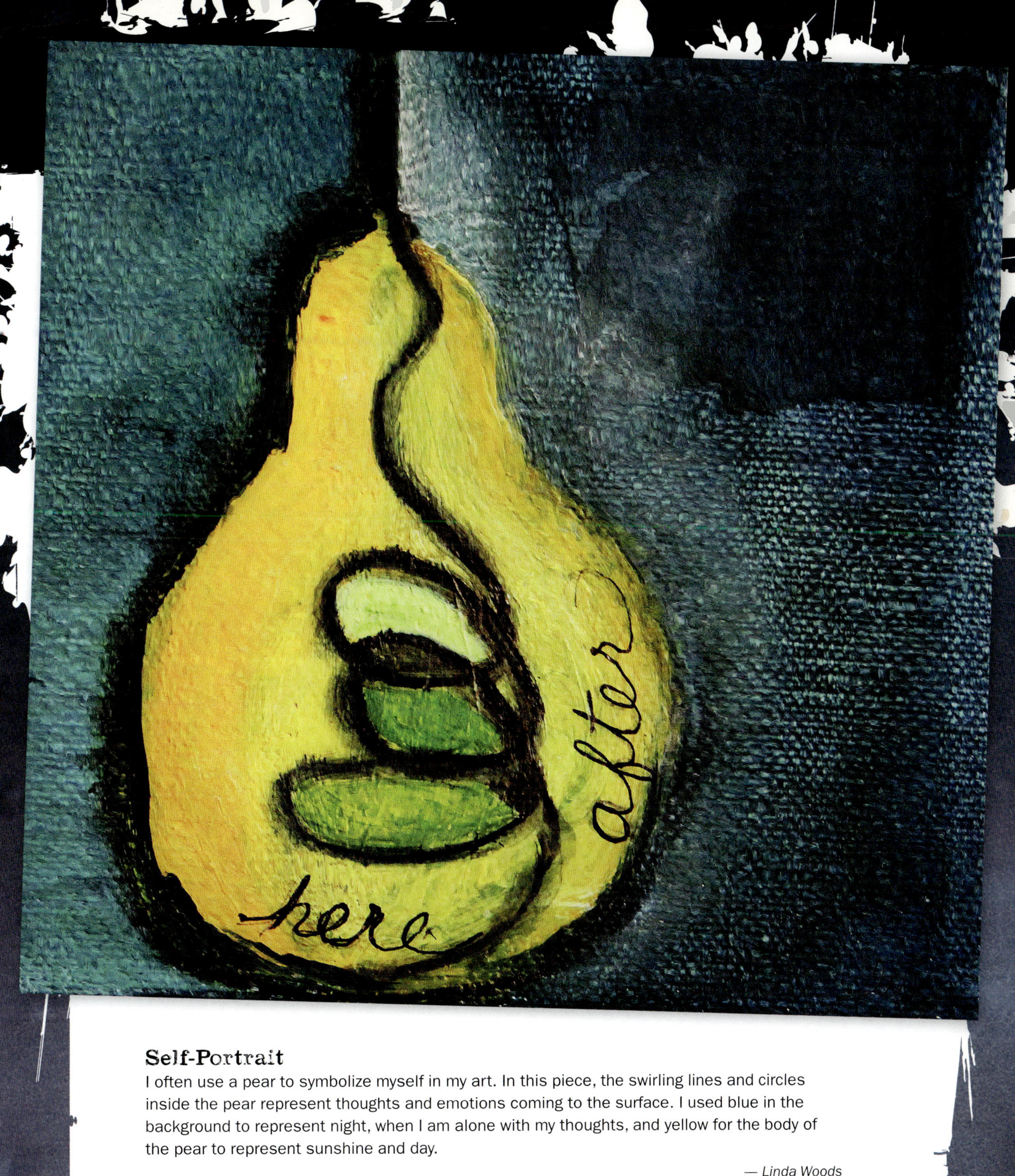

Self-Portrait

I often use a pear to symbolize myself in my art. In this piece, the swirling lines and circles inside the pear represent thoughts and emotions coming to the surface. I used blue in the background to represent night, when I am alone with my thoughts, and yellow for the body of the pear to represent sunshine and day.

— Linda Woods

If your artwork could talk, what would it say?

Popeye said it best: "I am what I am and that's all that I am."

—Angela Cartwright

"A little prayer for you." Aww, just kidding. They would be totally quoting the poet Henry David Thoreau: "The true harvest of my daily life is somewhat as intangible and indescribable as the tints of morning and evening. It is a little stardust caught, a segment of the rainbow which I have clutched."

—Sarah Fishburn

I have a feeling that some of the colors would scream out in protest to being covered up. If each paint color were a celebrity, they would all want their fair share of screen time. My paintings change so much that it's hard to know what layer will be covered and which layer will end up on top.

—Julie Prichard

"I'm finished now. Get on with something else." I have a tendency to think about a piece long after part of me has realized that it is finished. I want my art to say something else to others and tell a story to future generations.

—Leslie Marsh

"Take me back to the days of the sun, when time ran in circles and cycles, and meaning came from the moon and the stars. And the earth and the rain and darkness was just as important as light."

—Bridgette Guerzon Mills

"I wish to convey a feeling of ancient tribes with many stories to tell; a love for nature and connectedness to the land; a passion for gathering and squirreling all manner of found objects that have become symbols of my life in South Africa."

—Robyn Gordon

The artistic style and works have a fluidity. The mix of objects and style can certainly be termed eclectic; however the pieces are a reflection of a life. The viewer peels though the layers and symbology in order to make sense of and to place, in context, the story the piece is intending to portray.

—Judy Wilkenfeld

I try to make artwork that talks to people. My characters speak about vulnerability and sometimes sadness . . . about life's journeys and the lightness and darkness inherent in them. I hope my pieces also talk to people about the strength of storytelling.

—John Borrero

"Touch me. Ask me what stories I have to tell. Hold me 'til the metal grows warm in your hand. Turn the page. Turn me this way and that. Imagine. And do not be afraid to feel whatever emotions I've brought from deep inside to the surface for you."

—Nina Bagley

"Everything is beautiful. Take a minute to appreciate the world as it passes by you. The secret to happiness is all around you. Stop and smell, then draw, the roses. Stop and smell, then paint, the coffee. Art, like love, is for everyone to make."

—Danny Gregory

"Come back, don't leave, I'm not done yet!" I work in the small blocks of time that my day allows, so I constantly have to stop in the middle of something. Sometimes I swear I can faintly hear my artwork calling to me . . .

—Pam Carriker

"She is trying to be me. She wishes to live as though she is a visual journal . . . abundant, colorful, accepting, forgiving, open, mindful, explorative, expressive, contemplative, introspective, inspiring, layered, vibrant, gentle, playful and free . . . just like me, she still has a way to go."

—Orly Avineri

"Please don't hang me in the bathroom!"

—Robert Maloney

To me, art doesn't speak, it sings. I associate art with music. I can observe a piece of art and conjure up a tune for it. I tend to build art with a song or soundtrack in mind. If I had to pick one favorite lyric to define my work, I would choose "Soul on Fire."

—Michelle Ward

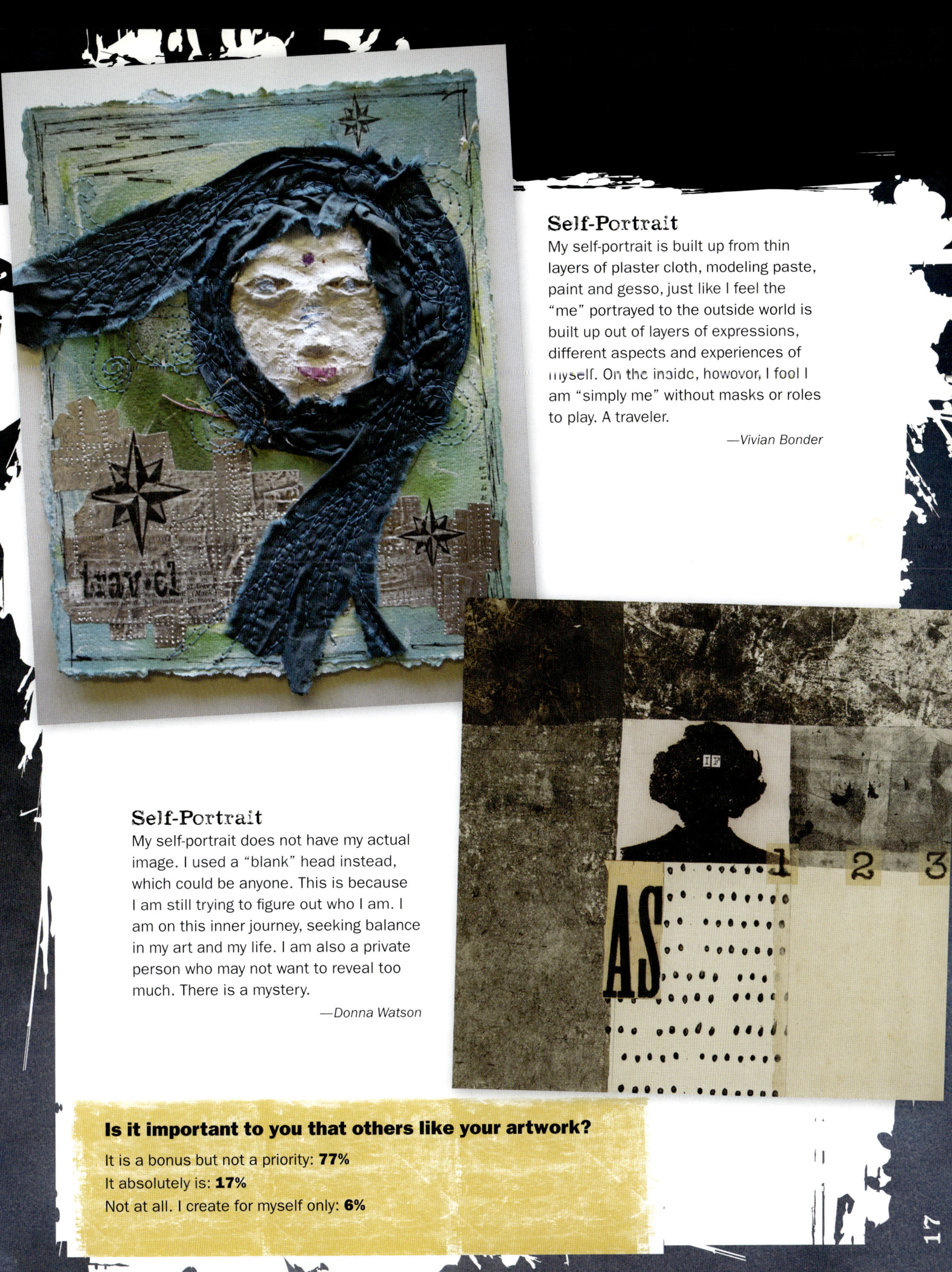

Self-Portrait

My self-portrait is built up from thin layers of plaster cloth, modeling paste, paint and gesso, just like I feel the "me" portrayed to the outside world is built up out of layers of expressions, different aspects and experiences of myself. On the inside, however, I feel I am "simply me" without masks or roles to play. A traveler.

—Vivian Bonder

Self-Portrait

My self-portrait does not have my actual image. I used a "blank" head instead, which could be anyone. This is because I am still trying to figure out who I am. I am on this inner journey, seeking balance in my art and my life. I am also a private person who may not want to reveal too much. There is a mystery.

—Donna Watson

Is it important to you that others like your artwork?

It is a bonus but not a priority: **77%**

It absolutely is: **17%**

Not at all. I create for myself only: **6%**

What three words do *not* describe your artistic style?

Describing one's own style can prove to be difficult for many artists. By comparison, defining what they are not seems simple. Despite the wide range of styles represented, nearly one third of the spotlight artists do not think of their art as cute. Many also said their style was not planned, suggesting that the artwork of this group is often intuitive and spontaneous.

Messy, loud, funny
—Pam Carriker

Humorous, frightening, comical
—Roxanne Evans Stout

Serious, linear, prissy
—Lisa Hoffman

Crafty, cute, adorable
—Karen Cole

Adorable, glitzy, whimsical
—Alicia Caudle

Whimsical, fluffy, cute
—Bridgette Guerzon Mills

Colorful, busy, unplanned
—Donna Watson

Cutesy, vintage, Americana
—Linda Woods

Messy, loud, funny
—Pam Carriker

Cute, sparkly, shiny
—John Borrero

Cute, formal, flat
—Leslie Marsh

Plain, restrained, predictable
—Angela Cartwright

Pretty, boring, meaningless
—Michelle Ward

Contemporary, superficial, contrived
—JoAnnA Pierotti

Disconnected, unemotional, discombobulated
—Judy Wilkenfeld

Feminine, plastic, cute
—Don Madden

Meticulous, preplanned, precise
—Patricia Larsen

Shiny, multiple, planned
—Nina Bagley

Realistic, conventional, cute
—Lynne Hoppe

Traditional, classical, realistic
—Robyn Gordon

Cute, modern, colorful
—Jen Crossley

Describable, artistic, stylistic
—Orly Avineri

Deliberate, fastidious, impersonal
—Danny Gregory

Dull, plain, unimaginative
—Jill Zaheer

Polished, urbane, minimal
—Judy Wise

Fun, quirky, feminine
—Julie Prichard

Minimalist, minimalist, minimalist
—Sarah Fishburn

Feminine, organic, cute
—Robert Maloney

Carnival of color
—Leslie Avon Miller

Planned, delicate, traditional
—Gary Reef

Are you comfortable sharing your art techniques with other artists?

Yes, always: **63%**
Sometimes: **36%**
Never: **1%**

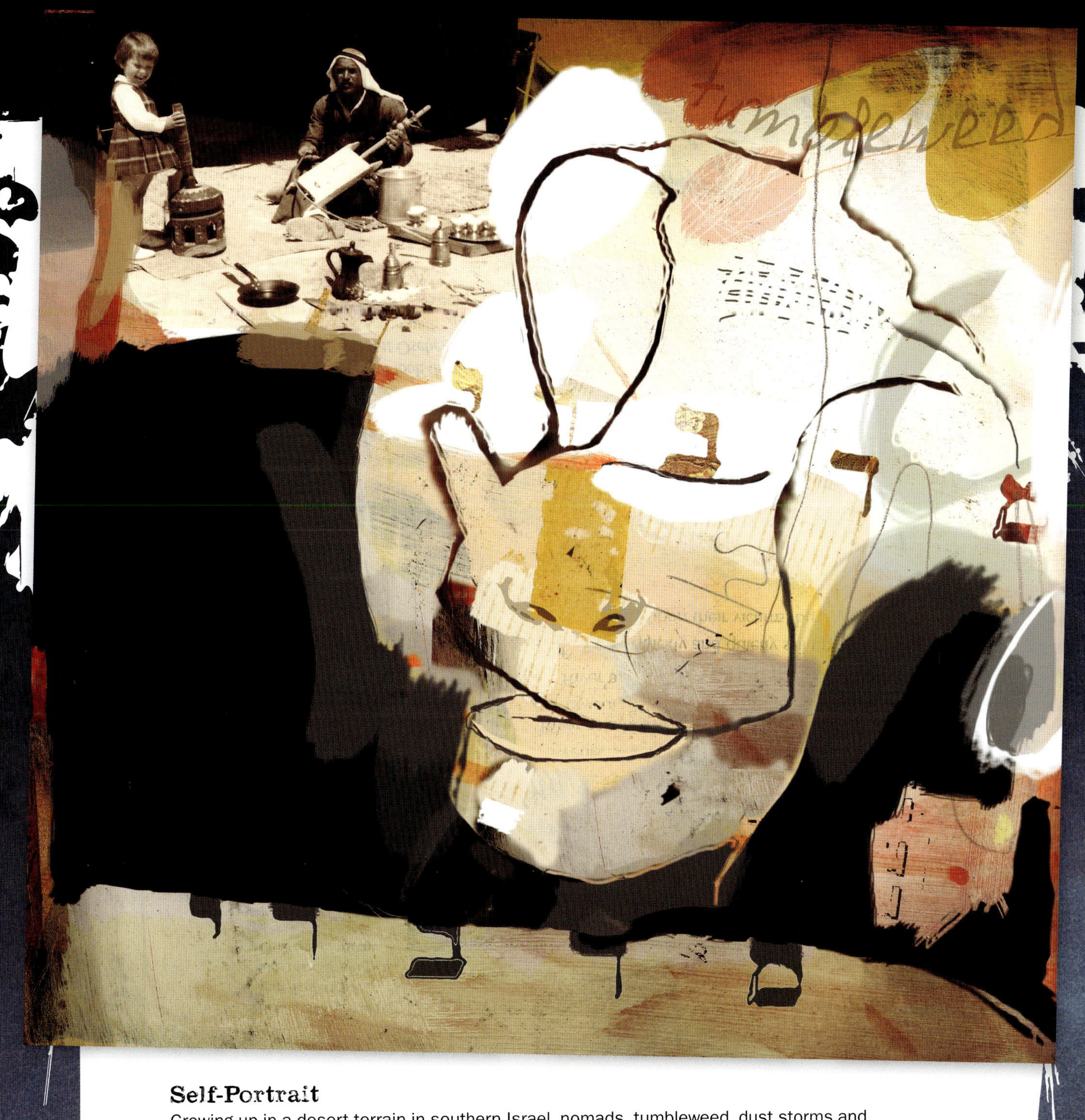

Self-Portrait

Growing up in a desert terrain in southern Israel, nomads, tumbleweed, dust storms and rain—among other things and less tangible ones—became a part of my emotional makeup. The desert is barren yet obscure. It is a land of contrasts, as I am. My constant interplay between concealing and revealing of visual information represents my growth process, and the act of veiling and unveiling portrays me.

—Orly Avineri

What shows up from time to time in your art that surprises you?

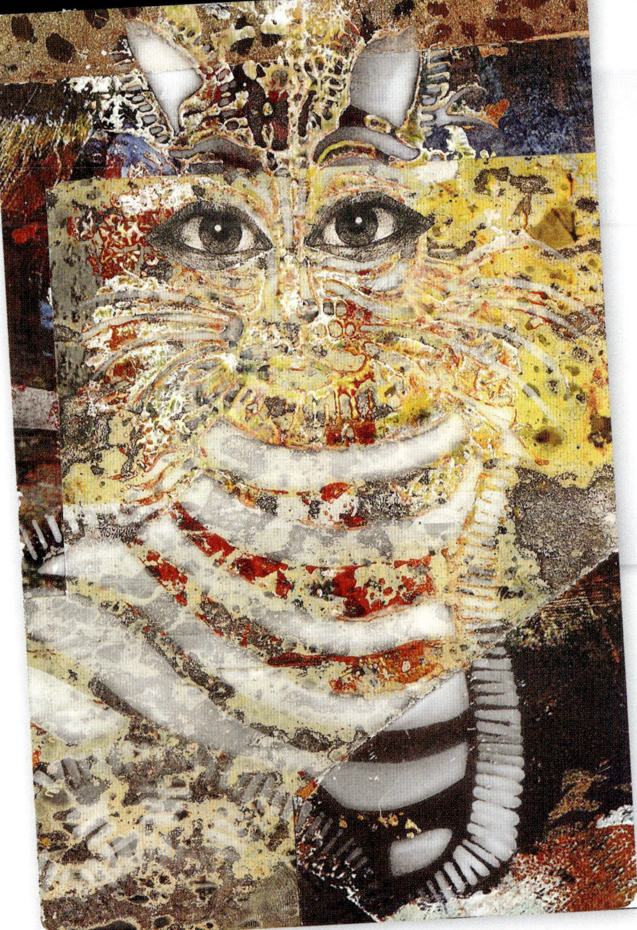

The Enchanted Feline

The Enchanted Feline began appearing in my work early on, but it never really completely appeared. I would often finish a painting and all of a sudden see her sitting quietly in the background staring right at me. I am always surprised and delighted when she turns up. I am not sure why she appears, but I get a sense that she represents an unknown force, which is all-seeing and wise. The Enchanted Feline is kind of my version of the Cheshire Cat from *Alice in Wonderland*. It is mysterious, has a mind of its own, appears rarely and is full of riddles and secrets. She can't be tamed or captured, so I just enjoy her when she decides to show herself.

—Gary Reef

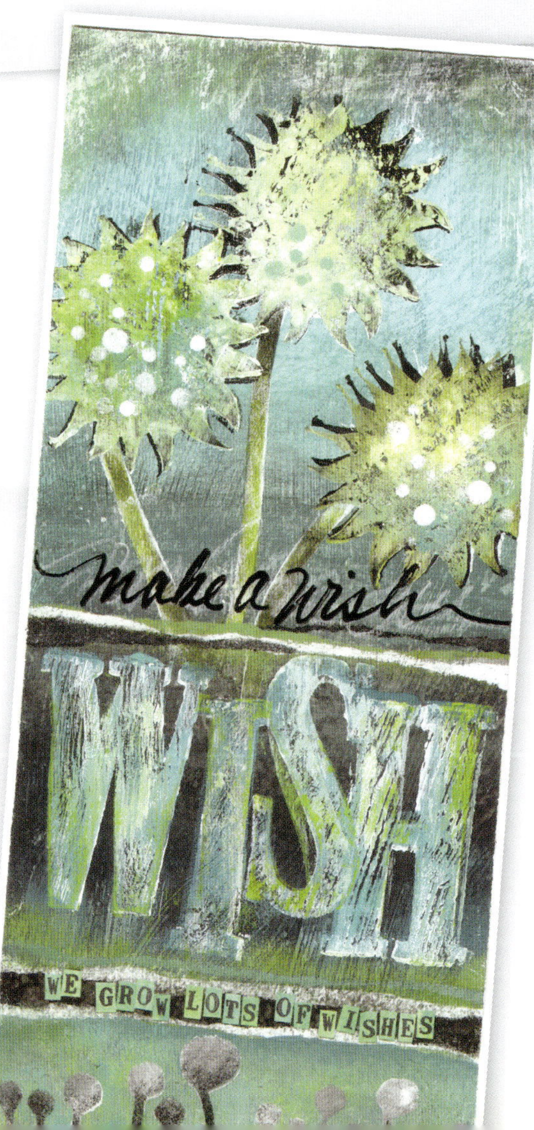

Growing Wishes

Nothing surprises me. Everything surprises me. I fully expect to be amazed every time I come to the table. While I often begin a piece with an idea in mind, I leave enough space in the plan for what happens in the process. I'm delighted when a cool texture or color mix occurs, or when an image or subject emerges. The fact that I am continually curious is the reason I go back to creating over and over again. It's the surprise element that keeps me interested in striving for more, pushing myself, redefining the limits.

—Michelle Ward

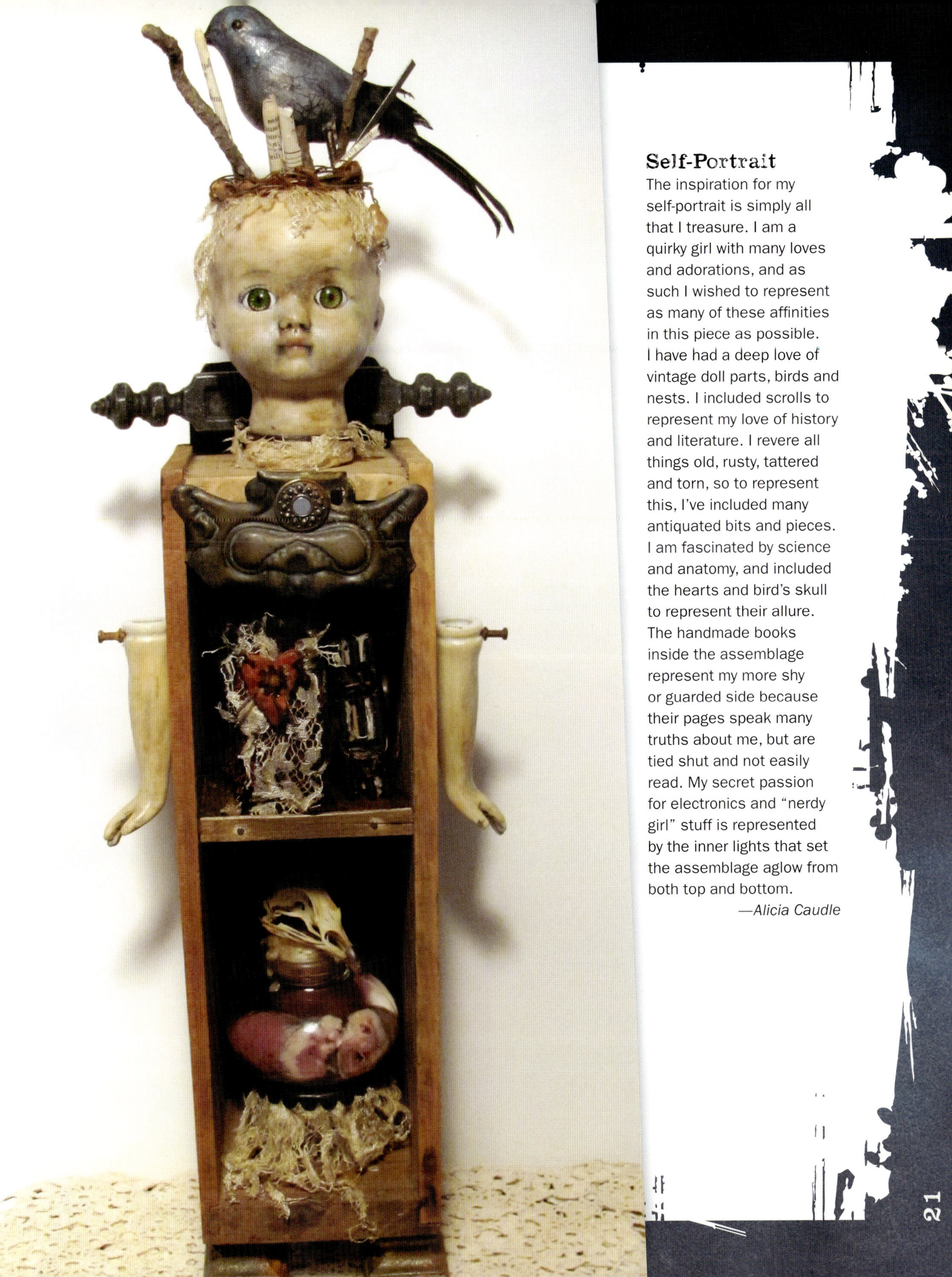

Self-Portrait

The inspiration for my self-portrait is simply all that I treasure. I am a quirky girl with many loves and adorations, and as such I wished to represent as many of these affinities in this piece as possible. I have had a deep love of vintage doll parts, birds and nests. I included scrolls to represent my love of history and literature. I revere all things old, rusty, tattered and torn, so to represent this, I've included many antiquated bits and pieces. I am fascinated by science and anatomy, and included the hearts and bird's skull to represent their allure. The handmade books inside the assemblage represent my more shy or guarded side because their pages speak many truths about me, but are tied shut and not easily read. My secret passion for electronics and "nerdy girl" stuff is represented by the inner lights that set the assemblage aglow from both top and bottom.

—Alicia Caudle

What art material or genre have you been hesitant about but have always wanted to try?

Although there is a small group of people who have already explored all their interests, the majority of artists have at least one art genre that they have thought about trying. Working with oils was the most desired choice, followed by encaustics and working on a large canvas. So what is holding them back? The primary reasons seem to include time, cost, space and fear.

Why hesitate? I have tried dipping into unfamiliar materials, out of interest in trying something different, but also because I enjoy the change. It's a valuable lesson to vary your medium, as there is always an opportunity to gain a new perspective that can be applied to your default art form.

—Michelle Ward

When I was little, my mother was an oil painter. I remember the smell of turpentine and the paint so vividly. I am entranced by the textures in oil paintings, but I am afraid of the health risks involved.

—Julie Prichard

I haven't tried egg tempera yet because of the cost. Someday, though.

—Lynne Hoppe

I've been thinking about creating a painting within the photorealism genre. I've recently been fascinated by the way this artwork involves multi layers of paint and mediums and has a depth and brilliance that can't always be captured in photos.

—Jill Zaheer

Animation. As a medium it blows my mind, but I don't have the patience or attention span to pursue it.

—Robert Maloney

Enormous abstract canvases. Space and time are issues, and I'm the sort of person who works best concentrating on one genre. I'm focusing on my carving because that is what gives me the most satisfaction, but one day I will do something with the huge canvas that is collecting dust in my garage.

—Robyn Gordon

I have always admired illuminated manuscripts. The intricacy of design—often in miniature form—fascinates and excites me. This skill done in the traditional way would take a very long time to learn. It is not that I am hesitant to learn it, but it is a question of life getting in the way. One day, hopefully!

—Judy Wilkenfeld

I have not spent much time working with watercolors. I usually apply color in heavy layers and was taught to make sure I "fill in" all of the space. But I was inspired by the Jamie Wyeth exhibit "The Seven Deadly Sins" where he applied watercolor paints thicker than I have ever seen.

—Karen Cole

Oil paints because of the chemicals involved and because I have allergies. Also, the drying time is much too slow for my impatience.

—Donna Watson

Does your art speak to you?

Yes: **95%**
No: **5%**

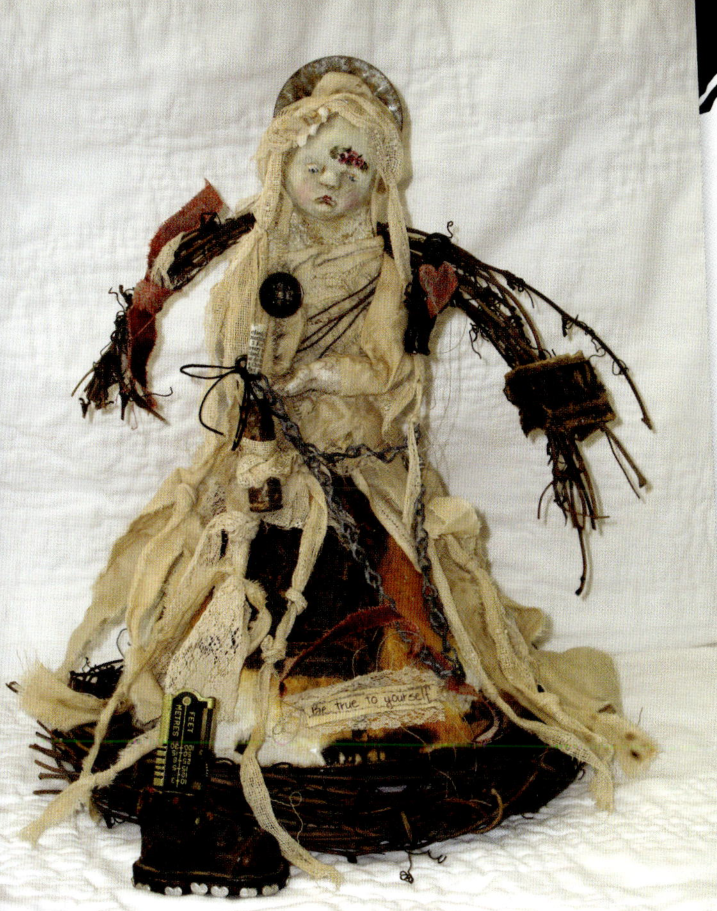

Self-Portrait

Be true to yourself, printed on fabric, is my motto for creating my assemblages. I depicted being a breast cancer survivor losing a body part, much like the dolls I find to use in my creations, using one old, cut metal button. The use of the vintage doll arm turned upward suggests my offerings of finished works to the world. Biblical scripture tucked in the bullet casing represents the spiritual armor I clothed myself with daily. The pewter Frozen Charlotte doll holding a heart shares that I wear my heart on my sleeve. Tucked into a bird's nest expresses that I am most comfortable at home for hours on end. The tarnished metal halo represents that by abiding in Christ, that only in Him do I stand accepted in the eyes of my Heavenly Father, not of my own righteousness. The grapevine used for my wings in a bowed-down fashion suggests that I am a sensitive person and sometimes I allow others or life's trials to weigh me down, stagnating my creativity. The little leather shoe says to the world, it is my journey; I have to walk it the best way I know how.

—JoAnnA Pierotti

Roxanne Evans Stout

Self-Portrait

When I started this canvas, my life was changing. My garden was in full bloom, the colors profuse and surrounding me, but still I was sad. My father had died earlier that year, and my son was about to embark on his journey to college. After being a mother for so long, what would be my purpose now? But as I continued to work on this collage, putting in it all the things that I love, my purpose became clearer. If I follow my heart each day, if I create, if I learn, if I am humbled by nature, if I love, only then I am true to myself.

—Roxanne Evans Stout

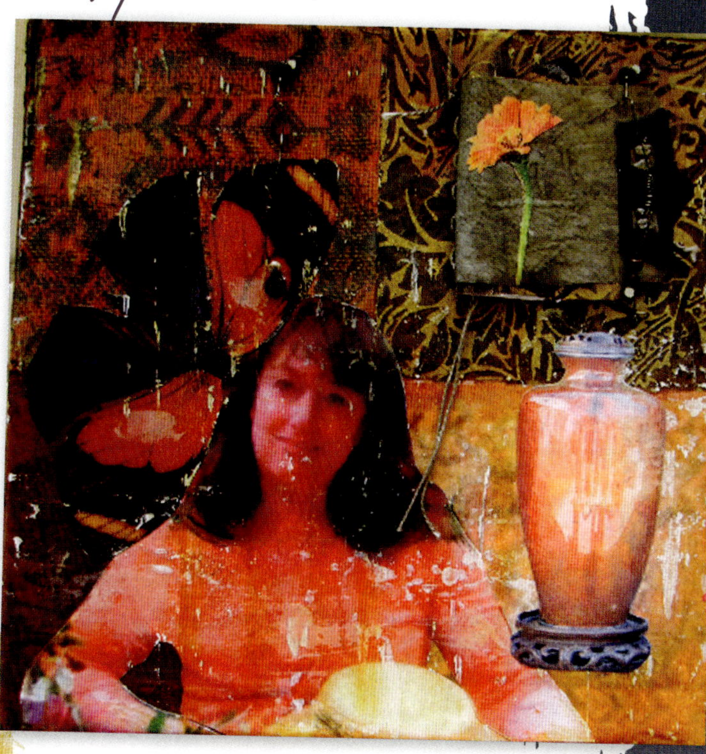

Do you see art as a compulsion or addiction?

Yes: **63%**

No: **37%**

What art material or genre have you been hesitant about but have always wanted to try?

I've been curious to work with encaustics for some time and have just not gotten around to experimenting with it. With encaustics there is a blurry quality that makes an image seem like a distant memory—a nostalgic glance back.

—*John Borrero*

I have been wanting to try throwing clay on a pottery wheel. Often I wonder about the reason I have never tried, and I believc it purely comes down to fear. Fear of failing, fear of succeeding, fear of not being able to find balance.

—*Vivian Bonder*

Oil sticks seem so creamy and bright, like big lipsticks skimming over a mirror. I would love to grab a handful and smear them on a wall. And yet I don't. I lack the cheek and confidence of Basquiat.

—*Danny Gregory*

Being an experimental artist, there is nothing I am hesitant about trying. I often find that working in different genres and using different materials helps me get across my ideas in new and exciting ways that I may not have achieved otherwise.

—*Gary Reef*

Sculpting in bronze. I think I am intimidated by the process. But I would love to learn how to make a bronze sculpture under the tutelage of an experienced artist in this medium—preferably in Italy.

—*Angela Cartwright*

I have mucked about in just about everything art related, so nothing comes to mind.

—*Patricia Larsen*

Oils. I tried them way back in high school. I love how they look and wish I had a bigger studio space to give them another try, but for now I'll stick with acrylics.

—*Pam Carriker*

I've always wanted to try making pottery but fear becoming addicted. I have visions of myself covered from head to toe with clay and glaze, and a backyard taken over by hundreds of garden gnomes holding plates.

—*Linda Woods*

Film making. Maybe I hesitate because of the time and money and the learning curve? And maybe the fact that I'd rather watch one of the *millions* of great ones already out there.

—*Sarah Fishburn*

I have been resisting a very strong pull toward sewing and art quilting because of the precision that is required. I am so much more spontaneous in my creative process. So instead I like to include small pieces of sewn fabric in my mixed-media work.

—*Bridgette Guerzon Mills*

Oil painting on large canvas. I don't have a proper studio to execute the painting, any of the supplies, and (mostly) the confidence in my ability to transfer a vision onto the canvas.

—*Nina Bagley*

I would love to try metal sculpture. What makes me hesitant is the fire! Those huge bursts of flames that fly out of the blowtorches completely unnerve me!

—*Roxanne Evans Stout*

Drawing. It's not that I have never tried to draw . . . it's just that I have never taken a studied approach to it. I would love to open a sketchbook and capture the world around me in paper and graphite.

—Leslie Marsh

Are there certain artists who you think are overexposed?

Yes: **82%**

No: **18%**

Printmaking calls my name! Although I do a lot of "pseudo printmaking" in my art practice, I have never been formally introduced to printmaking. I suppose I haven't done printmaking (yet) because I have been busy doing what I do, and I don't have ready access to a press or instruction.

—Leslie Avon Miller

Printing. I don't have enough time in my life (as measured in years, not in daily hours) to pick up a new art style and have it become a part of my art life. The heck with it, I'll just appreciate what printmakers do and leave it at that.

—Don Madden

I want to purchase a very large canvas and create an abstract mixed-media oil painting. I haven't in the past because I did not have the space, but I do now (a garage) and plan to do this soon.

—JoAnnA Pierotti

Encaustic. First of all, I am the world's clumsiest person. I just know that I'd be suffering third-degree burns in about five seconds, to say nothing of the ensuing house fire. I love the look, feel and smell of melted wax, but I think I'll leave this medium to the brave and physically adept.

—Lisa Hoffman

Materials unintended for art making excite me. There are complex and less near-at-hand materials and processes I'd like to explore. Encaustic, wax, pigments, gelatin and resin come to mind.

—Orly Avineri

I think I have plunged into every style and material that has ever held any interest for me. I am not a hesitant person, au contraire!

—Judy Wise

Since I was a small girl, I have always wanted to try my hand at metalsmithing, transforming a cold, hard piece of silver into something of astonishing beauty. I still, to this day, feel that pull, but being accident-prone as I am, I have been hesitant to do so.

—Alicia Caudle

I would love to try a hydraulic press as my next art adventure. I haven't gone down that road yet due to the cost factor of the press, but I can dream.

—Jen Crossley

Do you find it easy to title your artwork?

For some artworks, yes; for some, no: **61%**

Yes, it is never a problem: **31%**

I always struggle to find the right title: **8%**

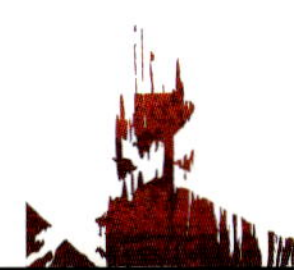

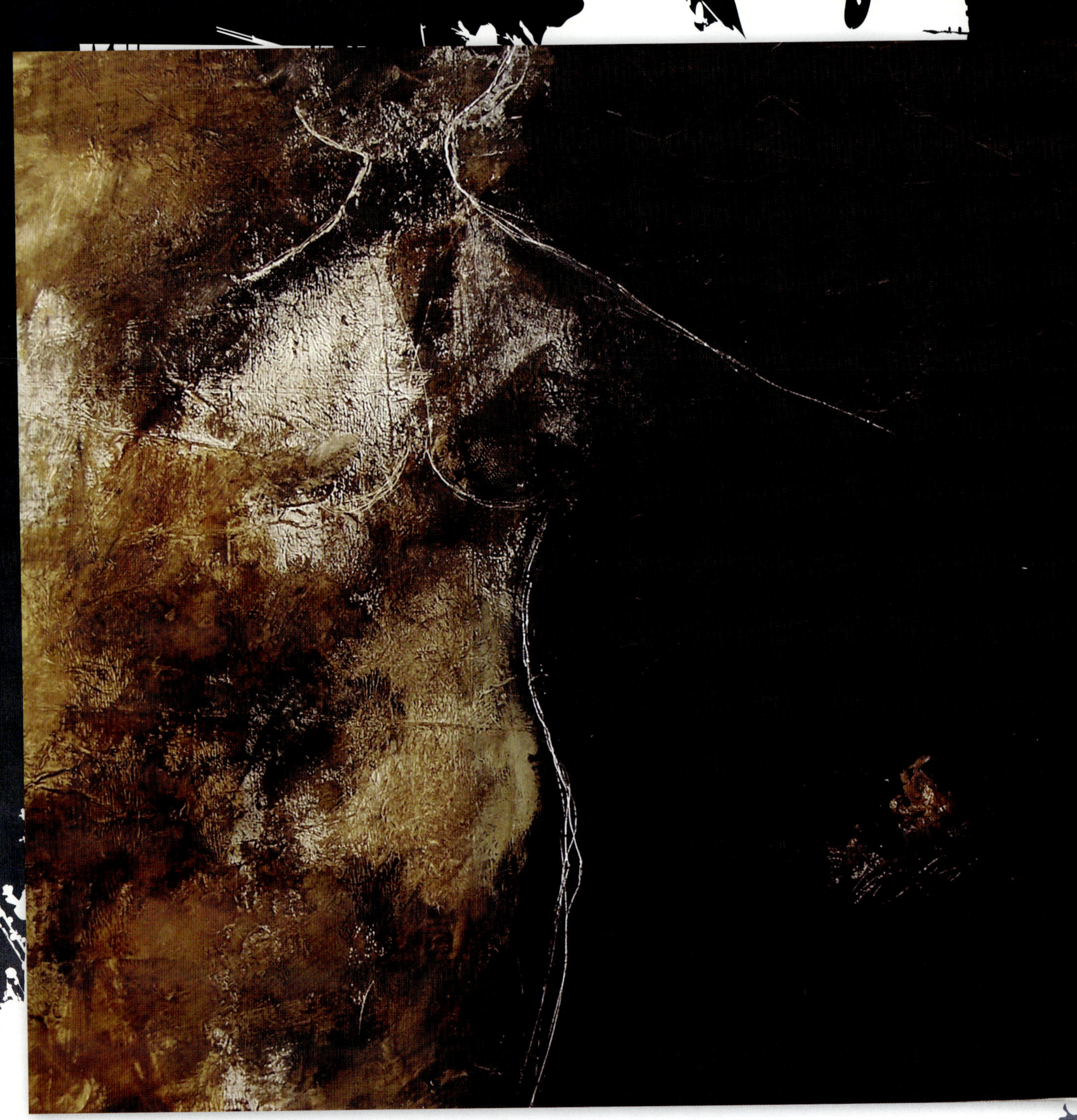

Self-Portrait

I am open to moments of exquisite connection with the earth, my life, the very essence of nature and my place within the circle. It is in the deeply still moments that I experience the ecstasy of being alive. This self-portrait is a reflection of the fleeting yet profound moments when I feel that connection most strongly.

—Leslie Avon Miller

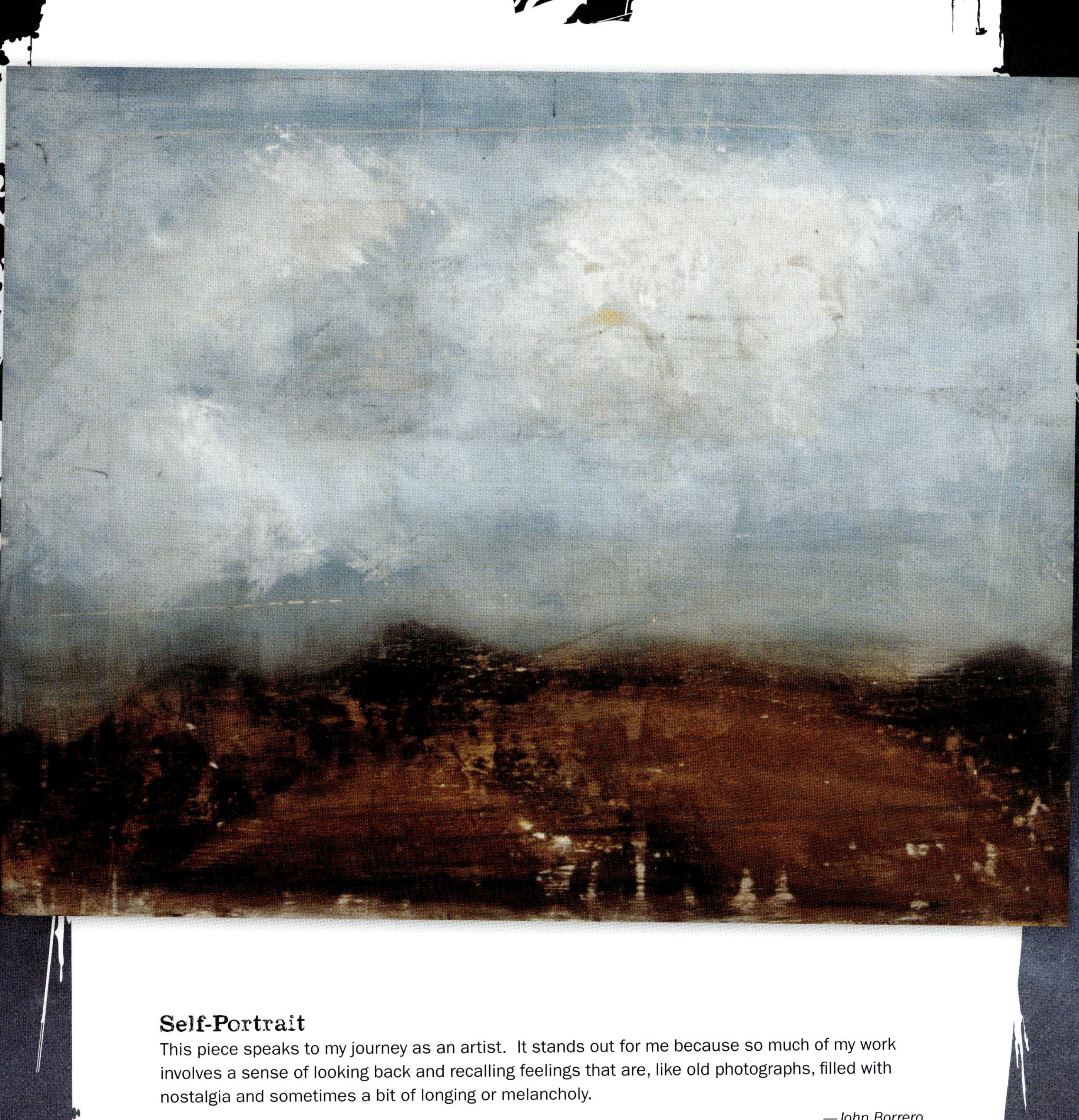

Self-Portrait

This piece speaks to my journey as an artist. It stands out for me because so much of my work involves a sense of looking back and recalling feelings that are, like old photographs, filled with nostalgia and sometimes a bit of longing or melancholy.

—John Borrero

What is the one secret ingredient that makes your artwork uniquely yours?

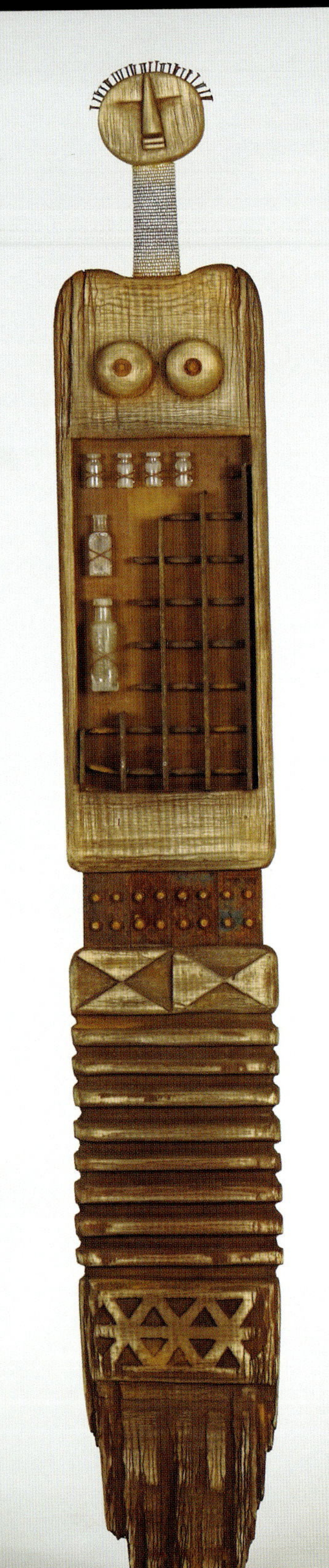

Running on Empty

It could be the natural stains that I make and use on my wood. By chance I discovered certain leaves and rust left wonderful markings on the wood, so I began to experiment with all sorts of natural stains. Rooibos tea is a base for many of my wood stains, and to this I add other concoctions.

—Robyn Gordon

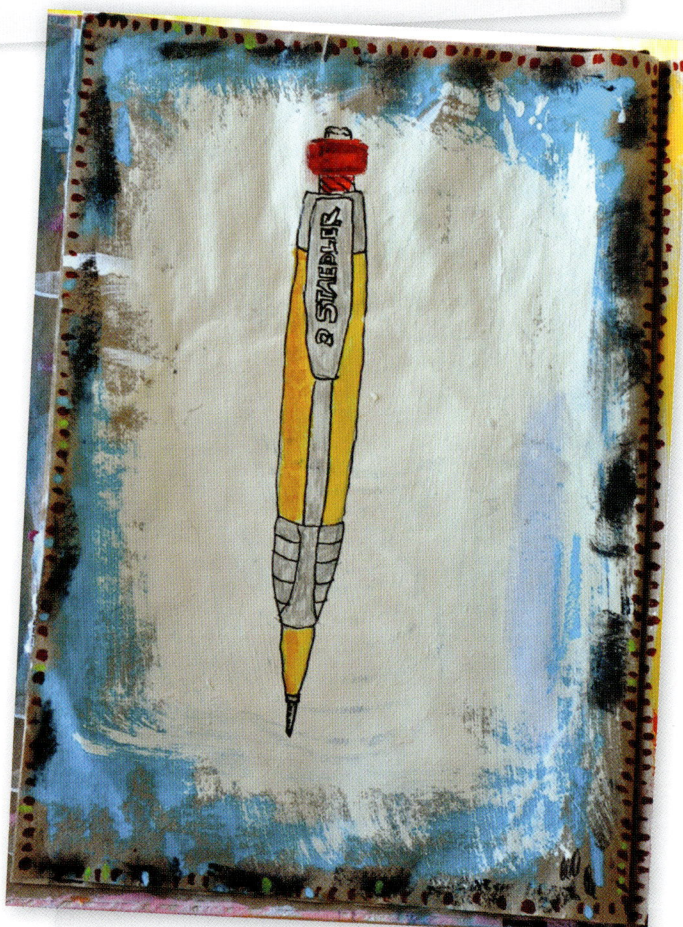

The Pencil

This is a tribute to my ugly-yet-irreplaceable mechanical pencil—long may it *not* be discontinued. . . all great ideas start with *this*.

—Lisa Hoffman

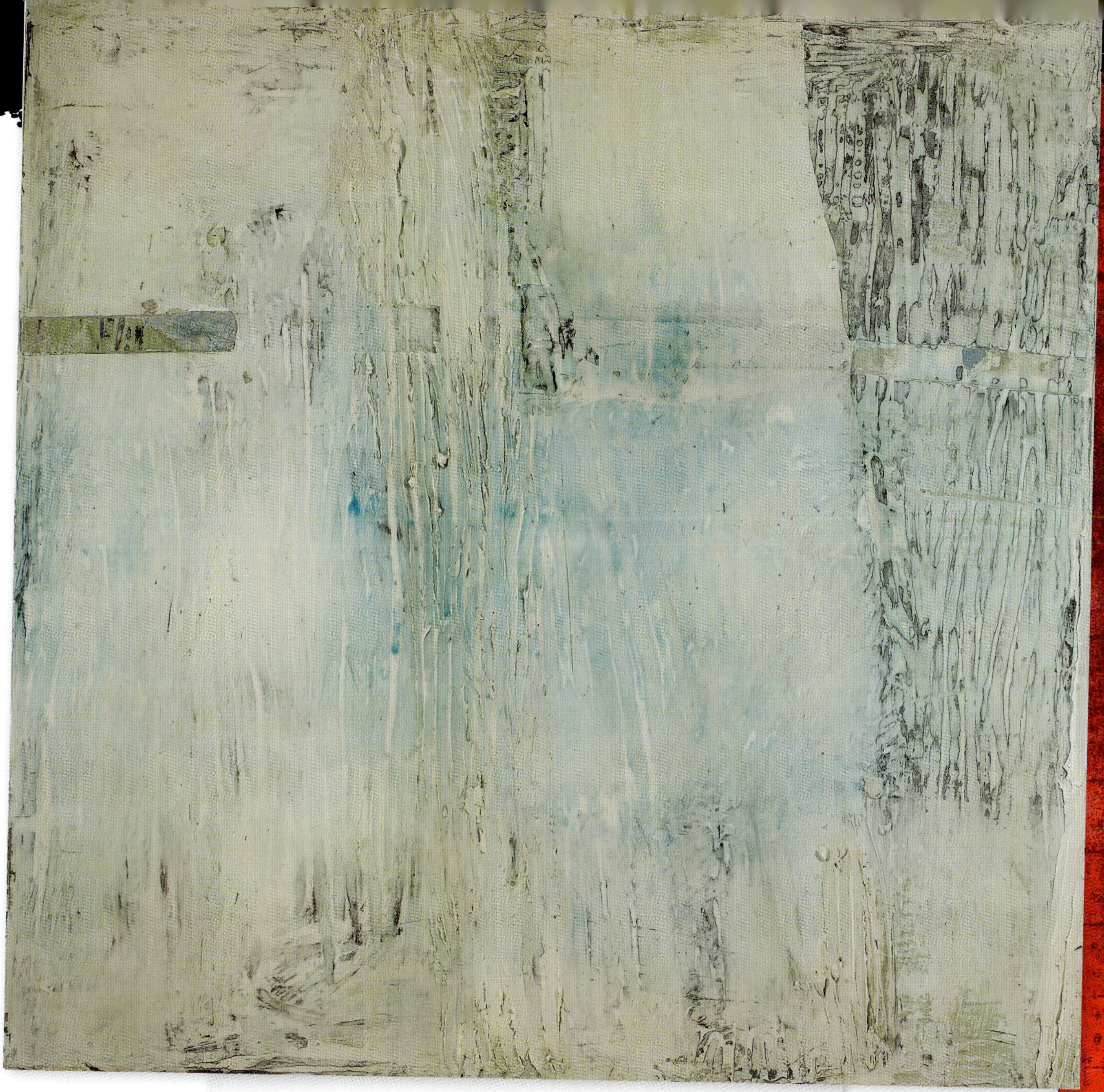

Remembering Blue

It is my intention that this painting, made from my favorite materials (plaster, stains and found objects), addresses the Japanese expression of *mono no aware*. Of the many translations, the two that I hope are imprinted in this piece are 1) an aesthetic awareness of the transience of all things and 2) the intangibility or evanescence of objects.

—Patricia Larsen

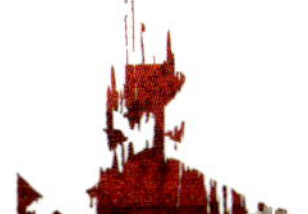

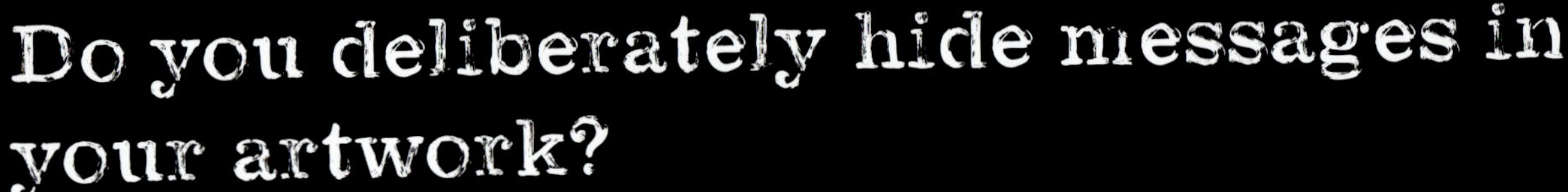

Secrets at the Beach

It's all about the mystery of art. I can't think of one piece I have ever created that does not have some hidden message. Sometimes these "messages" come to me while I am working, and I add things as I go. It could be a shape, a word, a color, a fabric. There are other moments where I do not realize until I am finished that there are all kinds of symbolic images in my work.

—Karen Cole

Worlds Blur at First Light

Once upon a time, there was a traveler who, though young, was seasoned. She had learned that the three essential items for making her way in the world with ease were a letter of introduction, a fresh set of paints and a comfortable pillow.

—Sarah Fishburn

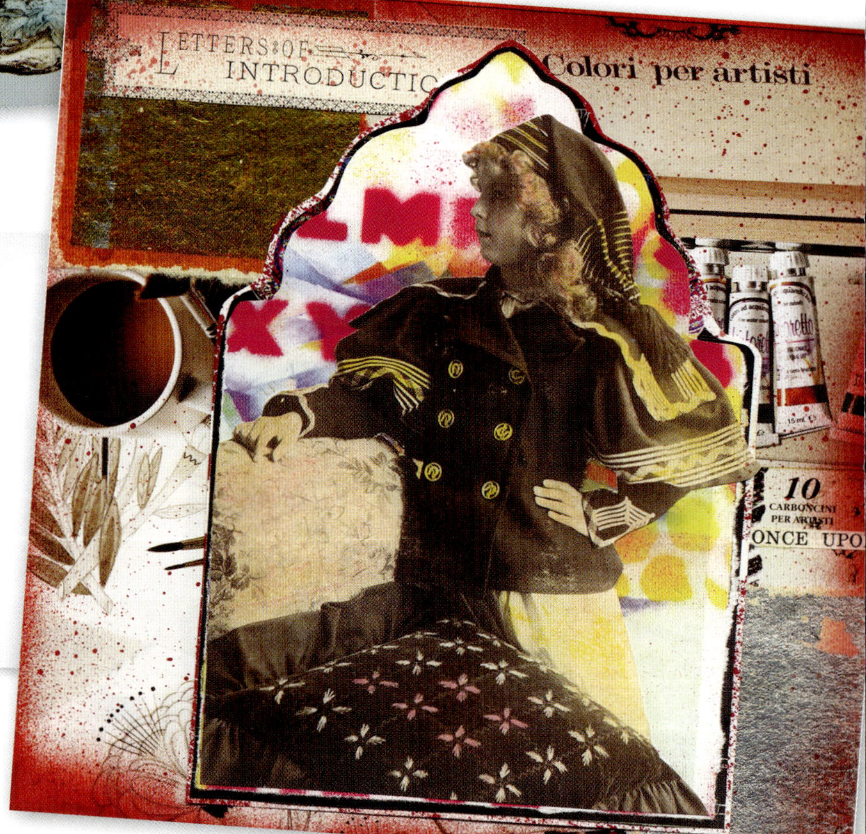

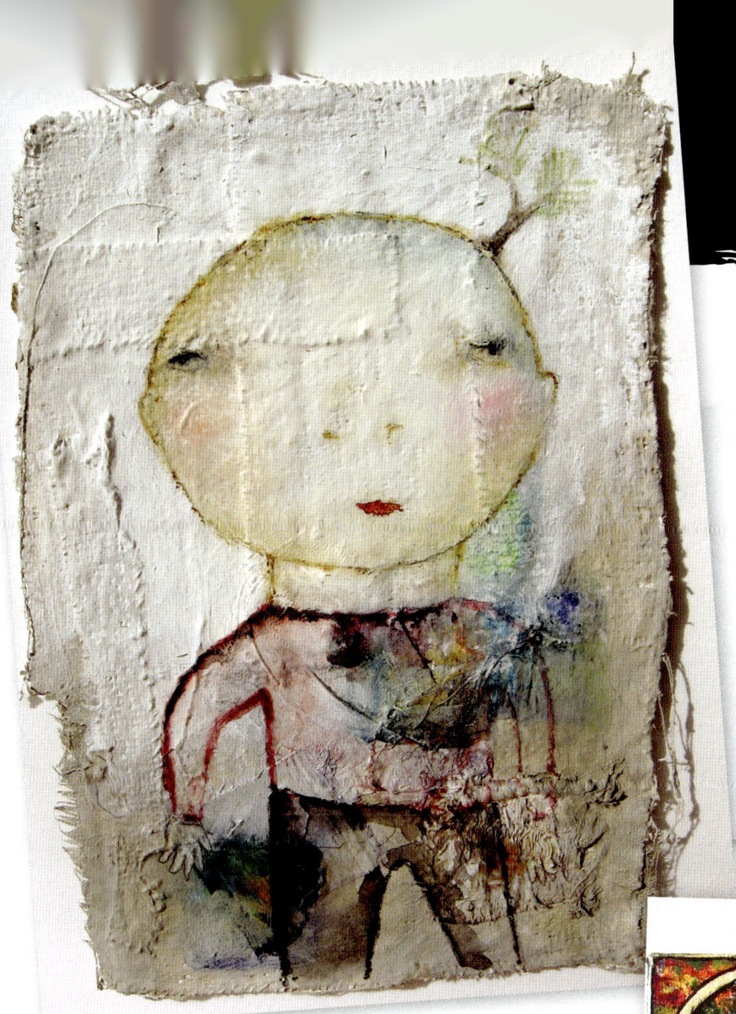

Small-Eyed Boy Passing Through

No, I don't. The messages (if there are any) show up on their own. I start out with a general idea of what I want to paint, and it goes from there with very little planning on my part. Once a piece is done, I rarely think about whether it contains a message or not. What's important to me is the process; if I'm to receive any messages, I feel like it will happen then.

—Lynne Hoppe

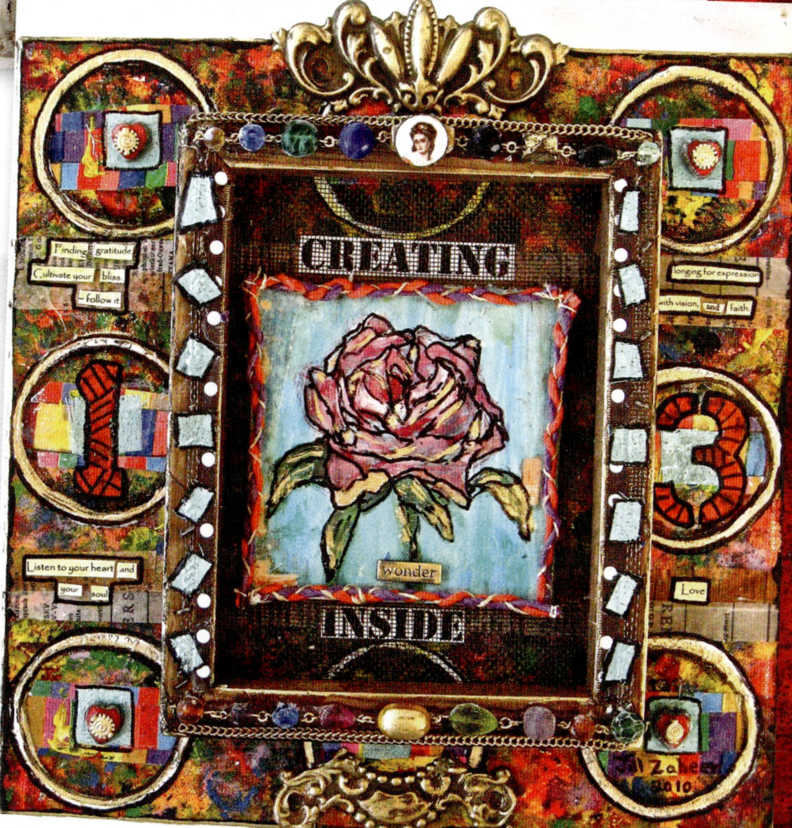

Creating Wonder From Within

Knowing that my past and future can be expressed in a work I'm creating, I often utilize words, colors, numbers and objects that have belonged to people precious to me and secret messages either hidden under layers or incorporated in a top layer that can be seen. I use mementos that can take me on a scavenger hunt to find just the right item to embody the precise emotion I'm trying to capture. I'm patient and forgiving–living in a state of continuous flowing energy filled with synchronistic events that always "wake" me, take me aback and never forsake me into thinking I'm alone in the world.

—Jill Zaheer

Is there a color that rarely shows up in your artwork?

Nearly every color of the rainbow and then some were listed. The least popular range of colors was the purples/pinks. The one color not chosen at all was green. Interestingly, the most popular response was that all colors were fair game and none were left out of the potential palette.

I think I'm an equal opportunity color employer for the most part.

—Lynne Hoppe

Color is the most important element of my work. I use a very subdued and limited palette because I am delighted by the subtlety of color.

—Leslie Avon Miller

No, not a one. I love all the colors of the rainbow as well as brown.

—Judy Wise

I rarely use black because you can get a much deeper color by mixing other pigment combinations.

—Gary Reef

Bright, clear colors. I like my pieces to look weathered and aged.

—Don Madden

Orange. After growing up in a house with an orange flowered couch, burnt orange shag carpet and even orange lamps, I got my fill of orange at an early age.

—Pam Carriker

I used to impose a ban on anything beige anywhere in my world. Just recently I decided to shut up and paint using the forbidden color. We're now engaged!

—Lisa Hoffman

I never meant to leave purple out of it, it just happened. I know that purple is associated with noble properties such as mystery and spirituality, but for me it is just too sweet, cute and girly.

—Orly Avineri

White. I don't really know why it rarely shows up in my work . . . I have nothing against it. It's very pretty. But kinda, well, white.

—Sarah Fishburn

Red. It is a difficult color to push to a point of subtlety.

—Patricia Larsen

Yellow rarely shows up in my work, much of which tells the story of victims of the Holocaust in WWII. Being the color of the enforced star worn by Jews throughout Europe, I am cognizant of the feelings of those survivors who may view the piece.

—Judy Wilkenfeld

Pastel colors rarely show up in my work. They don't seem to be enough to express the brightness, vibrancy and depth of the emotions and perspectives I am dealing with.

—Vivian Bonder

Yellow. I have never been comfortable with bright colors—even when I painted watercolor landscapes many years ago. I had yellow on my palette and never used it.

—Donna Watson

I use every color that I can get my hands on, even if it is just a pinch in a small area.

—Karen Cole

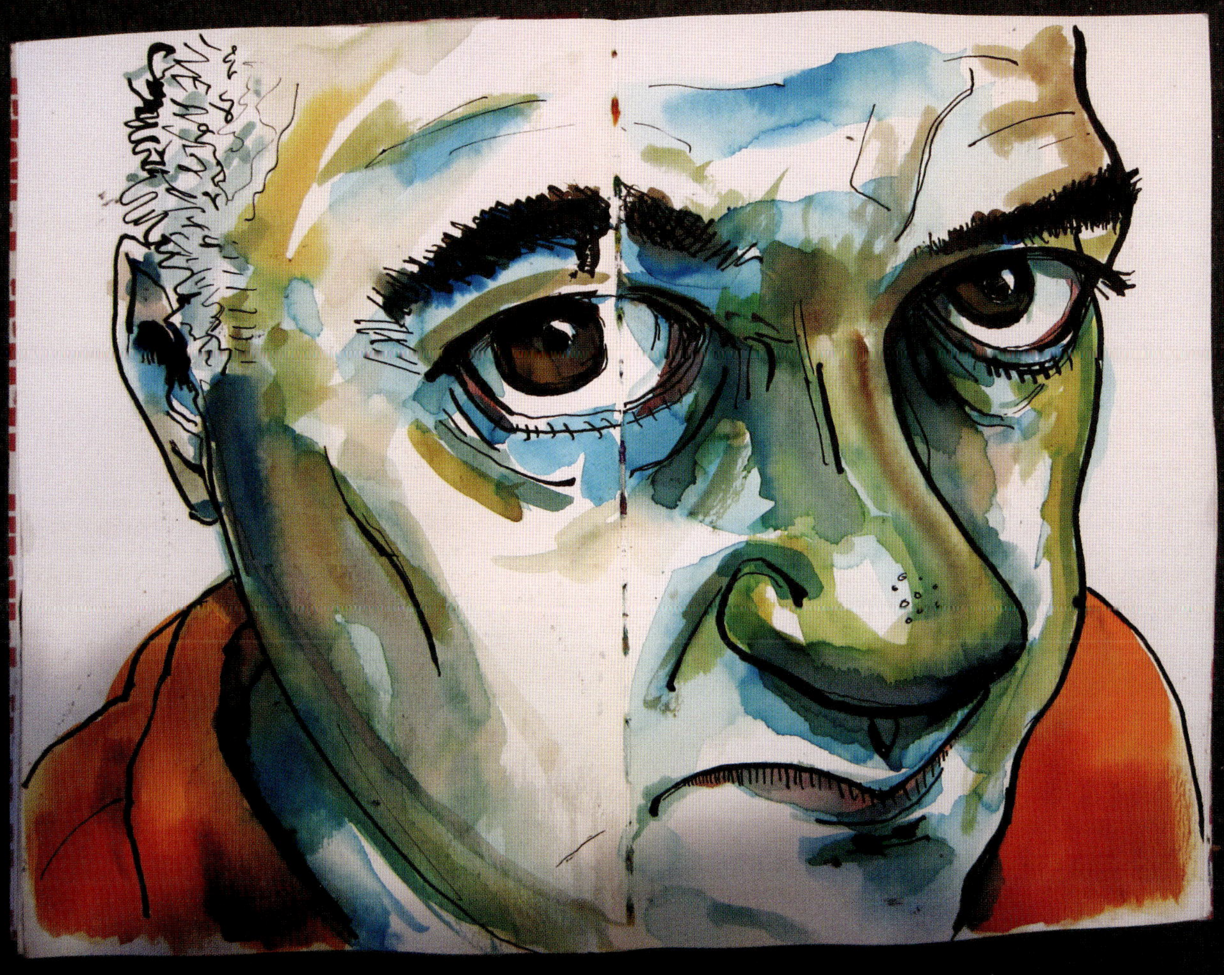

Self-Portrait

I draw and paint myself more often than any other subject—besides perhaps half-eaten bowls of cereal. Like my breakfast, I am always available to be drawn, willing and compliant. In this particular case, my subject seems a little more wary and reproachful than usual—or maybe I was just hungry.

—Danny Gregory

Do you sell your artwork

Yes, but only occasionally: **58%**
Yes, it is one of my activities as an artist: **23%**
No, but I hope to someday: **18%**
No, I do not create to sell: **11%**

Is there a color that rarely shows up in your artwork?

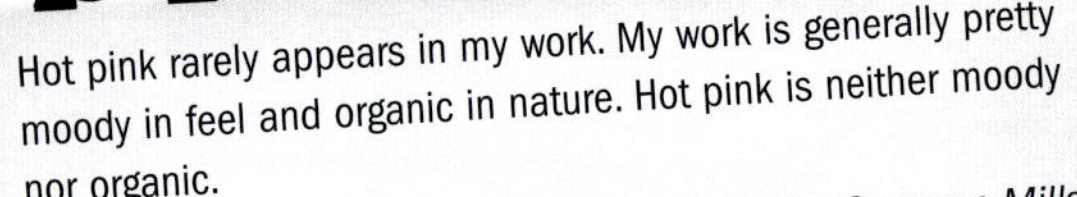

Hot pink rarely appears in my work. My work is generally pretty moody in feel and organic in nature. Hot pink is neither moody nor organic.

—Bridgette Guerzon Mills

Purple. I detest it, maybe because I was brought up in a house with no purple. Pink is a close second.

—Nina Bagley

I don't hold a grudge against any color, and I believe at one time or another I have pretty much used them all in my art.

—Angela Cartwright

Navy blue. I have reserved using this color in my art because it means something completely different than what I want to portray when I am creating.

—JoAnnA Pierotti

Acid yellow because I find it jarring.

—Robyn Gordon

Violet. Pinks and purples have never really appealed to me. I gravitate more toward tarnished and rusted colors in the green and red families.

—Robert Maloney

Gray is a color I always stayed away from. Growing up, I felt it was a color that never complimented my skin color. This must have carried out into my artwork.

—Jill Zaheer

Sepia. I just hate it. I feel annoyed when I see it and can't get away from it fast enough.

—Linda Woods

The entire range from pink to purple are my least favorite hues. Pink possesses a "little girly" feel to it; sweet and cute and totally unrepresentative of the type of art I typically like to create.

—Alicia Caudle

Boy, I don't think so. I am pretty lavish with all the colors in my box and layer them one on top of the other.

—Danny Gregory

The colors I mix are usually earthy or cool colors, so I think it would be unusual for you to see a bright pop of yellow in one of my paintings.

—Julie Prichard

I very rarely use bright colors. Almost everything that I work with is some shade of brown. When I paint, Raw Umber is my staple.

—John Borrero

Blue! I love blue, but in my own art, I am drawn to warmer colors, the colors of autumn, the colors of fields and trees, the colors of the earth.

—Roxanne Evans Stout

I hesitate to rule out any one color appearing in my work, but very rarely will I use pastels. I prefer a richer palette of gold, rust and browns, punctuated by turquoise, deep reds and green.

—Leslie Marsh

Most colors rarely show up in my work because I struggle with trying to make colors work together. I did have a friend over once to play with painting colored backgrounds, but after the play day, she told me to stick to sepia, so I got the message loud and clear!

—Jen Crossley

Blue. I have no blue paint in my studio. I do not connect with blue, but get dangerously close, because I adore the turquoise family of colors.

—Michelle Ward

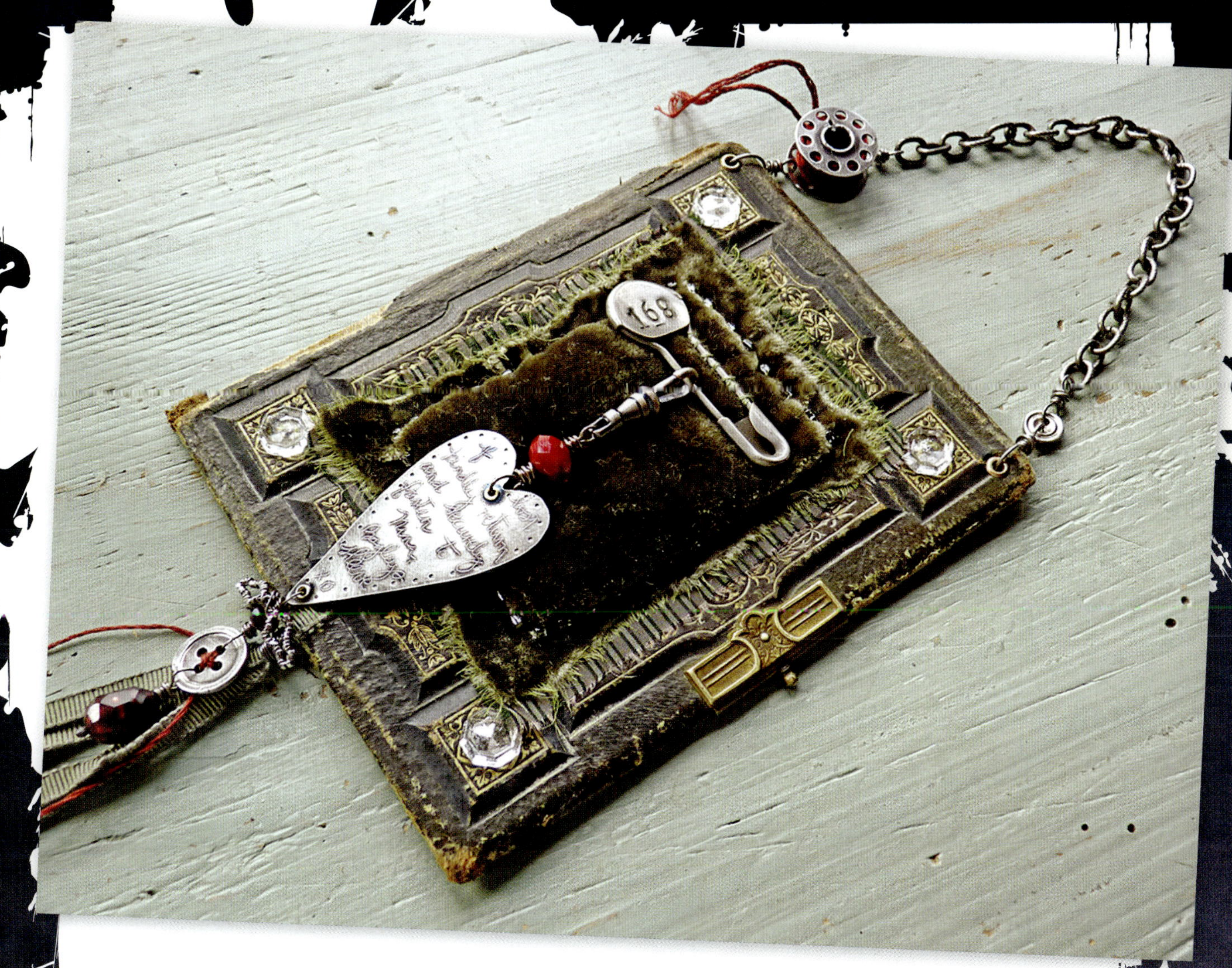

Self-Portrait

All my life I've been told that I wear my heart on my sleeve, because I am completely open (often to a fault) with what is on my mind and in my heart. This time around, I thought it might be nice to fashion a "home" for that heart, a place where it can always be pinned. The velvet-padded backing, to which the engraved heart is pinned, comes from a beautiful shirt that has been hanging, unworn, in the back of my closet for five years. I wore it to my brother's funeral and have not been able to ever wear it again. When cleaning out my closet prior to the making of this piece, I ran across the shirt again and thought it would be very fitting to use a bit of the cloth, taken from a sleeve, for my self-portrait piece. I can see my brother, Ben, smiling about this one, even as I write these very words.

—Nina Bagley

Do you worry about running out of ideas?

Not an issue at all: **58%**

Sometimes crosses my mind: **32%**

It is a constant fear: **10%**

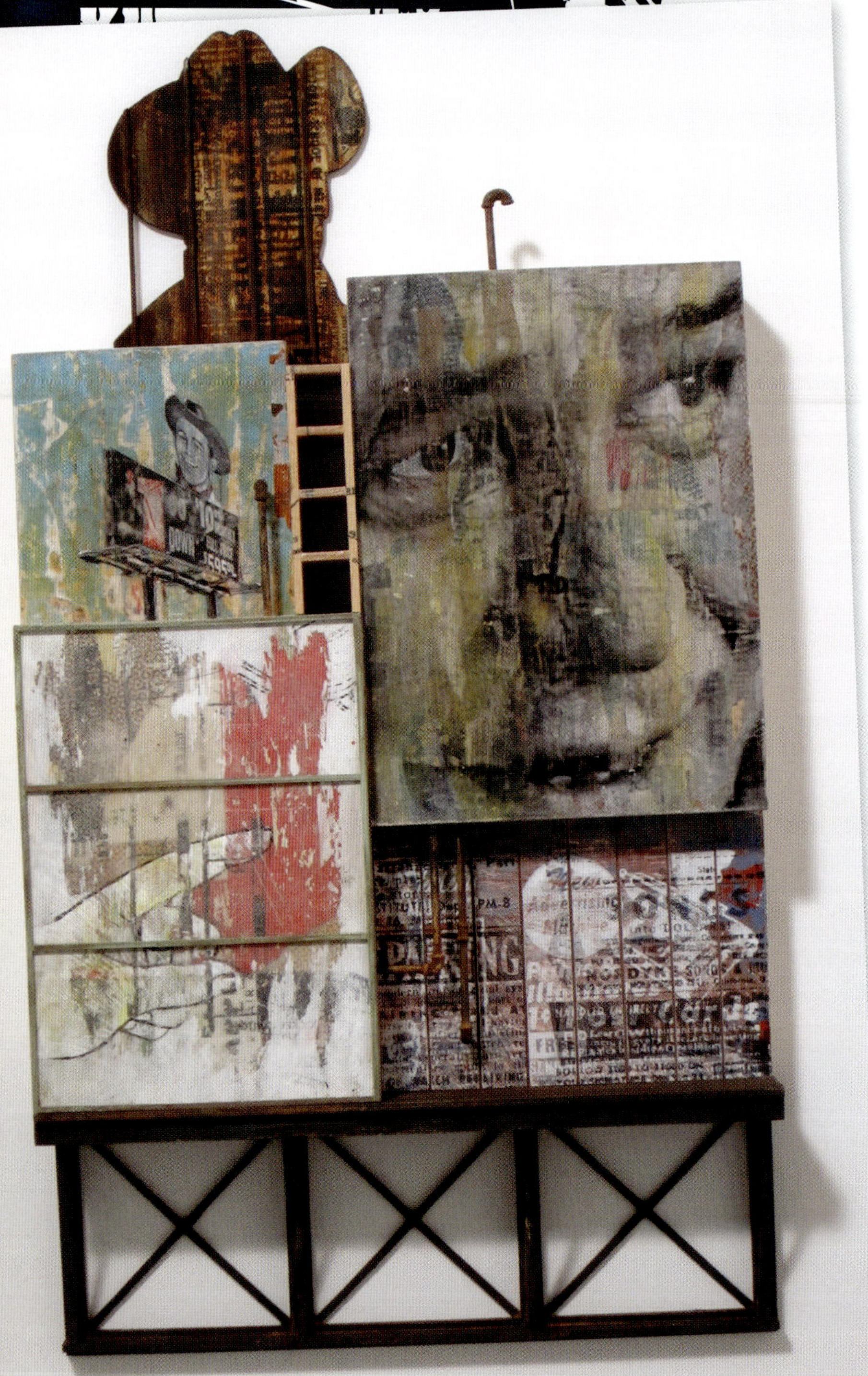

Self-Portrait

I realized early on that I didn't want to use an image of myself, so the main image is a face from a magazine from the '50s that I transferred onto a collaged surface. The rest of the piece sort of grew around it. I've been influenced lately by old advertisements and billboards that are layered over and over on top of each other. I've also been attracted to billboards that sit back-to-back and have extensions of the images that pop up over the tops of the billboards.

—Robert Maloney

Would you like to see more critical comments on the blogs?

Yes, if "constructively" critical: **60%**

No, I like it as it is now: **40%**

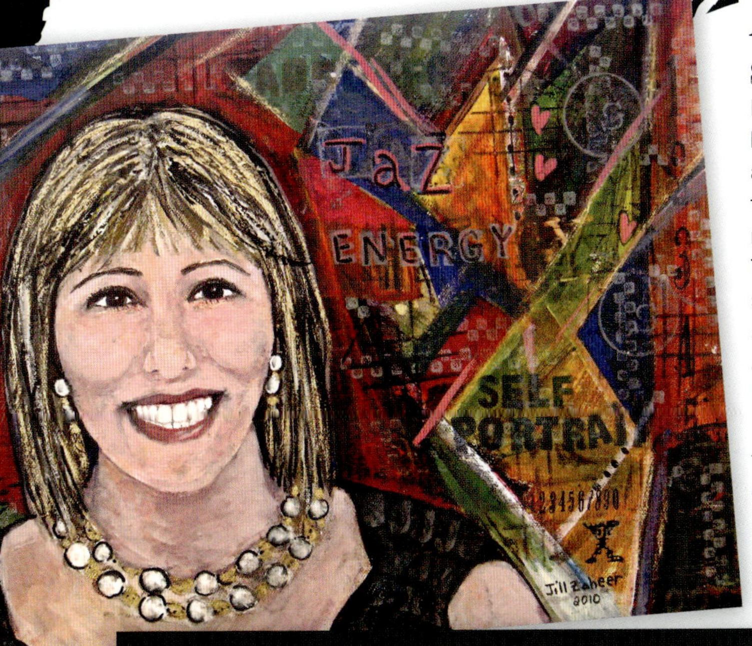

Self-Portrait

Life is filled with all sorts of challenges, so what better way to live life to the fullest than to create a self-portrait guided by both how I see myself and the essence and energy that is the force behind me—rich in color, patterns and personal meaning. The horns blow one by one, followed by the percussions and strings. I'm conducting to my favorite sounds—only my instruments are my artistic tools, and I'm the conductor. Colors are like music to me. Each note is a brushstroke until a full symphony of "artwork" is played before me. If it's not quite in tune, I will continue to tinker with it until it accurately conveys my song—my own wordless language that speaks for me.

—Jill Zaheer

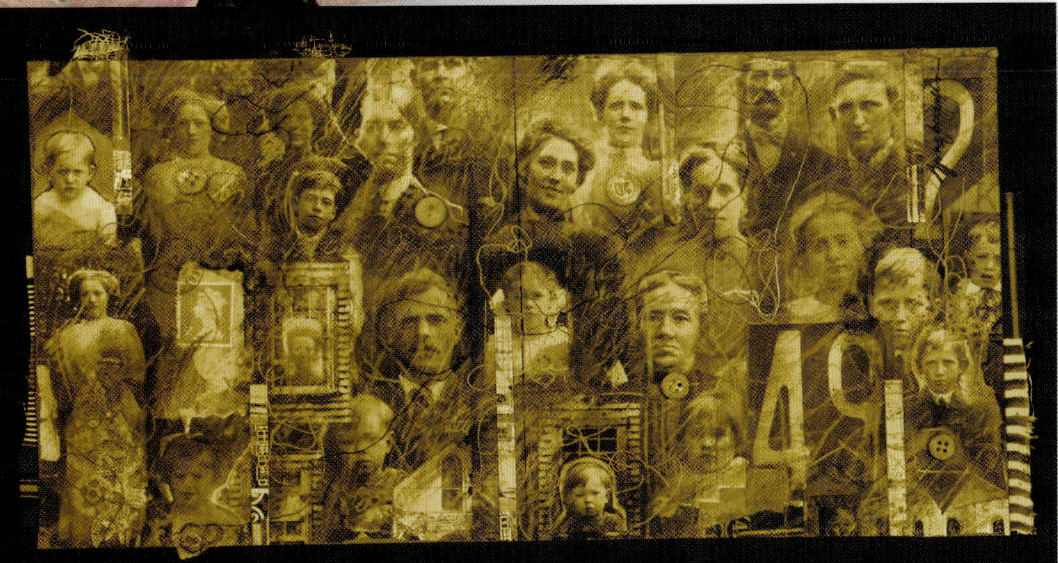

Self-Portrait

It took me too many years to become authentically interested in my family history, but in 1985 I attended a family reunion in Western Pennsylvania and finally met my "tribe" and chose to become thoroughly immersed in their history, images and lore. Making up for lost time, I wanted to hear every old story, listen to every tall tale, look at every old portrait and study every genealogy chart. That day I was given a large vintage group photo of my father's long-ago family, posing at a reunion. Dad sat with me and pointed to each face, telling me stories and remembrances about them. In fact, one of the little scamps sitting cross-legged in the front row is my dear dad. More than almost anything else I own, this photo has meaning, mystery, and deep importance. Each time I look at it, I have a sense of tradition and belonging. I connect to these faces and to their way of life. And, in a way, I mourn that I know comparatively little about them. The time I spend doing new works of art, using this old photo, is my way of paying tribute to my father's family and taking my place among them.

—Lynne Perrella

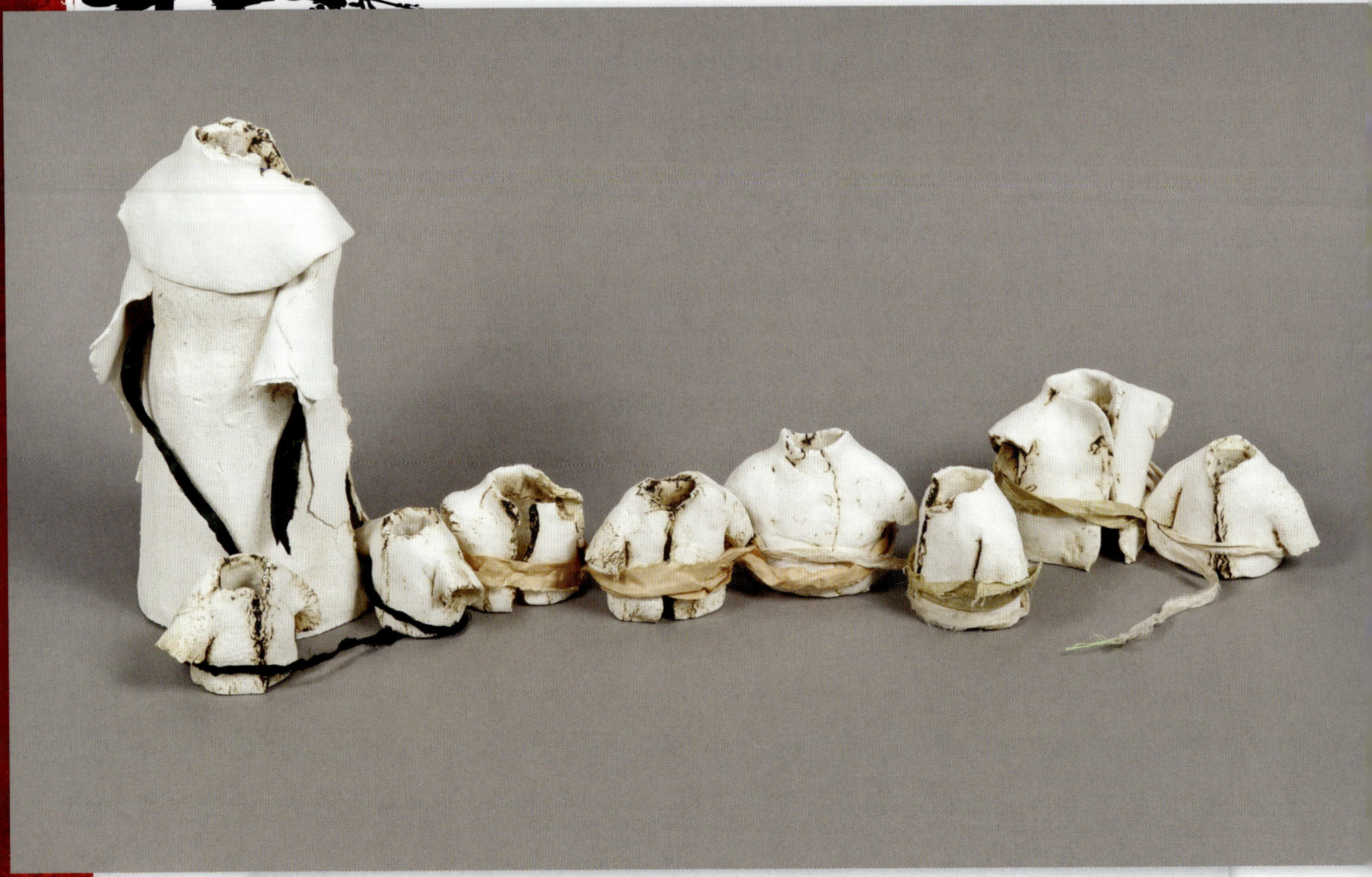

Lost Childhood: Galveston, 1900

My current art obsession is having my work look like it has been weathered and aged with time and has a history. I want you to feel that my work was unearthed after years and years, and wants to talk to you, to tell you a story. Can you hear the voices?

In 1900 a horrible hurricane tore across Galveston Island, Texas. On the west side of Galveston was St. Mary's Orphanage, established by the Catholic Sisters of Charity. The two dormitories were home to ninety-three children and ten nuns. As the winds increased and the water began to surge over the seawall, the nuns gathered the children and led them up to the second floor of the girls dormitory. They all heard the crash of the boys dormitory as it collapsed and was carried away by the floodwaters. Each nun took clothesline rope and used it to tie between six to eight of the youngest children to themselves, hoping to protect them. The death and destruction in Galveston was unbelievable. More than eight thousand died, and their bodies were littered throughout the city. All ten nuns and ninety-three children died in the storm. The sisters were buried wherever they were found, each with the children still tied to them. Today, where St. Mary's Orphanage once stood, there is a Walmart.

—*Don Madden*

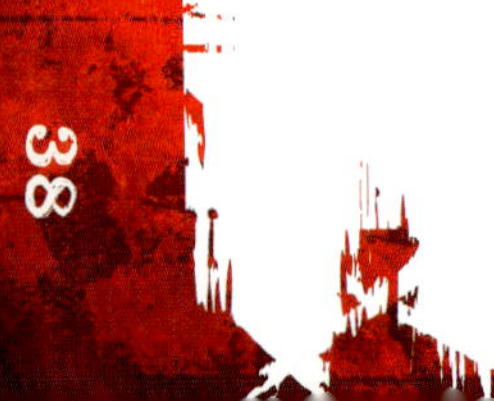

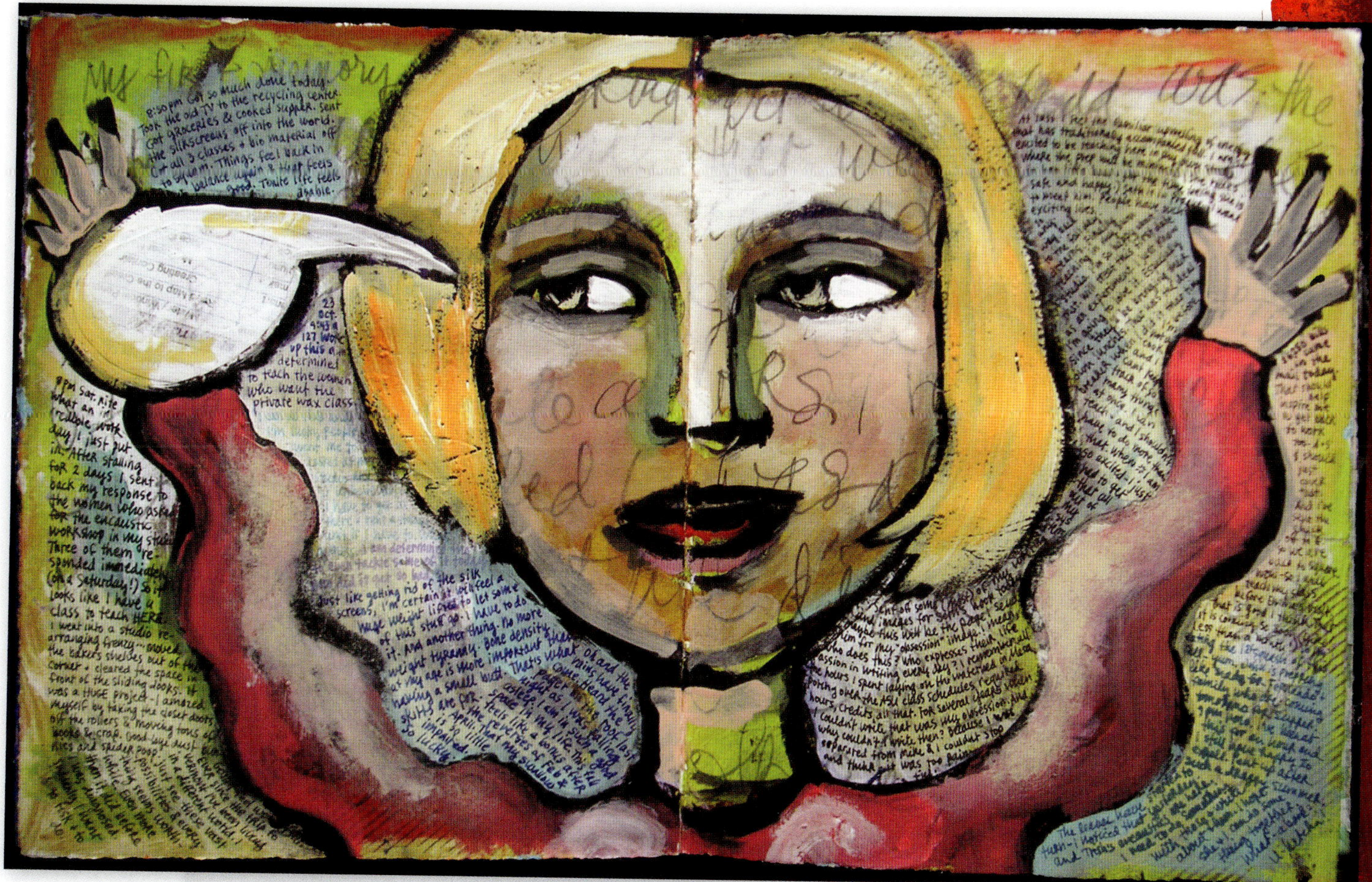

Boogly Woogly

This page is an example of my obsessive writing and image making. I am compelled to do it—to make things, to record the daily flotsam. I read once that artists have a type of epilepsy that causes their minds to fire rapidly; that image has stayed with me as a possible explanation for why I feel compelled to record, create and fill every moment. I would be very uncomfortable without paper and pencil or rudimentary art supplies.

—Judy Wise

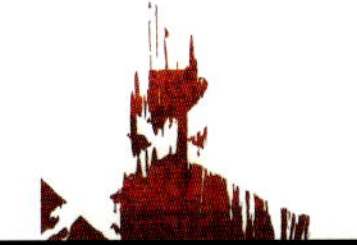

What is your current art obsession?

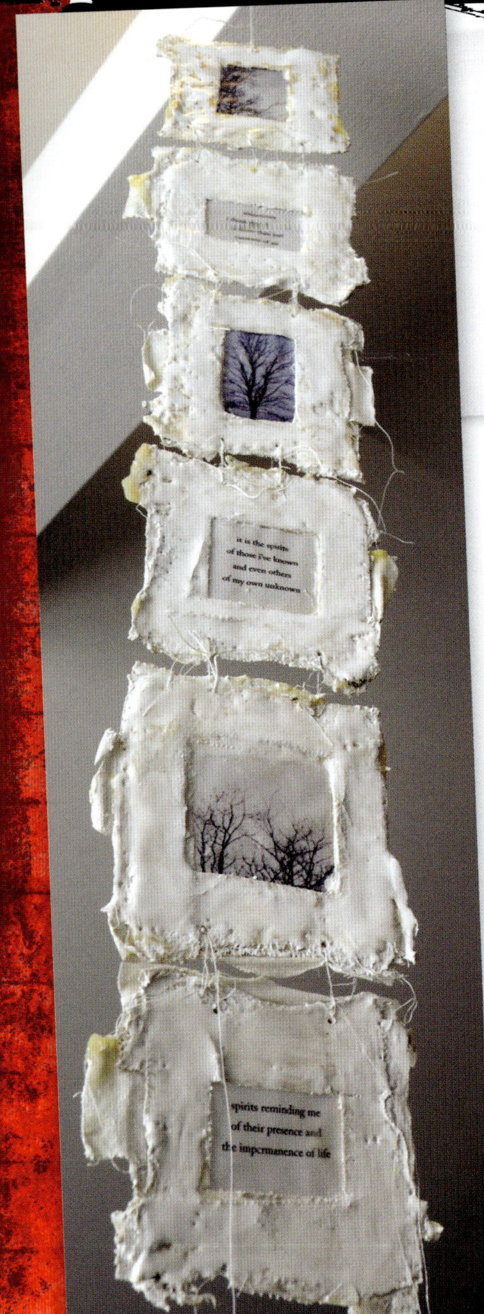

Spirits

Right now I am obsessed with incorporating encaustic with paper and, more specifically, book art. The combination of wax and paper is really beautiful because the paper absorbs the wax and becomes translucent if the paper is thin. You can also create three-dimensional forms with paper and wax. There are just so many possibilities. It is exciting to experiment with! This piece was made using plaster, paper and encaustic, and is meant to hang like a mobile.

—Bridgette Guerzon Mills

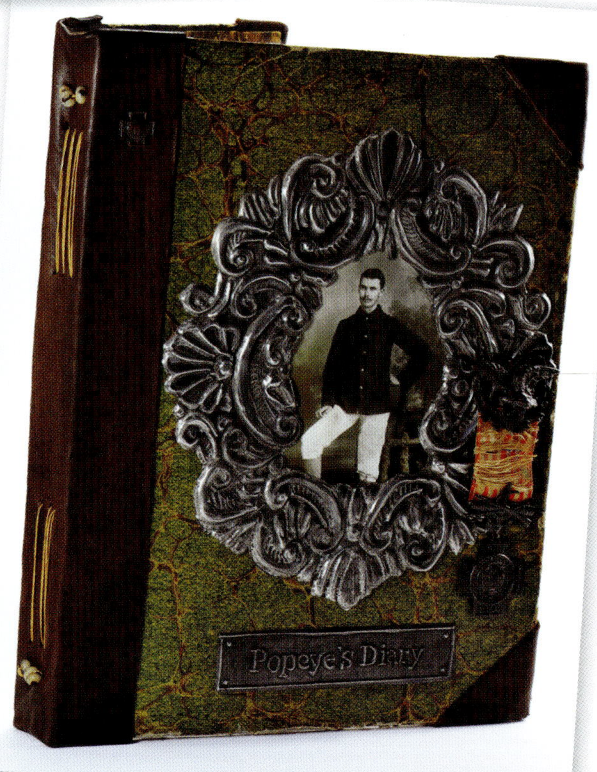

Popeye's Diary

My current art obsession is making books. Most of the books I make are blank journals that can be filled with memories, photos or thoughts. In creating these books, I generally aim for a theme, just because it gives the piece focus. But I especially enjoy producing more detailed books. Whether I am making a book that features a person's life or just a period in their life—like Popeye's Diary—I strive to pull a feeling from the viewer. These books are my interpretation of the event or the person.

—Leslie Marsh

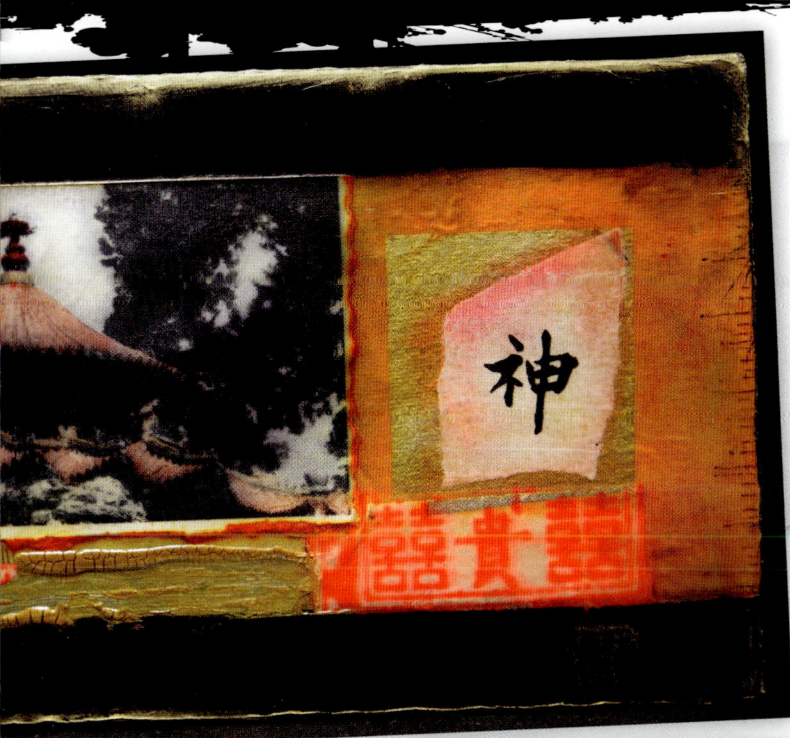

Spirit . . . Above the Fray
Acrylic matte gel. I'm having a love affair with it. I hand-paint my photographs with watercolors, oils, acrylics or inks, creating layer upon layer to build the story I want to tell. The gel fuses each layer together until it becomes one cohesive piece. On a recent visit to Asia, I was struck with a feeling of calm before the storm. On the surface there is a peacefulness . . . below the surface there is a crackling echo of a time past and a restraint that cannot be ignored.

—Angela Cartwright

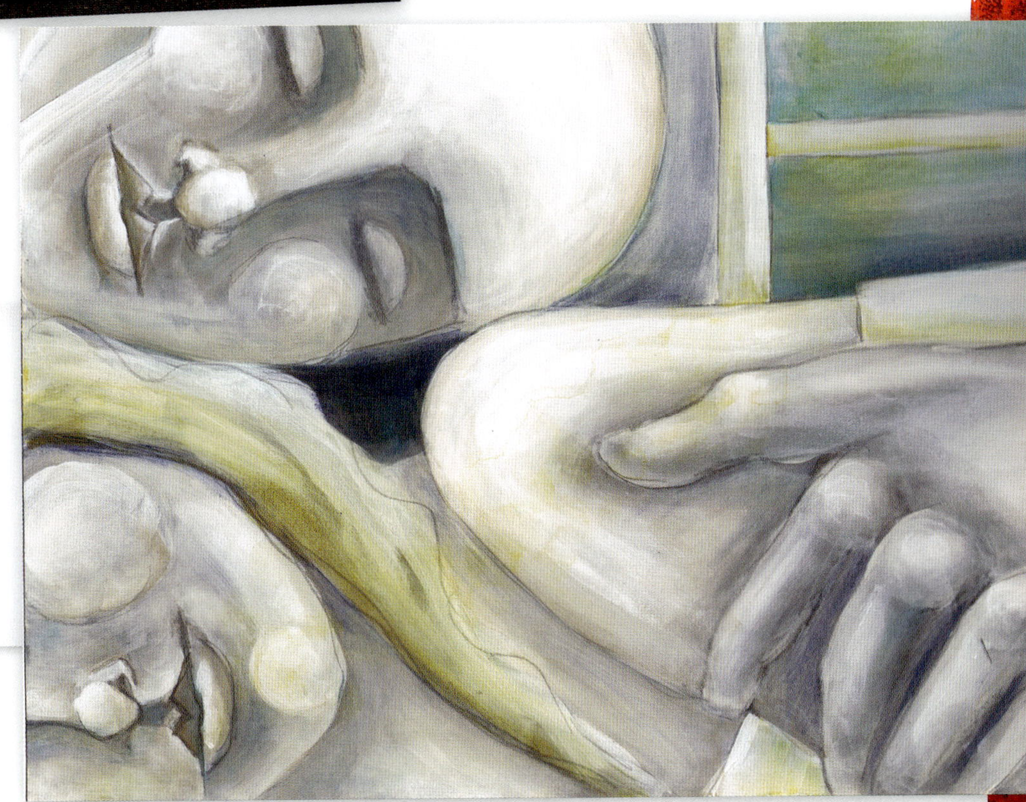

Morning Light
Conté Portrait Crayons. I've been sketching with them, using them under paint, adding them on top of paint . . . love them!

—Pam Carriker

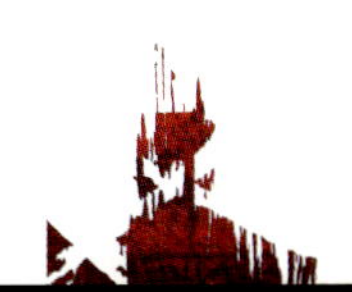

What is your biggest pet peeve in terms of art?

While some pet peeves focused on the practical, the majority were directed toward more personal, attitudinal issues. The biggest grievance related to snobbism in artists and the artist community. A close second was the often discussed topic of copying and imitation, with many artists highlighting the importance of people finding their own style and voice.

My biggest pet peeve would be snobbism. From a stranger, a relative or a friend or even from myself. As though there is only one type of art that is really art!?

—Roxanne Evans Stout

Flat-out imitation and the denial from the imitator that a piece of work is not an imitation. Inspiration is one thing, but blatant imitation of a style or a technique is something altogether different that upsets me more than anything else in my line of work.

—Nina Bagley

The monetary undervalue that artists place on their artwork.

—Judy Wilkenfeld

I would have to say that my biggest pet peeve in terms of art are people who need to know the explicit thought process and meaning behind every piece of art. I don't typically plan an art piece, so explaining the "why" to others just doesn't make sense to me.

—Alicia Caudle

Art "snobs" who believe, if you are not art school educated and are not trained in the fine arts (painting, drawing), you are not an artist.

—Karen Cole

Hearing people say that they can't do something. It's not true. You can.

—Julie Prichard

I wish all art could speak to me. It's a drag when I go to a gallery and I just don't get it because the work is all about references to other art I don't know or some intellectual notion I've never read or some sort of academic conceit. I want to appreciate what's being said.

—Danny Gregory

Eagerly looking for newness but finding oldness. Craving to be moved and energized by images that are novel, unorthodox, fresh, innovative, neoteric and unique, and seeing too many images out there that are clichéd, overwrought, overly adorned and tired.

—Orly Avineri

Time management. I have learned that while I may thrive on deadlines, I cannot function in freewheeling discoveries when a project or assignment has to get done. Honoring my commitments allows me to clear my head, and my table, and indulge in art-for-me.

—Michelle Ward

I am not overly fond of hyper-realism in painting. I find the obvious boring.

—Judy Wise

What is your preferred condition for creating?

Prefer to have music: **53%**
I need my silence: **31%**
TV in the background: **13%**
Love to have people around me: **3%**

When artists take themselves too seriously.

—*Patricia Larsen*

That a piece of art should "look" a certain way. There is nothing wrong with learning an artist's techniques, but then it's important to make it your own. The peeve is not believing in yourself enough to do your own thing.

—*Angela Cartwright*

I often wonder why some artists make it bigger than others. I see a lot of very talented people out there who go unnoticed, yet their work is so amazing and so unique. I just wish I could help everyone have their five minutes of fame and be appreciated for who they are and what they create.

—*Jen Crossley*

Art should be for everyone. The opportunity (time and place) and means (money) to make one's own art, and if one wishes, the opportunity (availability) and means (again, money, or trade goods) to procure works of art made by others.

—*Sarah Fishburn*

Do you consider rubber stamping a legitimate art medium?

Yes: **65%**

No: **35%**

Do you feel you have found your niche art-wise, or are you still searching?

Still searching for my artist's voice: **43%**

Found my niche, but just for now: **39%**

I have totally found my place: **18%**

One of my art pet peeves has more to do with my laziness. I often forget to clean my brushes and ruin them. Another check in the encaustics box—brushes used for encaustics never need to be cleaned!

—*Bridgette Guerzon Mills*

I don't understand the amount of time and energy people spend on the issue of copying. It seems counter to the creative process to me. I want to shout, "Wait a minute! Isn't it more important to just focus on what we're creating/doing *now*?!"

—*Lynne Hoppe*

Artists who only seem to care about sales and marketing. There is no personal expression or feeling in their work, and they only do work they think will sell. Unfortunately, they are often rewarded with shows and awards.

—*Donna Watson*

Copycats. I love to see true self-expression in art. It's such a powerful and personal thing. Seeing people copy someone else's truth to make a quick buck is offensive and rude.

—*Linda Woods*

It would have to be the notion that having an art degree makes you (1) a better artist and (2) a professional. At the end of the day, it is the artwork that should be judged, not the artist.

—*Gary Reef*

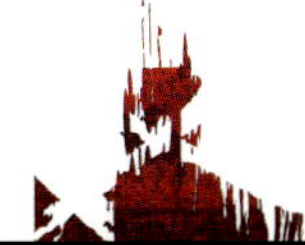

What is your biggest pet peeve in terms of art?

That everyday isn't a studio day!

—*Leslie Avon Miller*

I have purchased several pieces of art online because the picture and description of it drew me in. Several times I have received an item (especially jewelry) and find after a short time it falls apart. When I pay good money for a piece, I expect it to hold its value.

—*JoAnnA Pierotti*

People who look at my work and say, "Oh, how cute!" As far as I'm concerned, that's the kiss of death.

—*Don Madden*

I find it slightly annoying that there is sometimes such a snobbish atmosphere around art and that a massive difference is made between artists and crafters, and why exactly? We are all expressing various aspects of who we are, and isn't that just simply fine?

—*Vivian Bonder*

I don't enjoy art whose sole purpose is to provoke a reaction in the viewer. With a little bit of subtlety, art can lead us to deep places within ourselves, but I prefer for that process to be gradual and introspective.

—*John Borrero*

I'm always a big stickler when it comes to craft. When I see something that is barely held together with tape and foam core that says something about the artist.

—*Robert Maloney*

It's hard to understand how "great art" has historically been defined as "not worthy" by the values, political temperament or influential people who decided what was to be showcased and exhibited to the public.

–*Jill Zaheer*

I am the source of my own Peevedom. I'll have a unique and fresh idea. I'll file it away for later and bam—there it is. Someone else has not only thought of the same concept, but found the time to make it real. Dang. So I just cross it off the list since it's no longer an original idea.

—*Lisa Hoffman*

If I'm to be truly honest here, I'd have to say having my workshop materials copied/imitated. I put hours and hours of work into my class materials, so when I see a very similar class pop up, it does peeve me. When this happens, it's my signal to move on to create a new class.

—*Pam Carriker*

I see art as being a form of self-expression that requires a bit of effort. Not every thought is worth expression. Not every statement is profound. And while life is rife with art, not all of it is good art.

—*Leslie Marsh*

When do you do your best work?

No difference with or without a deadline: **39%**
With a deadline looming: **37%**
Without any pressure from a deadline: **24%**

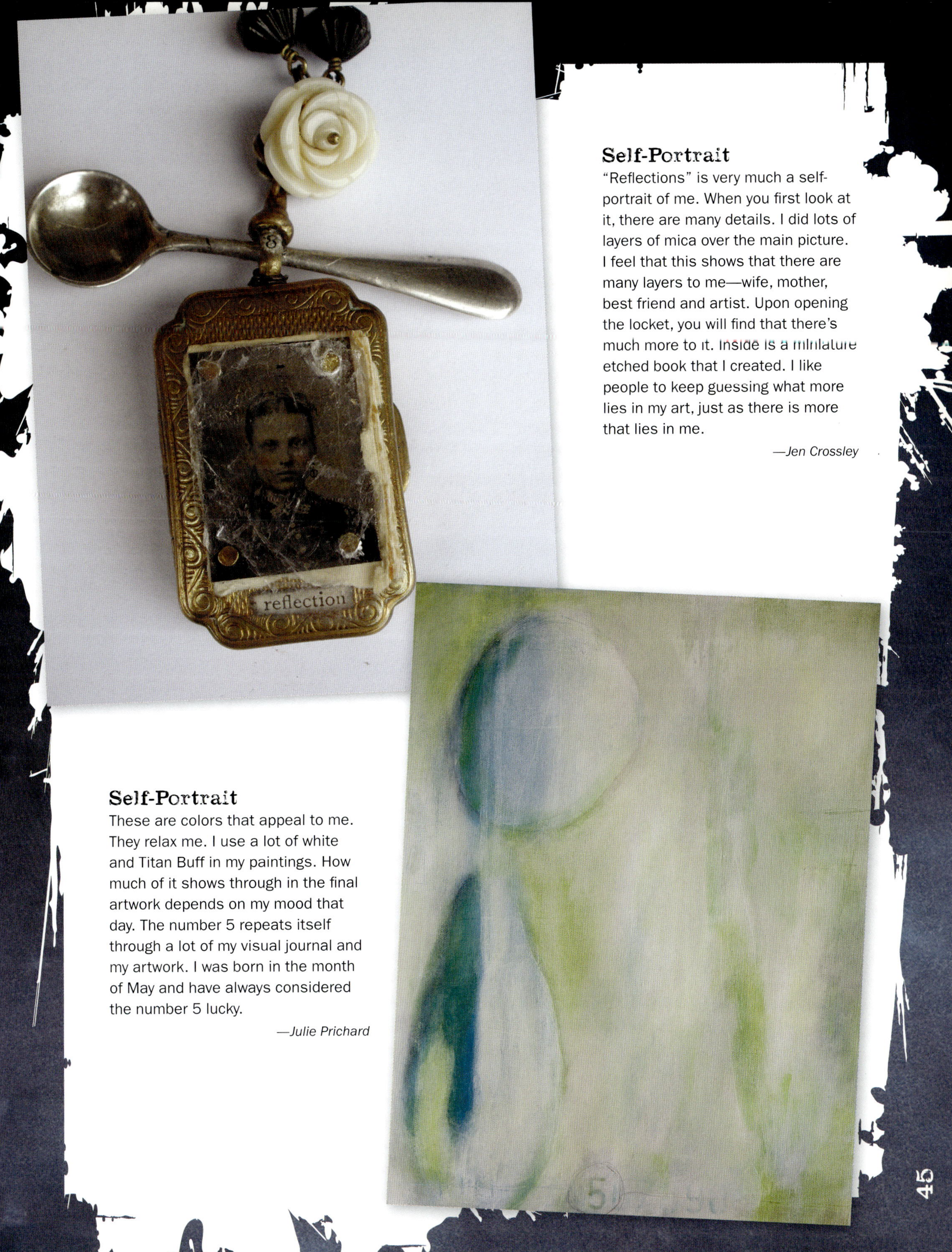

Self-Portrait

"Reflections" is very much a self-portrait of me. When you first look at it, there are many details. I did lots of layers of mica over the main picture. I feel that this shows that there are many layers to me—wife, mother, best friend and artist. Upon opening the locket, you will find that there's much more to it. Inside is a miniature etched book that I created. I like people to keep guessing what more lies in my art, just as there is more that lies in me.

—Jen Crossley

Self-Portrait

These are colors that appeal to me. They relax me. I use a lot of white and Titan Buff in my paintings. How much of it shows through in the final artwork depends on my mood that day. The number 5 repeats itself through a lot of my visual journal and my artwork. I was born in the month of May and have always considered the number 5 lucky.

—Julie Prichard

Is there one art material you couldn't live without?

Every artist has their one go-to supply that they would take to the proverbial desert island. Although there was a wide range of answers, most of the responses indicated that this group of artists went back to the basics. The three most popular materials were pencils, paint and acrylic medium.

Acrylic matte medium for collage. I have finally realized that I am a collage artist. I come from a painting background and have slowly added more and more collage to my work.

—Donna Watson

Antique lace, which reminds me of times past when folk really had a strong conviction about producing quality rather than cheap quantity.

—JoAnnA Pierotti

A graphite pencil because with just this one tool and any scrap of paper I can entertain myself for hours on end, it's cheap, you can find one just about anywhere, and it fits into the smallest of purses.

—Pam Carriker

I can't live without a camera. Any camera will do. I am a lazy artist. Taking photos is the effortless way of taking notes and doing research.

—Linda Woods

Acrylic paint. I can always find or make my own paper or other surfaces to paint on, or recycle my clothing if I wish to sew. I create my own inks and dyes and oftentimes fashion my own paintbrushes. Paint, however, is not something that I have ever created on my own (yet!).

—Alicia Caudle

A piece of charcoal may seem like a dusty, dirty stick with little value, but in the hands of an artist, it can become something magical, solid, dark and mysterious, pale and dreamy, transcendent.

—Karen Cole

I couldn't live without my stencils. I use them so often to create layers and a sense of history in my work.

—Gary Reef

Plaster. I never seem to finish exploring the possibilities that this medium offers.

—Patricia Larsen

Clay. I build with it. It's solid and sturdy, and it lets me push it around, punch it, shape it, mark on it, texture it, glaze it, fire it, and sometimes it gives me great satisfaction to hear the crashing sound it makes when I toss out a piece that stopped talking to me.

—Don Madden

My collection of brushes is one supply I wouldn't want to be without. I've grown to love and appreciate real paintbrushes versus the disposable foam brushes that used to be my staple.

—Michelle Ward

I consistently love to prowl through sheaves of my old drawings, defunct paintings and journal pages, and use slivers and bits of them in new collages. The tattered bits never fail to yield something fresh.

—Lynne Perrella

People! My artworks are about people, human stories and the history of them. Were they not present, it would be impossible for me to tell their stories.

—Judy Wilkenfeld

Ink. A drawing done in pencil just seems like a cheat, a doodle, a vague notion to me. I need the definiteness of black India ink.

—Danny Gregory

I am a huge fan of Golden's Acrylic Glazing Liquid; I never make anything without it. I frequently refer to it as "secret sauce."

—Julie Prichard

Oh, this question is cruel. Where do I start? I guess pencil. I love to write and draw so much.

—Judy Wise

Without a doubt my all time favorite supply is Caran d'Ache Neocolor II Watersoluble Crayons. In my humble opinion, they are the most vibrant, versatile, easy-to-use, take-it-along-on-my-journeys sort of color-in-a-stick!

—Vivian Bonder

The quick answer is that I couldn't live without a paintbrush, though I know I could create a tool to apply paint with. The real answer would have to be some kind of paint—watercolor, acrylic or oil.

—Jill Zaheer

Wood. I've been carving wood for many years so I'd feel lost without it.

—Robyn Gordon

I could not live without epoxy. When you are combining wood and metal and porcelain and antique items, sometimes a strong epoxy is your best friend.

—John Borrero

Words. I use them in almost every single piece of artwork I create, which is why I say that my designs are narrative, that every piece tells a story. Why? Because I am a writer, I suppose, and because I am in love with words and all that they imply.

—Nina Bagley

Gesso. I use it as a paste, paint and an embedding agent; you can add color to it, make it thinner or thicker, and it cleans up with soap and water.

—Angela Cartwright

Photographic images, for the simple reason they're the heart and soul of every piece I concoct.

—Sarah Fishburn

It sounds completely dramatic to declare that I could not live without encaustics. Even though I work in a variety of media, encaustics is just the perfect vehicle to express my complete inner vision.

—Bridgette Guerzon Mills

Acrylic medium. I use it all the time for collaging, protecting surfaces, adding texture, doing medium transfers, etc.

—Robert Maloney

A pencil *with* an eraser. I know that *real* sketchers discourage erasing, but I *love* erasing. I have an eraser that's so big that you need a crane to lift it.

—Lisa Hoffman

Graphite pencils. It wouldn't be easy to do without paint, oil pastels and colored pencils, but the one thing that I always use is a graphite pencil.

—Lynne Hoppe

Paper. Just like most of the human body is made up of water, most of my work is made up of paper. I wouldn't like to be stranded on an island without my papers to busy myself with.

—Orly Avineri

Metal almost always finds its way into my work. I love the texture and dimension added to a piece when metal is introduced. Metal can be cut, bent, hammered, engraved, patinaed, etched and melted. And it is enduring.

—Leslie Marsh

Found objects. These give me the biggest buzz in my art process. I find something unusual and I want to make it come to life once again.

—Jen Crossley

I couldn't live without water media—particularly acrylic paint. It plays well with other mediums. It slathers, it flings, it drips, it runs, and when dry, it stays put. I like that!

—Leslie Avon Miller

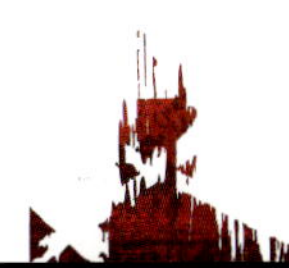

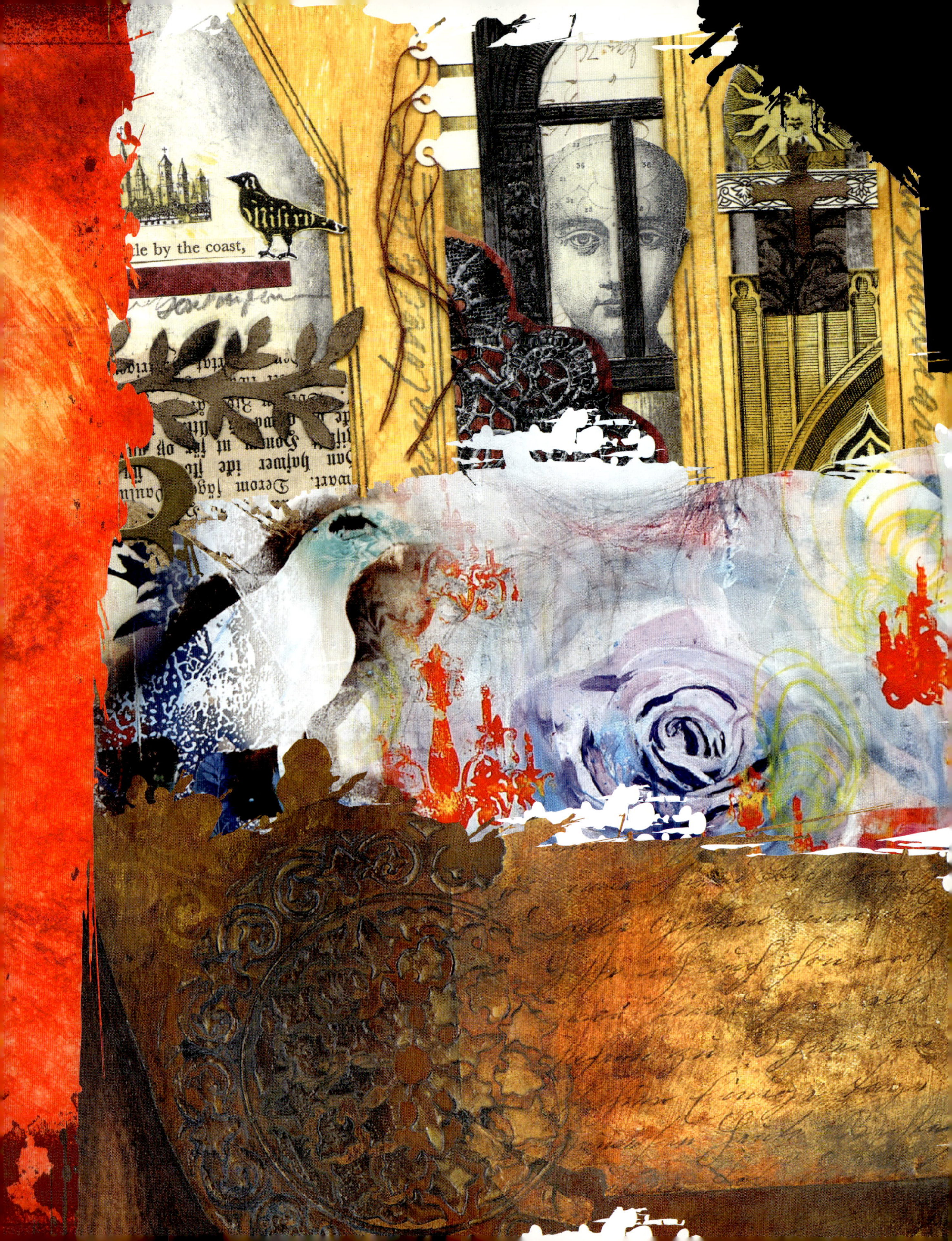
tle by the coast,

section two

Passion in Action

The first section of this book focused on the key ingredient that goes into the creation of every artwork: the artist. In the pages that follow, the journey takes you further into their hearts and minds. Within every artist, amateur or professional, is the drive to create. The successful artist finds a way to mine their inner emotions and reveal these through their art in a way that is compelling, moving and ultimately meaningful to the viewer. I believe the force behind this process is passion.

The passion of the artist is fueled by life experiences, creative influences, and hopes and dreams. Intimate emotions and feelings, such as anger and vulnerability, underlie the desire to create and are expressed in works of art. The obstacles that are faced and the regrets that may occur serve only to push each artist forward.

The thirty-one spotlight artists you have already come to know continue to share their passion to create in Section Two. Here they have all openly and generously shared personal thoughts about their own beliefs, wishes, doubts and challenges. There are questions and answers to read, artwork to see, and more intimate self-portraits to observe. You will also find additional survey responses from the larger group of participants. Read along and enjoy the trip into the artist's soul.

Who has had the most impact on your creative life?

For creative impact, family comes first. Well more than half of the spotlight artists listed family members, such as spouses, parents, grandparents, aunts and cousins, as having the most impact. Not surprisingly, mothers were number one. For the other half of the group, creative impact comes from friends, other artists and even themselves.

My mother, my sweet mother. Her subtleties, her intricacies, her sorrows, her absences, they all became mine and fueled my creativity. They still do. Through her beauty, I found mine. Through her silence, I found my voice.

—Orly Avineri

God.

—Patricia Larsen

It's me. Everything I express in my art is based on what I am feeling. It's the hardest part and the greatest benefit of being your own boss. Whether I am creating art for myself or for a client, I always start with how I feel or what I want to say. It always comes back to me.

—Linda Woods

My father. He's a retired art director and successful landscape painter. Growing up I always had some good exposure to both art and design.

—Robert Maloney

Definitely my mum. She has always allowed me to express myself freely and encouraged me to simply be me, forming an excellent basis for creativity.

—Vivian Bonder

My husband. This is my second marriage, and the last eleven years have helped me to grow so much. I never had the confidence before to stick my neck out. My "Fly-boy" gave me wings and taught me to fly, and for that I'll be ever grateful.

—Pam Carriker

My cousin Diane was ten years older than I. From the age of eight or so, I watched her artistic talent blossom, and from that moment I knew. Later in life, I met Paula, a ceramic artist, who lived a life that was full of style and creativity. It would have to be both women.

—Karen Cole

It was a friend of mine who said, "Ever heard of altered art?" Those words took me in the direction to alter my photographs. I always knew that photography was a part of me, but to step into a world of altered art . . . well it opened doors, and I'm glad I walked through them.

—Angela Cartwright

My parents. It was my mother's creativity that placed me in the art store when I was little. On the other hand, watching my dad fix everything himself has made me more inquisitive. My parents have instilled the strong sense of "do-it-yourself-itis" that I have today.

—Julie Prichard

If you keep a journal, do you keep it private?

Yes, all of my journals are for my eyes only: **20%**
Some journals I share, but some are private: **68%**
No, I am an open book and share all my journals: **12%**

My wife, Susan. Sometimes she sees beautiful things in my work that I never noticed until she talked about it. Sometimes I lose my momentum, and she has to tell me to put my Big-Boy Boxers on and get back to work. She's my best fan and my toughest critic. She's my soul.

—Don Madden

It would have to be my mother! She saw the potential in me at an early age, and she nurtured that creativity. "Follow your heart, follow your passion and believe in yourself" were words spoken to me often. Thanks, Mum!

—Gary Reef

Definitely my mother. She came over from England as a young woman and was an artist in every way. My mother had her own unique style. To me she was different from all the other mothers, not only because of her accent, but because she was an artist.

—Roxanne Evans Stout

My mother. From as far back as I can remember, she was always creating something and selling whatever she made to boost the family income. When I was a child, it just seemed natural to create art. It wasn't something that we thought about. It was a lifestyle.

—Robyn Gordon

As a child, it was my Aunt Anetta. She is a wonderful artist and always made me feel that all of my artwork was wonderful. As an adult, I would have to say that it came through contact with a series of people—all of whom helped me find my inner voice.

—Jill Zaheer

I can*not* pin this down on a single person—sorry! My mother, her parents, books and movies, Sarah Bernhardt, the Pre-Raphaelites, Emma Goldman, Joseph Cornell, Marc Chagall, Billie Holiday, INXS, Keith Haring, my kids, everyone whose world collides with mine, every day of my life.

—Sarah Fishburn

I cannot really attribute one person to this. The ebb and flow of my creative life is dependent upon and influenced by those about which I am making a piece of art. Influences of time, place, those who enter my life's path and journey subsequently have and have had an impact on my creative life.

—Judy Wilkenfeld

That would have to be my father, although it's not easy to choose just one person. Growing up with someone who creates whatever they need from scratch (and it turns out beautifully) gives you a "can do" attitude about making stuff.

—Lynne Hoppe

I am lucky to have a small circle of friends with whom I share the love of art. We each have a different approach, yet we respect and appreciate each other's styles. I think this creative life wouldn't be nearly as rewarding if I didn't have these friends to share the enthusiasm, the passion, and the vision of how good it feels to be plugged in as an artist.

—Michelle Ward

My grandmother, Josephine Sansone, who passed away several years ago at ninety-one. Nana created all her life. I love that even though she is no longer on this planet in human form, her spirit lives on, and her creations left behind remind us of her beautiful spirit and passion she had to create.

—JoAnnA Pierotti

My husband. He has always believed in me and my work, and has been the one to push me in getting my work out into the world. He believed in me when I did not. He inspires me to be the best that I can and to keep going.

—Bridgette Guerzon Mills

My mother. She and my father always encouraged me to follow my love of making things, drawing and painting. My mother in particular gave me a strong sense of being loved and treasured.

—Judy Wise

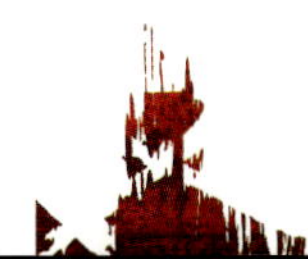

Who has had the most impact on your creative life?

My wife, Patti, always encouraged me in many ways. She was my inspiration when I first started making art, and she always gave me lavish praise and shrewd direction. She was a great reader and a great editor, too, and would gently prod me in new and exciting directions, always making my work better and more daring.

—Danny Gregory

Can I say "people" instead of "person?" I have a tight group of Magical People who believe in me and cheer me on every step of the way. There are some heavy-hitter role models in my life for sure, but honestly, I think that it's the people who talk to us and love us *every day* who make the difference.

—Lisa Hoffman

Teesha Moore. She began publishing my artwork in her Studio zine back in 1999, and hired me to teach my very first class, in 2001, at the first Artfest. She and her husband Tracy were godsends when I was going through a divorce and I will forever be grateful for their encouragement and support.

—Nina Bagley

Actually, it's me. I'm the one who has made my art a priority, who has invested many hours and resources into being an artist. Of course, I feel a deep sense of gratitude to my supportive husband, the many workshop instructors who have shared their love of creativity, and my closest artist friends.

—Leslie Avon Miller

My husband. Over the years, he was always supportive of whatever decisions I made dealing with marketing and sales, even when I decided to take a few years off to develop a new medium and style of painting. Even now, he helps me frame and ship paintings.

—Donna Watson

My dear friend, Yves Le Meitour. When we met a dozen years ago, I was very shy and quirky. He would often present me artful tasks to complete. This really helped me out of my shell, making it easier for me to share my work with others, which had previously been impossibile.

—Alicia Caudle

I got my creative side from my mum, who was always making things, but someone who has impacted my creative life would be my dear sis (not related by birth but by choice), Linda Lynch. We met online many years ago. Linda always encourages me and makes me strive to be a better artist and person.

—Jen Crossley

My grandmother was a prolific crafter. She sewed quilts, embroidered dishtowels, tatted doilies, made afghans, Christmas ornaments, baby booties, etc. She often asked for my input for patterns, incorporating them into her design, building my confidence, making me feel like I was an artist.

—Leslie Marsh

My community of friends and family has been extraordinarily supportive of me and really pushed me to explore my own art. Probably the single most significant step that I've taken as an artist was joining an online artist community. If I am an artist today, I have that community to thank for it.

—John Borrero

I never know which of my Influences will guide me on any given day. Perhaps the inspired lust for color of Romare Bearden? Or the fondness for tattered, weathered and scratchy materials, a la Hannelore Baron? By crediting and acknowledging our Influences, we are consciously honoring all the enthusiasms and inspirations that feed our spirit every time we enter the studio.

—Lynne Perrella

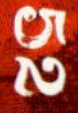

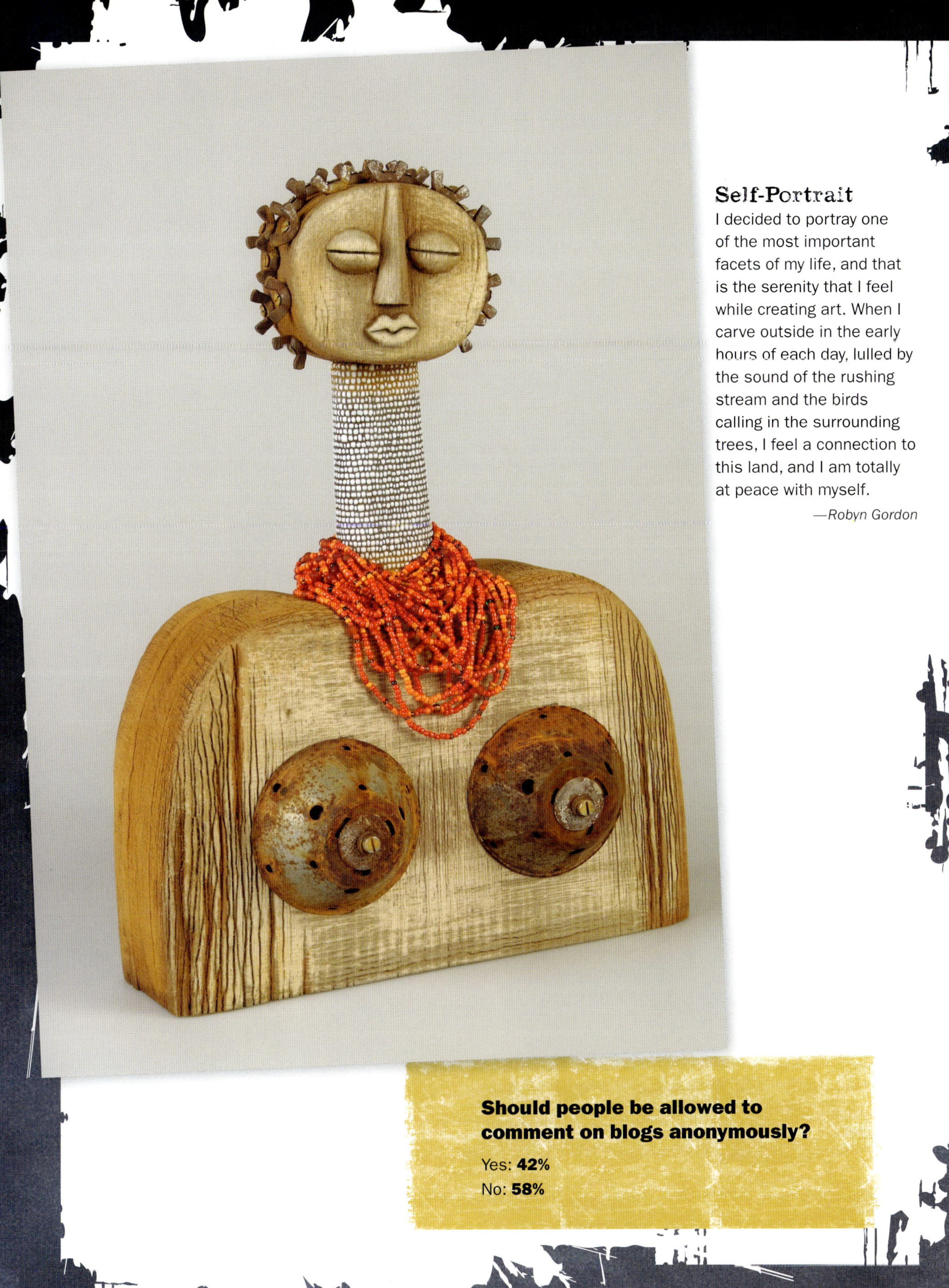

Self-Portrait

I decided to portray one of the most important facets of my life, and that is the serenity that I feel while creating art. When I carve outside in the early hours of each day, lulled by the sound of the rushing stream and the birds calling in the surrounding trees, I feel a connection to this land, and I am totally at peace with myself.

—Robyn Gordon

Should people be allowed to comment on blogs anonymously?

Yes: **42%**

No: **58%**

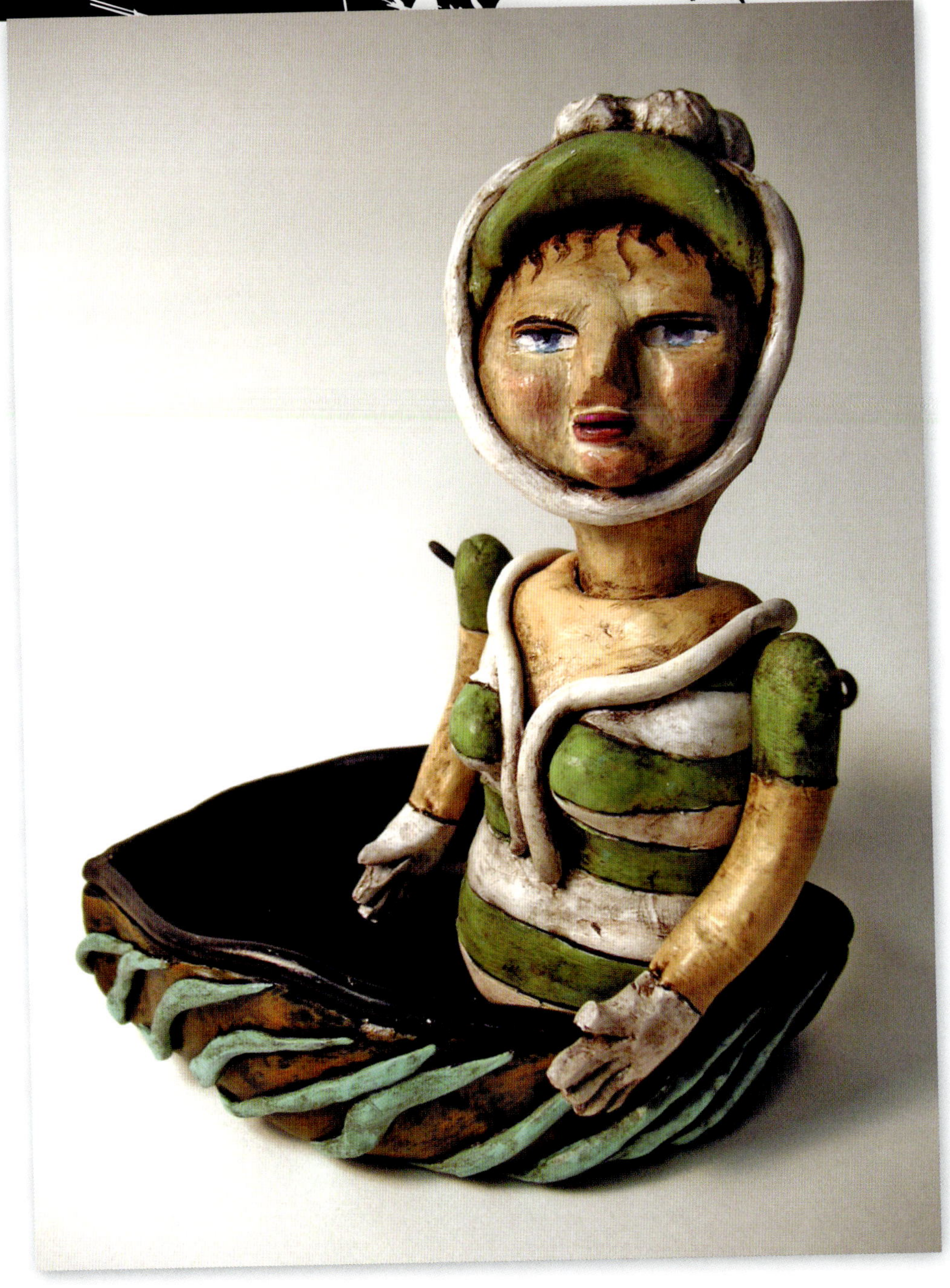

Self-Portrait

The boat has appeared in my work for over a decade now. Maybe because I live in the Pacific Northwest it feels like the perfect metaphor for safety as I make my way through the perilous currents of life. A little, fragile boat, crafted with my own hands, protection enough against the elements. Sometimes I have company in the boat (a house, a companion), but in this piece I do not.

—Judy Wise

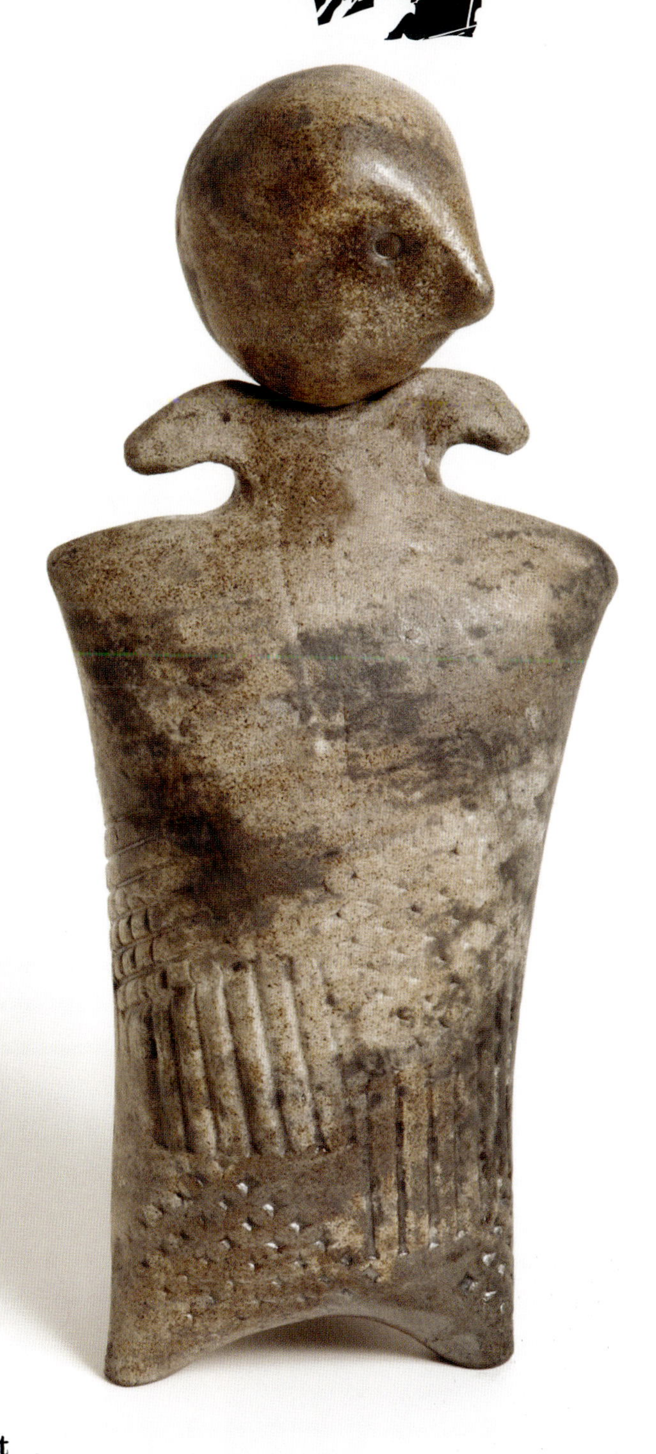

Self-Portrait

I've been around for a while. My hair is disappearing, my belly is growing, and my body is showing the past wear and tear of too many years in the corporate world. There are days when my hands refuse to play nicely with the clay. In spite of all that, I'm looking on down the road ahead.

—Don Madden

How do you express passion in your artwork?

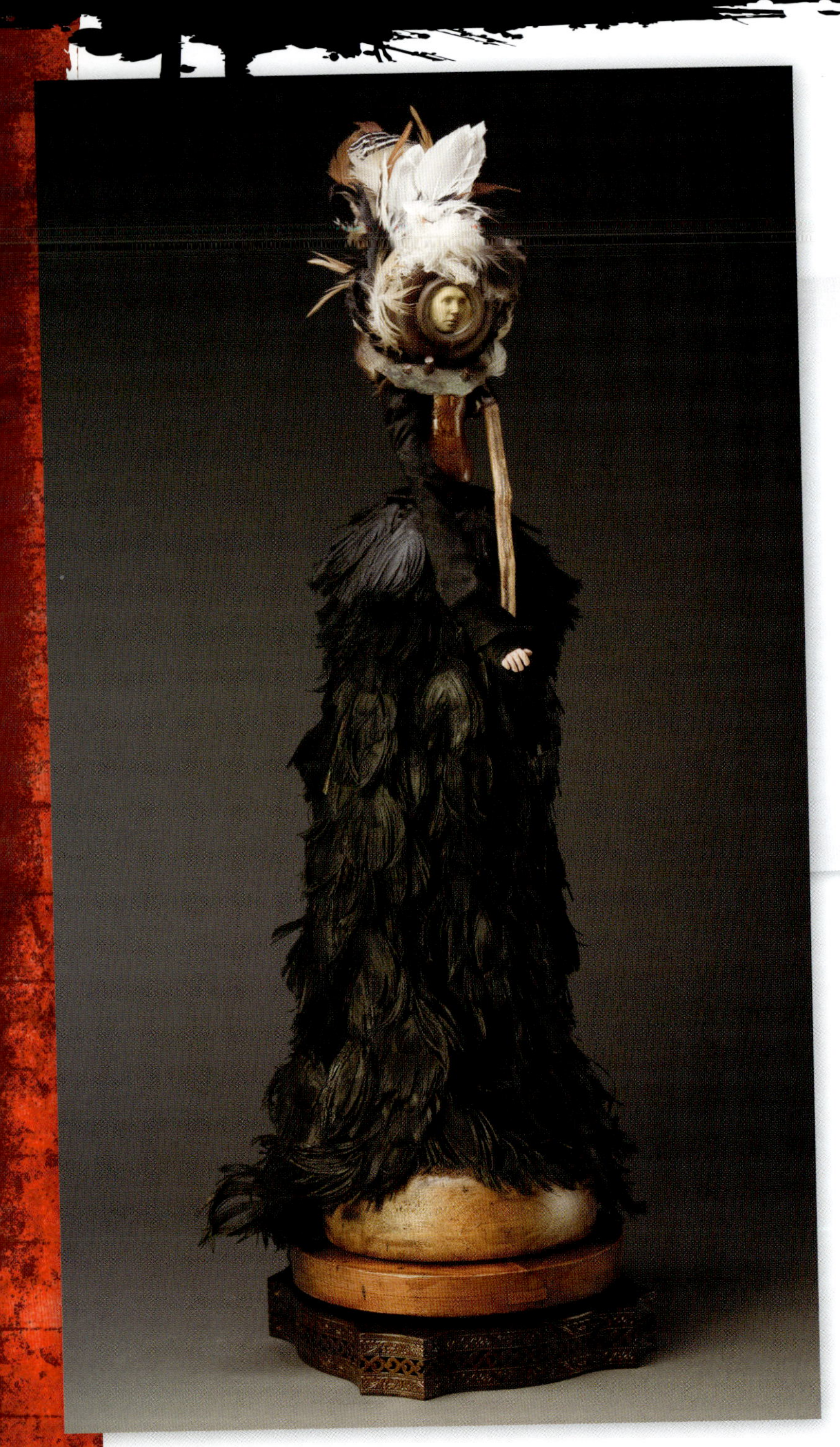

Persephone

In making my sculptures, the passion comes through in my ability to bring energy to my pieces and to give them a sense of emotion and movement. My goal is to make my pieces feel alive to people . . . full of human character. When people see my work and feel drawn to a piece, or even when people find my pieces to be "intense" or engaging, I know that the piece has achieved that sense of personality. If, in the end, there is enough of a human voice in a 22" tall assemblage of repurposed materials for people to be engaged emotionally, then I feel fulfilled—and genuinely relieved and happy.

— John Borrero

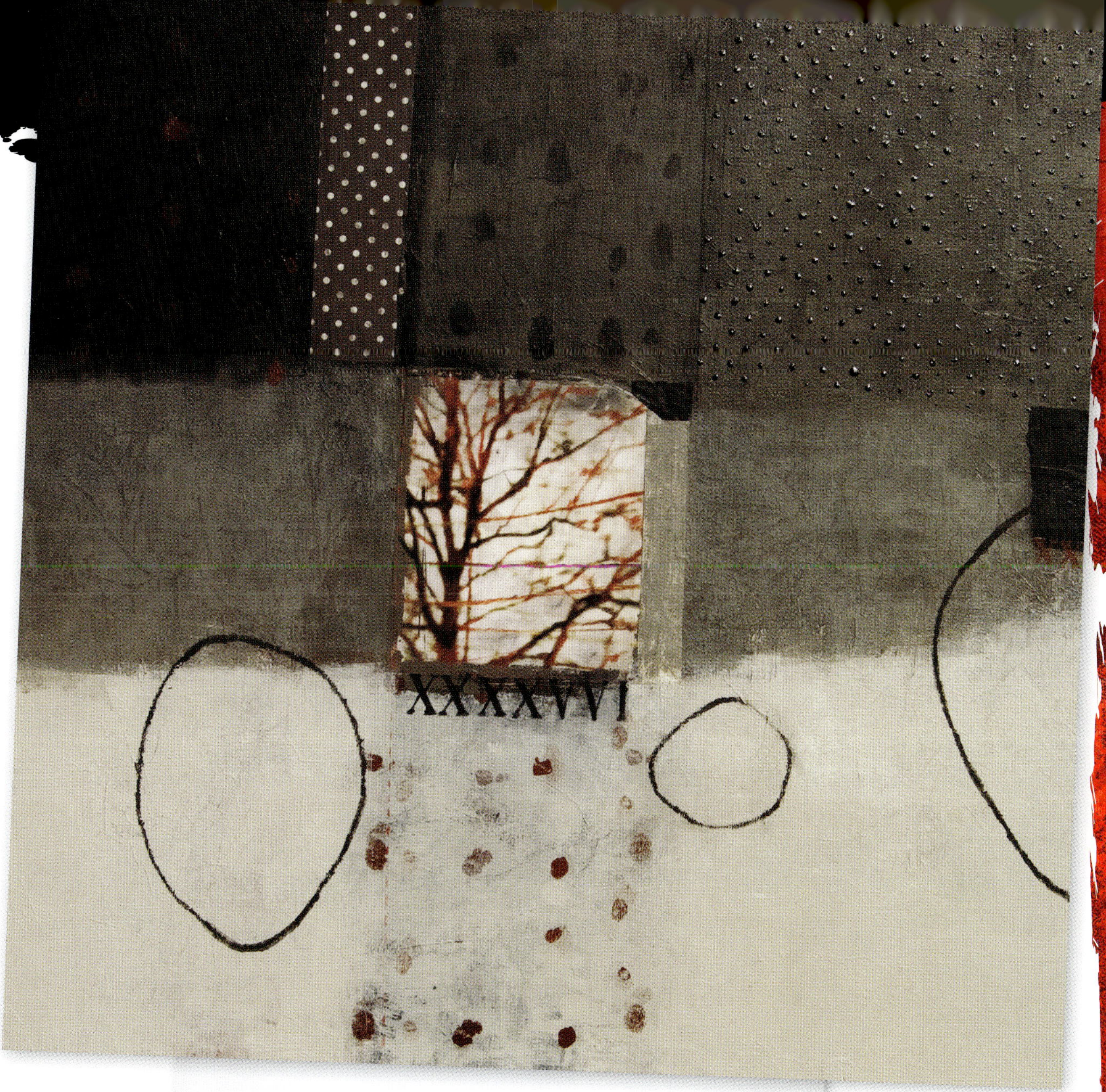

Endless Cycles

One of my passions is nature-based images. Another passion I have is for textures. I see dots, dashes, circles, letters and numbers as textures, as well as surface textures which I create with paint and textured papers. I build up layers of paint and papers, trying to achieve different textures. A black or white surface with lots of textures can really turn me on.

— *Donna Watson*

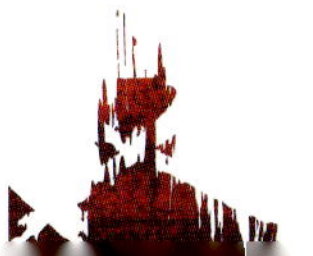

How do you express passion in your artwork?

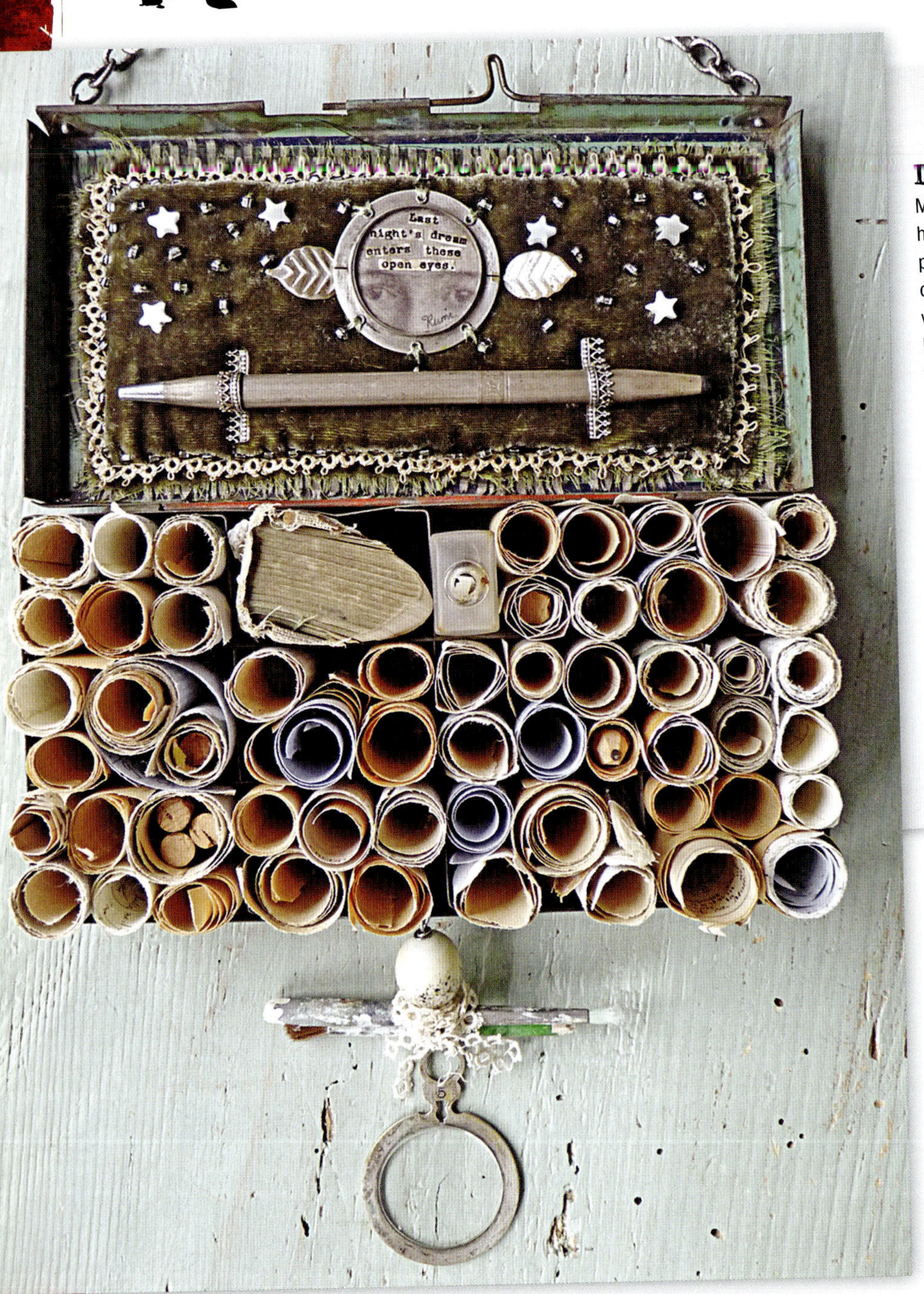

Last Night's Dream

My artwork is focused expressly on the human emotion, and never do I create a piece without an image, a few words or a combination of the two. The base of this work is a wonderful vintage mechanic's hinged tin box with metal dividers inside that form a grid. The papers are tightly rolled and stacked upon one another. Within several, I've written a few very strong passions, wishes and dreams of mine, with the intention of taking papers throughout the years and writing down additional dreams, then tucking them back into the collection. Honored here, then, are my passions of writing, of art, of friends . . . and of wishes and dreams.

— *Nina Bagley*

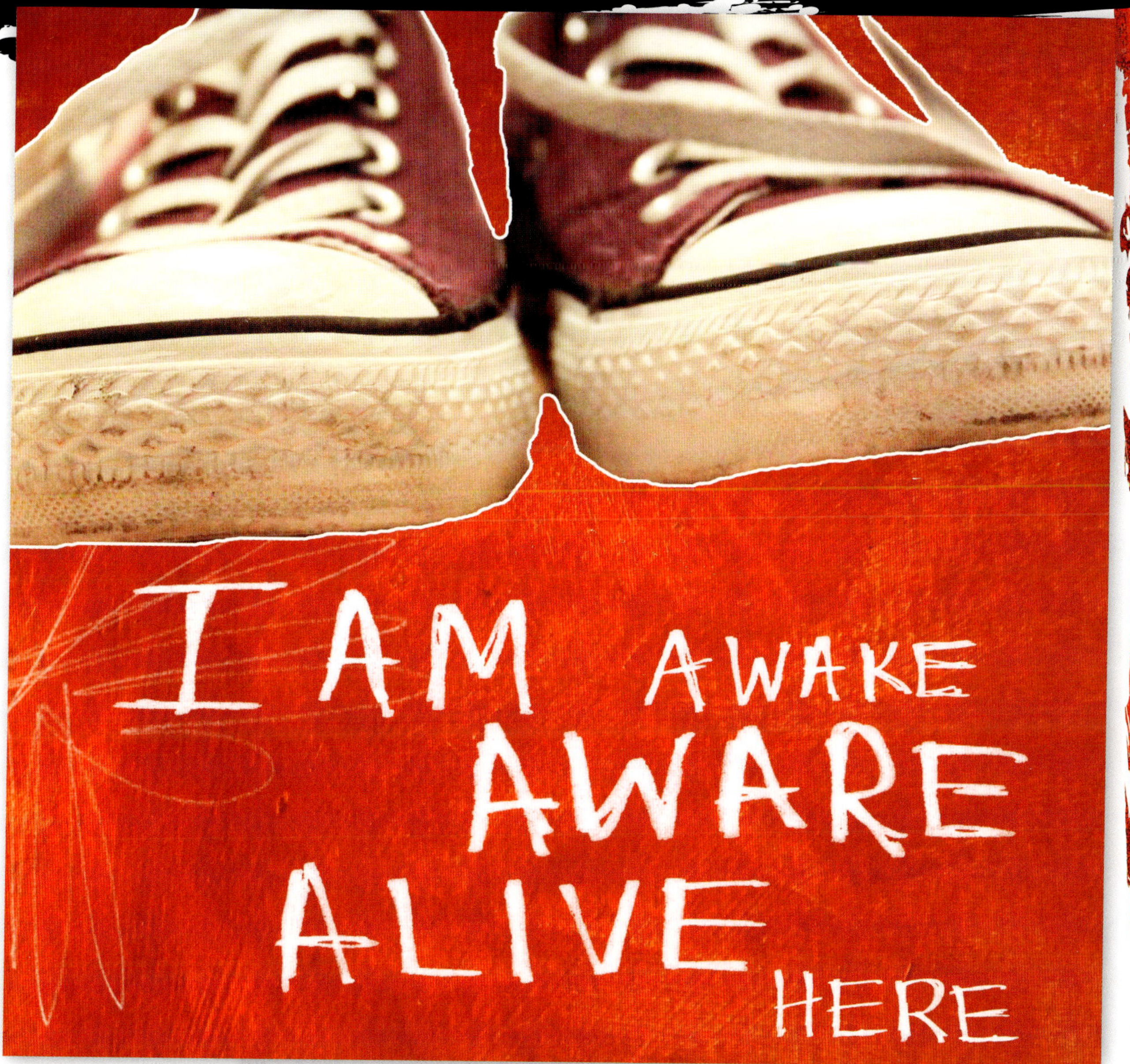

With My Shoes On

I express passion in my art by showing up and being present. I express passion by expressing myself passionately in bold colors with confidence and simplicity. In this journal page, I have captured the moment of my feet firmly on the ground and being ready and excited to explore what life is about to offer me.

— *Linda Woods*

If you had your choice of fame versus income as an artist, which would you choose?

By far, the majority of artists chose income. The main reason given was that income would allow them to continue to pursue their artistic passion. Fame was also chosen by some, primarily because that would indicate that they were respected and appreciated as artists. And for quite a few, neither fame nor income was a focus in their artistic pursuits.

Tough one. I guess somewhere in between. Living comfortably doing the things I love in my own way while gaining some recognition along the way.

—Robert Maloney

I have always imagined that with fame comes income . . . but if I had to choose one or the other, I would choose income. With income I would be more relaxed knowing that my family would remain comfortable even during uncertain economic times.

—Julie Prichard

I have seen that if I'm genuine in my art, people find me and follow me. If I can continue producing art that feels honest and have it still appeal to people, I can ask for nothing more. So I suppose that means a moderate income with a modest amount of recognition and I'm happy.

—John Borrero

Fame is nice, and I've had a little taste of it, but if I had to choose between the two, I'd always go for being able to support myself as an artist. For the past twenty years, I have been able to sustain a full-time career on my own. What a gift that has been from the universe!

—Nina Bagley

My first impulse is to choose fame. It is a wonderful feeling to be appreciated and know that people can relate to your work and be touched in some profound way by what you, as an artist, have created. That being said, many famous people have said that their fame has impacted their lives in a negative way.

—Karen Cole

The part of me that sees being an artist as work is also the part that has a growing family and would love to have steady income come from my art. The part of me that feels that being an artist is a calling doesn't necessarily want fame, but rather respect from my peers and the outside world.

—Bridgette Guerzon Mills

Actually I would choose neither. What I seek is the thrill of experimentation, the joy of resolution and the satisfaction of creating. By not particularly seeking fame or income, I am free to focus on creating my art. It's my gift to myself.

—Leslie Avon Miller

I would pick getting my art exposed to more people rather than making lots of money. Because I have income from my job as a teacher, I don't need my art to be my moneymaker. Mostly I just want to stay true to my art.

—Roxanne Evans Stout

Income! Having an income would allow me to continue creating art and to bring some of those grand ideas into reality occasionally.

—Gary Reef

What would boost your creativity the most?

More time: **51%**
More space: **37%**
More supplies: **12%**

Income. I need the income more than I need fame, and I don't think fame would bring me what I'm searching for in life. I love creating art in solitude, and I love seeing all the details of nature that thrive in stillness. Perhaps fame would clash with these ideals.

—Robyn Gordon

I'd be less than candid if I said that the monetary rewards aren't a perk. However, I do not make my artistic decisions based on economics.

—Angela Cartwright

I'd choose income. Fame would mean more social engagements, which would mean less time for art, and I wouldn't like that.

—Lynne Hoppe

At the chance of sounding really lame I am going to choose neither. I am not sure if I were famous and/or making income from my art that I would be able to keep doing what I love best in my own unique way without thinking of the consequences.

—Vivian Bonder

Fame. I like the responses from people when they "get it." However, if you want to give me some money, I won't turn it down.

—Don Madden

I would choose income. In this way, I would be able to pursue all the art dreams I can't currently fulfill because of lack of time.

—Jill Zaheer

I don't really want either. My goal is simply to catalogue my experiences, to understand them better, and if I have any influence on others, it's simply to encourage them to do the same. My artwork is the by-product of my experience and observation of life. I can't imagine it attracting fame or fortune.

—Danny Gregory

I doubt that with my artwork I would seek either fame or income because that does not reflect what my work is about nor what I am about as a person and an artist. My art speaks to social justice issues, but for me, if one person is affected positively, then the recognition of a job well done has been achieved.

—Judy Wilkenfeld

I would choose income over fame. Being able to depend on a steady and respectable income from making art would open up a lot of new directions that would be a dream to explore. There are destinations and events I would love to visit that would fill me with inspiration.

—Michelle Ward

Fame is a mirage. I don't think I could handle the demands or loss of privacy. I'm better at spending money.

—Judy Wise

Definitely my answer would be income. Fame is not important to me, and I do not seek after it. Validation comes when someone purchases my art. Because I have a passion for finding various objects to use in my work, income gives me the opportunity to purchase more supplies.

—JoAnnA Pierotti

As for fame? I can now leave the desire for fame in a smoldering heap, crushed under my boot heel. Now seriously, who cares? As for art income? Smart people always have a Plan B.

—Lisa Hoffman

I think we all want to be famous in our own little way, but I find the income helps me pursue my art more. It gives me opportunities to buy more supplies, to take classes from other artists I admire and to learn new techniques to help my art to evolve. So it's income for me.

—Jen Crossley

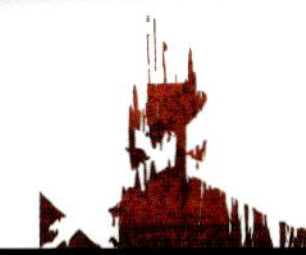

If you had your choice of fame versus income as an artist, which would you choose?

Fame, because who acquired one of my paintings would mean more to me than how many paintings I sold. Fame would mean that others respect my work.

Donna Watson

Income, most definitely! I am the type that gets a bit anxious and awkward around others, and I really, really despise attention being drawn to myself. Plus, you can't really spend fame at a flea market.

Alicia Caudle

Fame, because with fame comes opportunity to share on so many different levels. Having artwork and a book published has allowed me to teach in many venues. Nothing makes my day more than getting an email from someone who found one of my articles or workshops helpful.

—Pam Carriker

Call me pragmatic, but I would choose Income (with a capital I, and a steady one at that). Then I wouldn't always have to weigh keeping a roof over our heads or filling the bare cupboards against buying a batch of Prismacolors—always deciding what we will have to do without.

—Sarah Fishburn

I would choose necessity over luxury. I would make sure there is abundance of yummy food on my table and a terra-cotta roof over my head, maybe even a vegetable garden visible through my kitchen window. Once I have that taken care of, I wouldn't mind at all being noticed.

—Orly Avineri

Income. I can't buy a flexible shaft with fame. Then again, if one had enough fame, it should be fairly easy to parlay that into income. I am unable to see myself as famous; I can more easily see myself as rich.

—Leslie Marsh

Money so I always have the funds to keep making art.

—Patricia Larsen

I would choose income. I like the security of a roof over my head and food on my table. I like the security and comfort of being an observer. With fame comes the loss of anonymity, and as soon as you become the one everyone is looking at, your perspective changes.

—Linda Woods

Overall does your family support your life in art?

Yes, 100% behind me: **59%**
Sometimes yes, sometimes no: **34%**
No, they just don't get it: **7%**

Have you ever told another artist that you like their work when you actually didn't?

Yes, that happens often: **5%**
Yes, but only occasionally: **38%**
No, I just don't offer any feedback: **52%**
No, I always share my opinion even if negative: **5%**

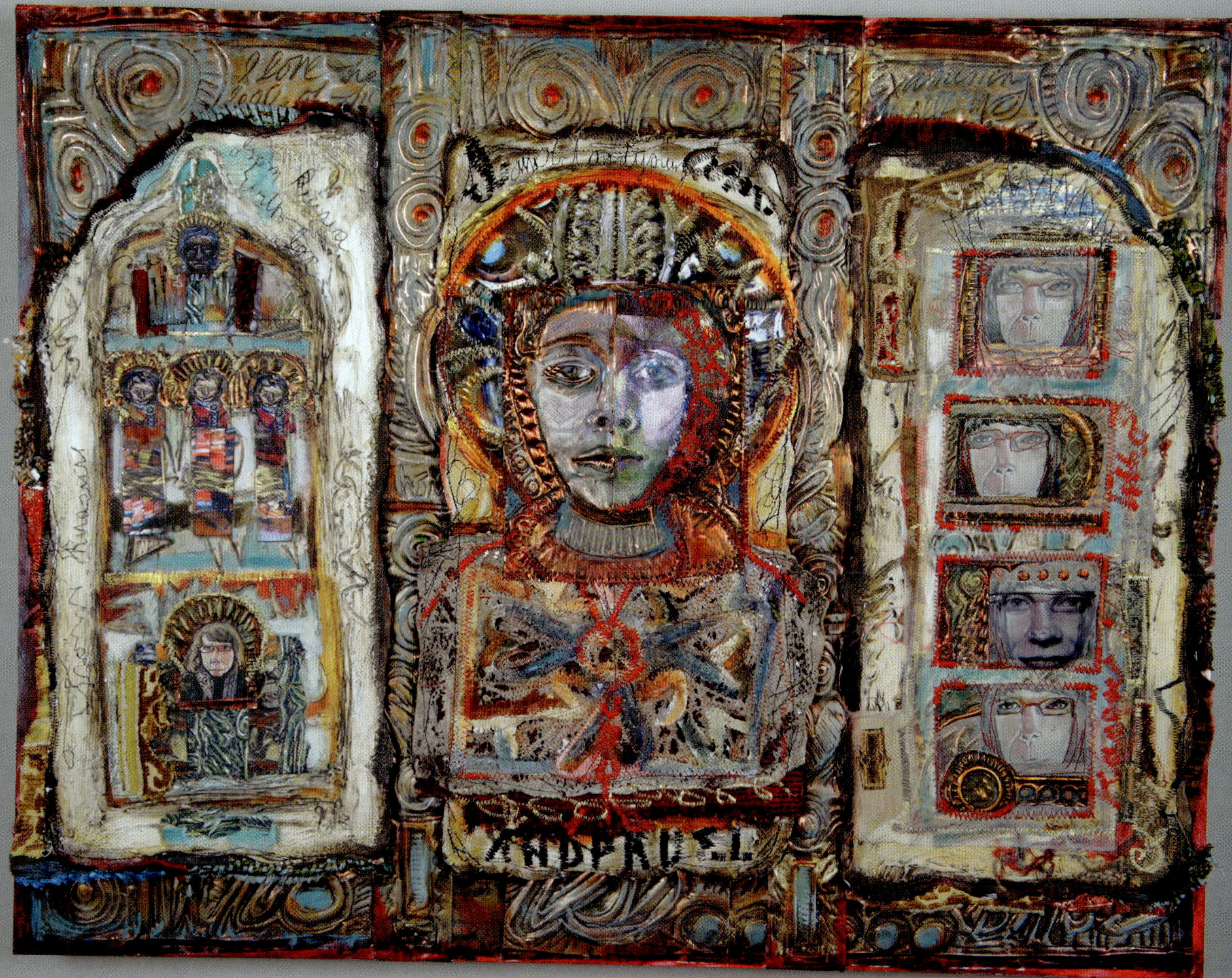

Self-Portrait

I remember sitting cross-legged in front of a three-sided mirror in college painting my first self-portrait, wondering which side of the mirror was the real me. Red shirt, torn jeans with dried paint marks, unsmiling, trying to be an artist, full of angst. The inspiration for this work stems from a most amazing weekend spent with ten artists—led by Lynne Perrella—in Clinton, Massachusetts, where we had a tour of the Museum of Russian Icons. I chose to create a triptych, in a way re-creating the first self-portrait (there is an actual piece of that very painting in this new self-portrait). I have attempted to record the passage of time. This work carries the memory of both parents and my aging process.

—Karen Cole

What is your most quirky creative habit?

Quirky comes in all colors of the rainbow, and each of the spotlight artists seems to have their own unique hue. Many consider their actual technique as quirky. For some, their quirkiness relates to the habits they have before they begin to create, whether that is cleaning their workspace, dancing, meditating or leaving their canvas out in the light of the full moon.

I have to (*have to*) clean my worktable off beforc I can start a new project. It clears my head and helps me to focus on the task at hand. I feel absolutely frustrated if I have to work amidst a mess from a previous project.

—Pam Carriker

Multiple journals: One in which I glue printouts of artwork of artists and photos of color combinations that I like; one that I call my "Collection of Words;" a third that is a visual journal where I collage, paint and write; and yet one more journal that I bring to lectures or workshops that I attend.

—Bridgette Guerzon Mills

Picking up anything that catches my eye—whether on a city sidewalk, beach or deserted road—and putting it in my pocket for some future art project.

—Patricia Larsen

Does drawing with my nondominant hand count? If not, it certainly makes my art look quirky!

—Lynne Hoppe

I love dots and circles. There are dots or circles on my socks, scarves, some home decor, tote bags, dishes and cups, even dishtowels. Dots and circles invariably end up in my paintings and collages.

—Donna Watson

Prior to creating when using fabrics, I must have order, or at least attempt it. I like little piles of fabric stacked by the same color. Unfortunately, before I know it, the little segregated piles become one huge disassembled mess. But I never give up and start the process over every time.

—JoAnnA Pierotti

I start off using a brush, but always end up using my fingers to paint. Then I end up having to wash a brush with globs of paint on it but needing to turn on the taps with my hands full of color. Sometimes I also paint my hands on purpose to find out the effect of the color on my state of being.

—Vivian Bonder

Do you think of art as therapeutic?

Yes, art is my form of therapy: **45%**

Sometimes art can be therapeutic for me: **49%**

No, art is just art: **6%**

Do you consider digital art to be equal to hand-done art?

Yes: **29%**

No: **35%**

Too different to compare: **36%**

I get a kick out of carving outside with monkeys peering down at me.

—Robyn Gordon

If I am about to start a new piece or work on a new project, I will find any excuse to avoid my studio. "Honey, can I take out the trash?" Once I have started something, stay out of my way. Creating is my only form of meditation, yet it is so difficult to begin. I wish I could explain that.

—Karen Cole

I have a ritual when preparing a stretched canvas. Before I can begin working on it, I must leave it to be exposed to the light of a full moon. I guess I believe that the energy and light from the moon somehow breathes life into the canvas. Weird, I know, but mine is not to question, but to do!

—Gary Reef

My compulsion to write everything down. Going back to childhood—journals that have followed me around most of my life like ducklings.

—Judy Wise

I only draw in books—it's a limitation, but one I like. I can't frame this work or display it, and people need to sit down and look at it intimately, one-on-one.

—Danny Gregory

I can't throw away the paper I use as a table protector. The random, layered, messy craft paper that lines my work surface is evidence of the art process that I cannot discard. I attach these palettes in my journal, and I have made use of them by incorporating them into a piece.

—Michelle Ward

When I feel that I'm finished with a painting, I sign the piece and know that it's done. Invariably, I seem to always go back to rework parts of the painting—starting by taking my name off the painting until, again, I feel that it is really finished. At that time, I re-sign the painting.

—Jill Zaheer

I love to dance to African or South American music between projects or when I take little breaks from my current painting or collage. And when something good happens on my canvas, my heart beats fast as if I am newly in love! Maybe this happens to everyone.

—Roxanne Evans Stout

One quirk would be starting forty-three projects in unison. I don't know why, but I cannot work on just one or two things at a time. A second quirk would be making my house look like a tornado passed though it with the way I have to spread things out all over the place while amid my numerous projects.

—Alicia Caudle

When I am doing art, I consume large amounts of caffeine and eat lots of junk food, and I do my best work from 8P.M. to 6A.M. I am on sort of a vampire's art schedule.

—John Borrero

My entire creative process is a bit fragmented. I first art-journal on my wild and super messy table in one room, then move to another to scan my journal pages and further work on them. And I cannot settle down to work on a piece if the kitchen is a wreck.

—Orly Avineri

Hoarding. I can't help myself. Things I have dragged in from the woods are tucked into every corner of the house, propped up over picture frames, in jars, tucked between pages of books. Some things I eventually use; others simply gather dust.

—Nina Bagley

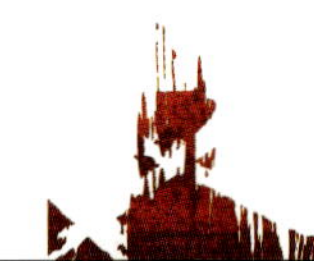

What is your most quirky creative habit?

I love things that make texture in clay because they make me look at my world in a different way. A typewriter ball becomes a secret language. A golf tee becomes an eye. I always get strange looks when I'm gathering stuff up at garage sales.

Don Madden

I keep a freakishly clean work area. I can easily tell you in which plastic tote even the smallest scrap of ephemera is located. When people see photos of my studio, they think I have just cleaned for the photo-op. Nope. I am a neat freak.

—Julie Prichard

I find myself going into a deeper meditative state while working on a piece. In order to achieve the correct placement and finding of objects to convey my story, going into this state seems to bring the right energy to it.

—Judy Wilkenfeld

I keep papers with coffee stains or paint spills, feathers I find and the smallest slivers of photographs that I have cut up. And sometimes . . . I use them.

—Angela Cartwright

I think everything I do is normal! I suspect some of my friends might say one of my quirky art-related habits is related to the one supply I can't live without—the camera. I take photos of everything, especially in places where there are big signs that say NO PHOTOS.

—Linda Woods

Overly-enthusiastic erasing.

—Lisa Hoffman

Maybe it's quirky that I have a large studio with three separate workspaces, and they are generally so covered with stuff that I work on the island in my kitchen.

—Leslie Marsh

I love having my iPod up full blast while creating and singing out of tune at the top of my voice with my children telling me to turn it down. Revenge is sweet, I say. It makes me feel happy, and the creative juices flow away. A happy mum makes happy art, I say.

—Jen Crossley

In the process of creating, I take as much paint off of a piece as I put on. However, I have learned how to recycle/re-use much of that paint in an effort to be respectful of the planet and our resources.

—Leslie Avon Miller

When I go to a museum or gallery, I always enter the door and navigate through the space by going to the right and continue going through the rooms always going to the right until I've seen every room and return to the door I started with. I seldom miss a room.

—Robert Maloney

What is your most creative or productive time of day?

Morning: **41%**
Afternoon: **22%**
Evening: **22%**
Middle of the night: **15%**

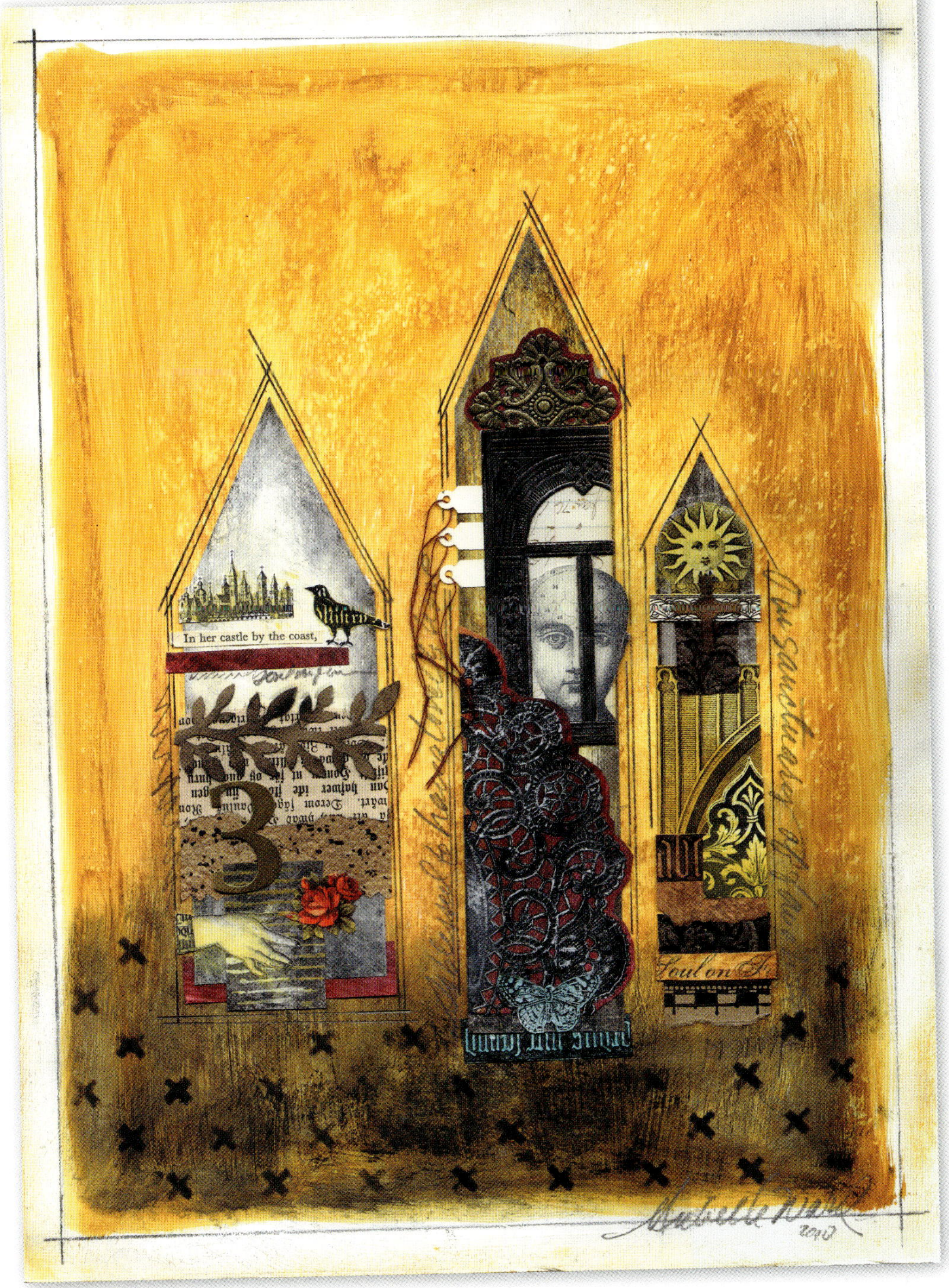

Self-Portrait

My interpretation of "self-portrait" is any expression that gives you an insight to the person. This piece illustrates my interests, both past and present, and includes many of my favorite images, patterns and colors. I prefer to rely on the mystery of meaning with layers of secrets embedded within, versus presenting an imitation or reproduction of my likeness.

—Michelle Ward

What is the one choice as an artist that you regret having made or not made?

Nearly all the responses to this question fell into four categories. The most common regret was not having had more formal education or training. A close second was actually not having any regrets at all but instead embracing life as it is. Close behind that was the regret of not pursuing art earlier in life. And in fourth place was wishing that there had been more opportunity to travel.

I wish that I had allowed myself to make art earlier. I had a long dry spell from my mid-teens to my late thirties when I did not commit to making things. It would be nice to have illustrated journals documenting those lost years, a record of what I was doing and seeing and feeling.

—Danny Gregory

I wish I had given up my day job ten years earlier and concentrated on creating the art that makes me happy. It always comes down to income and yet I have found that no matter what medium or genre I am passionate about, it has always generated a fairly regular income. If only I had had faith in myself earlier.

—Robyn Gordon

There are no regrets. It's all a journey. Each decision you make informs the next step in the process.

—Michelle Ward

I regret not going to art school. Art school ensures one will spend time focusing on art, and for many, defines the graduate as an artist. So much time saved on that question. I think it would have been wonderful to learn at the hands of experts, and to study with others who had the same compulsion.

—Leslie Marsh

Finding the time and money to travel more.

—Patricia Larsen

I regret that while I was young, single and ambitious that I did not attend art school somewhere in Europe. Knowing what I know now and the desires within, I would have made that choice early on. Knowledge and experience helps add depth to creating art.

—JoAnnA Pierotti

I do not like to hold on to regrets and "what-ifs," because I feel that everything happens for a reason. But if I had to pick one, I would say that I regret not studying art in college. I would love to have the academic background, not for status or legitimacy, but for the knowledge base.

—Bridgette Guerzon Mills

Every choice I made while on my way to becoming the artist that I am today brought me closer to the profound realization that we are all innately creative and eager, that I don't belong to an elite group, and that I am part of a wondrous community that's called Humanity. I truly wish I understood it earlier.

—Orly Avineri

Would you describe yourself as talented?

Yes, I recognize my talent: **49%**
Yes, but I don't always admit it: **38%**
No, I just don't feel that way: **13%**

I believe that I have no regrets so far. Timing sometimes plays a part though. I'm trying, and have been trying, to make my dream come true to teach in the United States. It's difficult to break in, but it is my one dream.

—Jen Crossley

While living in Europe, I have never made the effort to go to Barcelona to admire Gaudi's stunning and inspiring architecture.

—Vivian Bonder

I have no regrets. Sometimes, though, I wish that life would reverse itself and the adults would go to college. I did not know what the value of my art college education was when I was there.

—Karen Cole

I regret not having enough time to spend going out to look at more art and traveling to see more art. Often I end up cooped up in my studio or tied up with responsibilities and not getting out to museums, galleries and open studios as much as I'd like.

—Robert Maloney

I can't think of any choices that I regret. Even so-called bad ones taught me something, so I wouldn't change them.

—Lynne Hoppe

As an artist, I probably should have stayed in school. As a person, I don't actually care.

—Sarah Fishburn

I haven't regretted anything yet. Every choice I have made led to different experiences or opportunities, and each one had a lesson or purpose. Even the things that hurt me were worth it because they enabled me to look at things differently. I can't regret that. It's what fuels my art.

—Linda Woods

Not pursuing it sooner. It took me reaching the age of forty to kick myself in the rear and put my work "out there." I wish I'd been brave enough years ago, but life's a journey, and everything happens for a reason.

—Pam Carriker

I took classes from some artists whose work and style I admired. Some of the teaching artists helped steer me in an appropriate direction. Unfortunately, other teaching artists couldn't see my individuality, and I wasted a lot of time unlearning their style in order to develop mine.

—Don Madden

I wish, I wish, I wish I had taken art classes in high school and in college.

—Leslie Avon Miller

Many years ago I chose to concentrate on one medium. I regret that I did not begin to experiment and try different mediums for so many years. I feel that my artwork has grown and matured because I have opened my mind up to so many new mediums and experimentations.

—Donna Watson

I would have to say that one thing I regret is having never taken any art classes in my life. I am never short on ideas or inspiration when creating my art, but that does not make up for the fact that there is a vast and undiscovered world of skills and techniques out there for me to learn.

—Alicia Caudle

I wish I had continued to make art when I was a child. At eleven years old, my drawings got very small and eventually vanished. At fifteen, my artistic expression exploded again with a camera. But I didn't pick up a paintbrush again for many years. I wish someone had encouraged me to at least draw in a journal at the time.

—Angela Cartwright

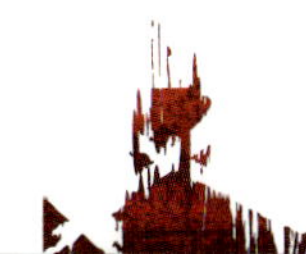

What is the one choice as an artist that you regret having made or not made?

I used to regret not going to school for art. I've since reconsidered that. I don't have any regrets today. I feel extraordinarily blessed for what I have and where life has brought me. If anything, I wish I had more of an eye for business!

—Julin Dorroro

I regret not continuing my interest in art throughout the years I was raising my children. I think it would have enhanced their childhood as well as have been an artistic and creative venue to express my energies and feelings in life.

Jill Zaheer

I regret not being more aggressive and assertive with my own career, and I regret not having a state-of-the art computer knowledge and savvy to better my online networking.

—Nina Bagley

I always wish I could have majored in art when I first went to college. However, my parents were completely against this idea. I probably would have been an art teacher long ago if I could have pursued my dream. But thankfully, I ended up going back to school to be an art teacher later anyway.

—Roxanne Evans Stout

I regret not doing more workshops or classes in order that more techniques could be applied to my works. Being self-taught, I always regretted not going with my gut and studying art full time.

—Judy Wilkenfeld

Sometimes I regret that I dropped my photography major. That regret is promptly dismissed when I remember the awesome career I had and the friends I made with my backup plan as a Graduate Gemologist. I no longer think of dropping the photography major as a regret—it was only a detour.

—Julie Prichard

Honestly, I cannot think of any. I didn't choose to be the way I am, and the way I am is at the root of all my choices. I am stubborn in my choices, in making them as well as defending them, and I suspect many artists are the same. That's why no one can ever tell us anything—ha, ha.

—Judy Wise

Easy. Not moving to New York City in the '70s when I could have afforded it! I can still see my imaginary apartment: small yet stylish, where I could cram in an army of unique individuals on Friday nights for a full-on salon.

—Lisa Hoffman

Not finishing my bachelor of visual arts degree. I started and then met the love of my life, who had to return home to Norway after a year. I was left with a tough decision, and my heart won out in the end. Although I don't regret my decision as such, I kind of do in a half-weird way, if that makes sense.

—Gary Reef

Which statement best describes how you felt when you sold your first piece?

Thrilled, and I had no problem letting go: **40%**
Thrilled, but it was hard to let go: **29%**
Surprisingly sad: **7%**
Have not sold any of my artwork yet: **19%**
My first sale? Who can remember??: **5%**

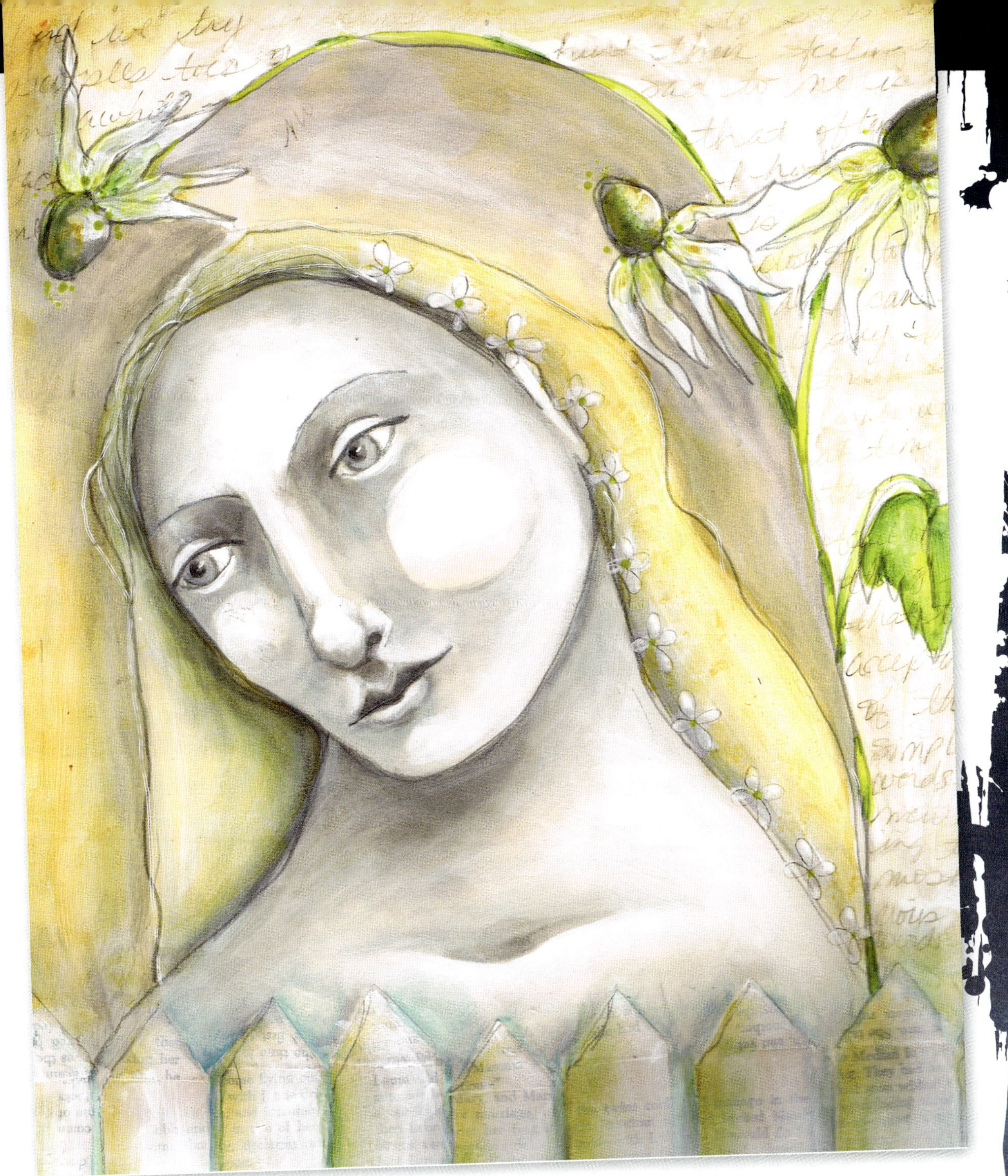

Self-Portrait

My portraits are always self-portraits of sorts. Although they may not look exactly like me, they contain my emotions through journaling, both visible and hidden, and some facial characteristic(s) e.g. cheekbones, nose, etc. Creating self-portraits is a great exercise in self-discovery and the processing of emotions.

—Pam Carriker

Is there an emotion that shows up more frequently than others in your artwork?

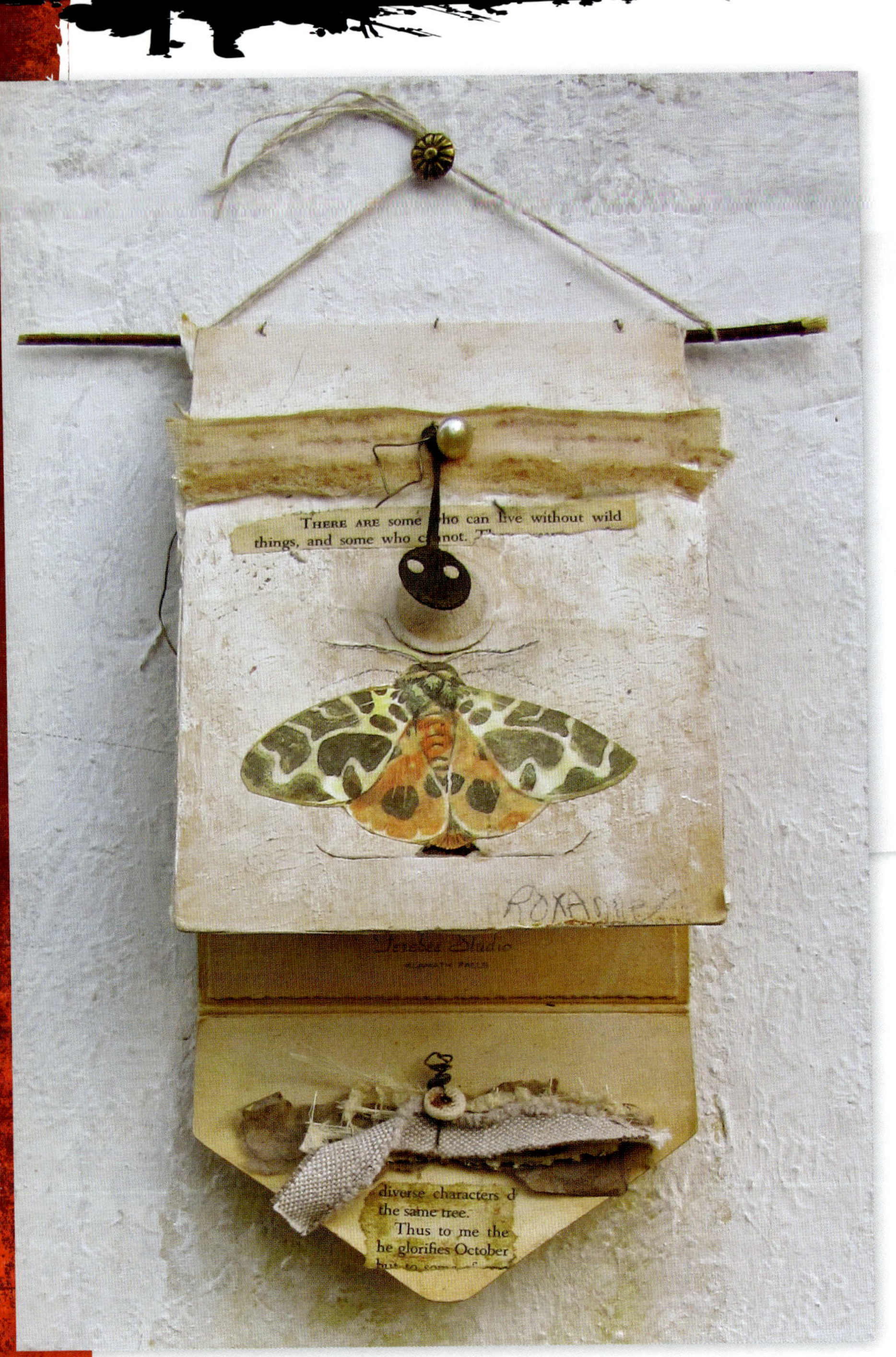

Thus to Me

The feelings that show up in most of my pieces are wistfulness, a sense of connectedness and longing. With these words in my mind, I created "Thus to Me." My project began with a little photograph booklet. I love books and paper and opening something that reveals a new piece of art. I began by texturing the surfaces with tissue paper and gesso, then spontaneously adding found objects that seemed to tell my story. While I was working, other parts of "Thus to Me" became focal points as well; words, images and scraps all told their own story. So the story continues, of connecting with the natural world, of longing for tranquility and wistfulness of adventures not yet taken.

— *Roxanne Evans Stout*

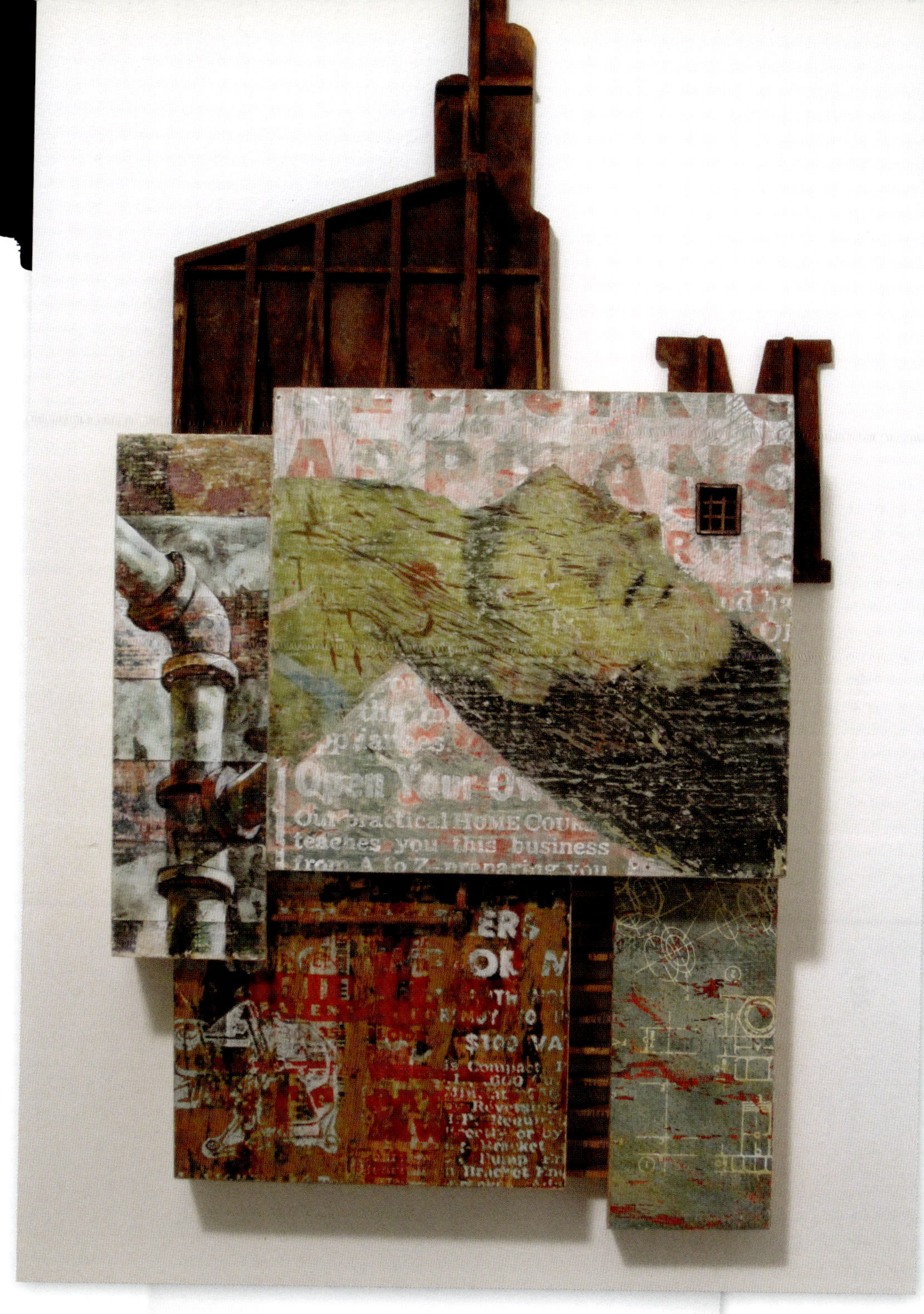

Menthol

I normally don't think of my work as being very emotive, but the theme of exhaustion came up as I was working on "Menthol." I wanted to capture that feeling of the passing of time with a weathered and worn-out look.

— Robert Maloney

Is there an emotion that shows up more frequently than others in your artwork?

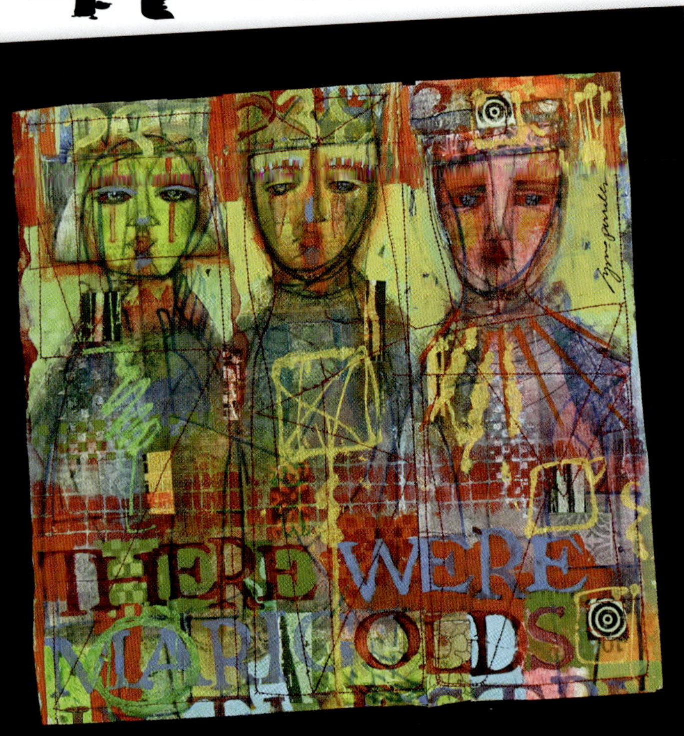

Marigolds in the Stream

Traditions are very important to me. I am an inveterate researcher and museum hound, and I love to steep myself in images that have historical significance and meaning. However, I strive to make my artwork look fresh and distinctive—not merely "vintage." This work of art was done in France, in a wonderfully sunny studio full of kindred artists working with anything at hand. A sewing machine was set up nearby, and I heard the hum of the machine, the quiet chatter of the artists, the outdoor sounds of breezes and birdsong, and rushing water. I heard one of the artists say, "Did you notice? There are marigolds in the stream." She said it quietly, with deep appreciation of our beautiful surroundings. I worked on three Icon figures and used stamps to imprint the quote about the marigolds onto my painting. To me, the image would not be complete without the words. The painting is a reminder of the moment—it not only reminds me of what I saw, but what I felt.

—Lynne Perrella

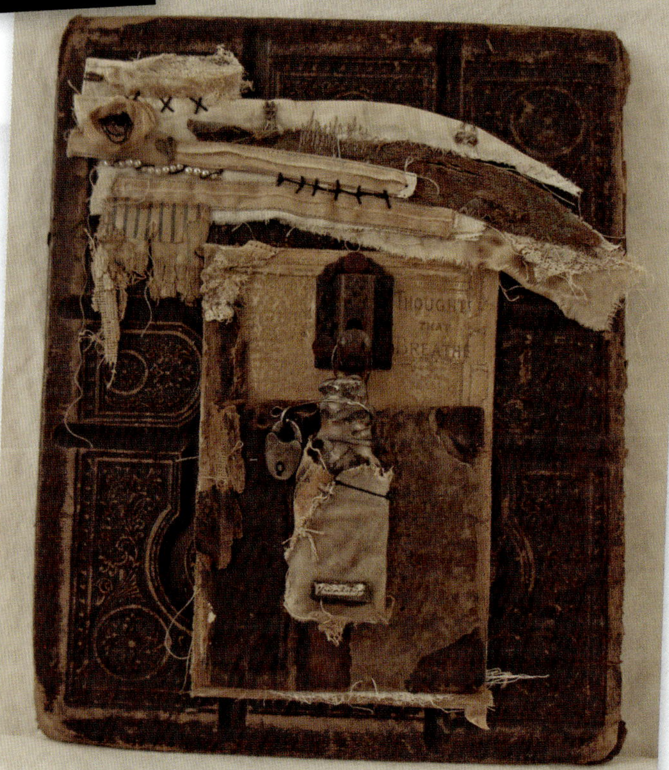

Thought That Breathe

The emotion that shows up frequently in my work is a passion to encourage others. So many of us face difficult situations along the journey. The fabric collage on the top of my piece represents my life journey thus far, depicting the obstacles and the pearls found along the way. The glass bottle represents the hope contained in my heart. The lock and key remind me to unlock my heart and encourage others with the comfort I've been comforted with from my Creator.

—JoAnnA Pierotti

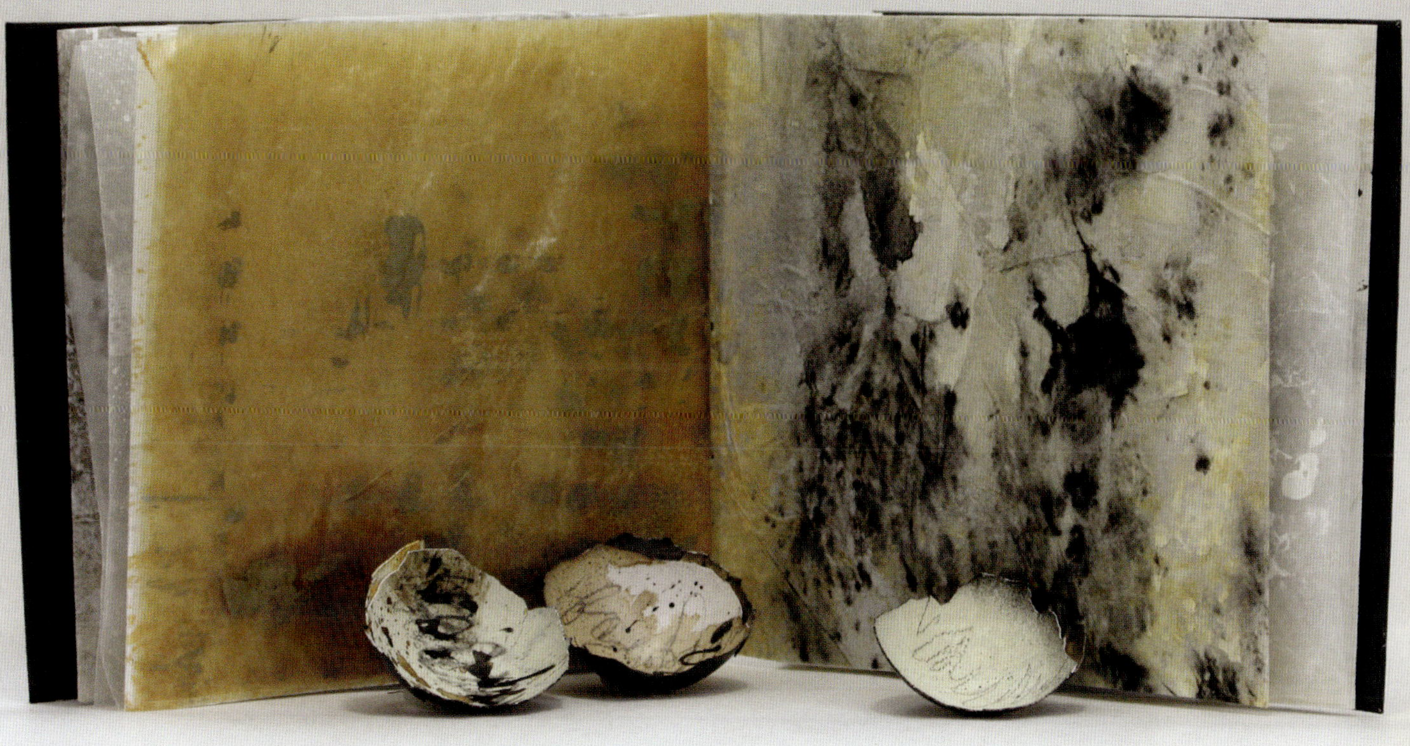

Breathe In; Breathe Out

The emotional nature of my work is about seeking peace and stillness so I may really feel my love for the world and feel the world's love for me. My art practice is tied to being aware of the joy and privilege of being alive. My work tends toward minimalism, toward simplicity, and toward depth expressed through the use of texture. My work is often void of imagery to allow myself and the viewer to go beyond words, beyond thinking and beyond the concrete. The work is a pathway to beingness in a moment of stillness. It is a breath in and a breath out.

—Leslie Avon Miller

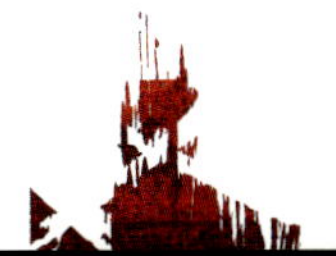

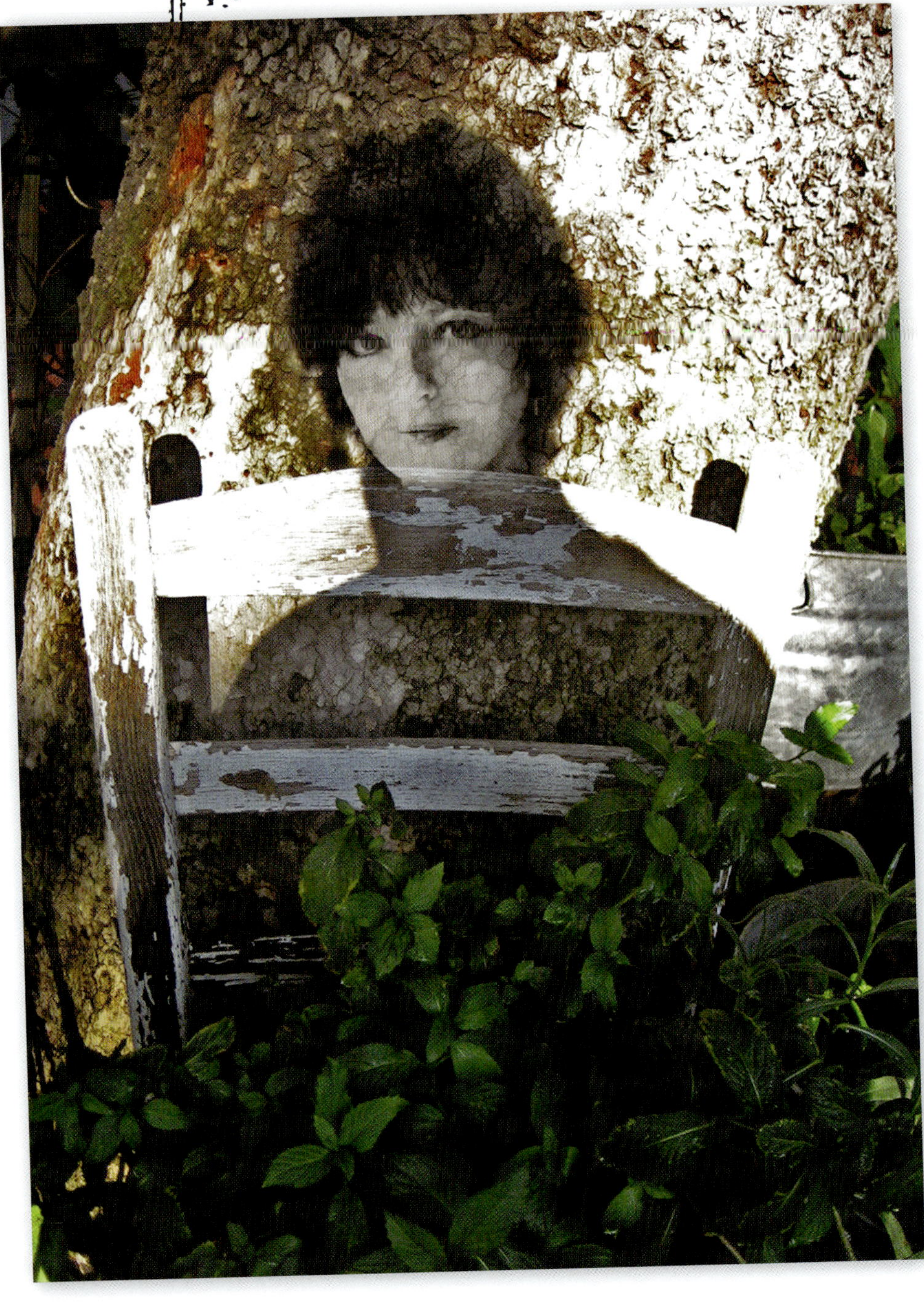

Self-Portrait

Shadows. I have been using my own shadow in my art for years now. Sometimes you see them; sometimes they are hidden under layers. Because my art is a reflection of my personal experiences, my shadows are the perfect way for me to be a part of what I have created.

—Angela Cartwright

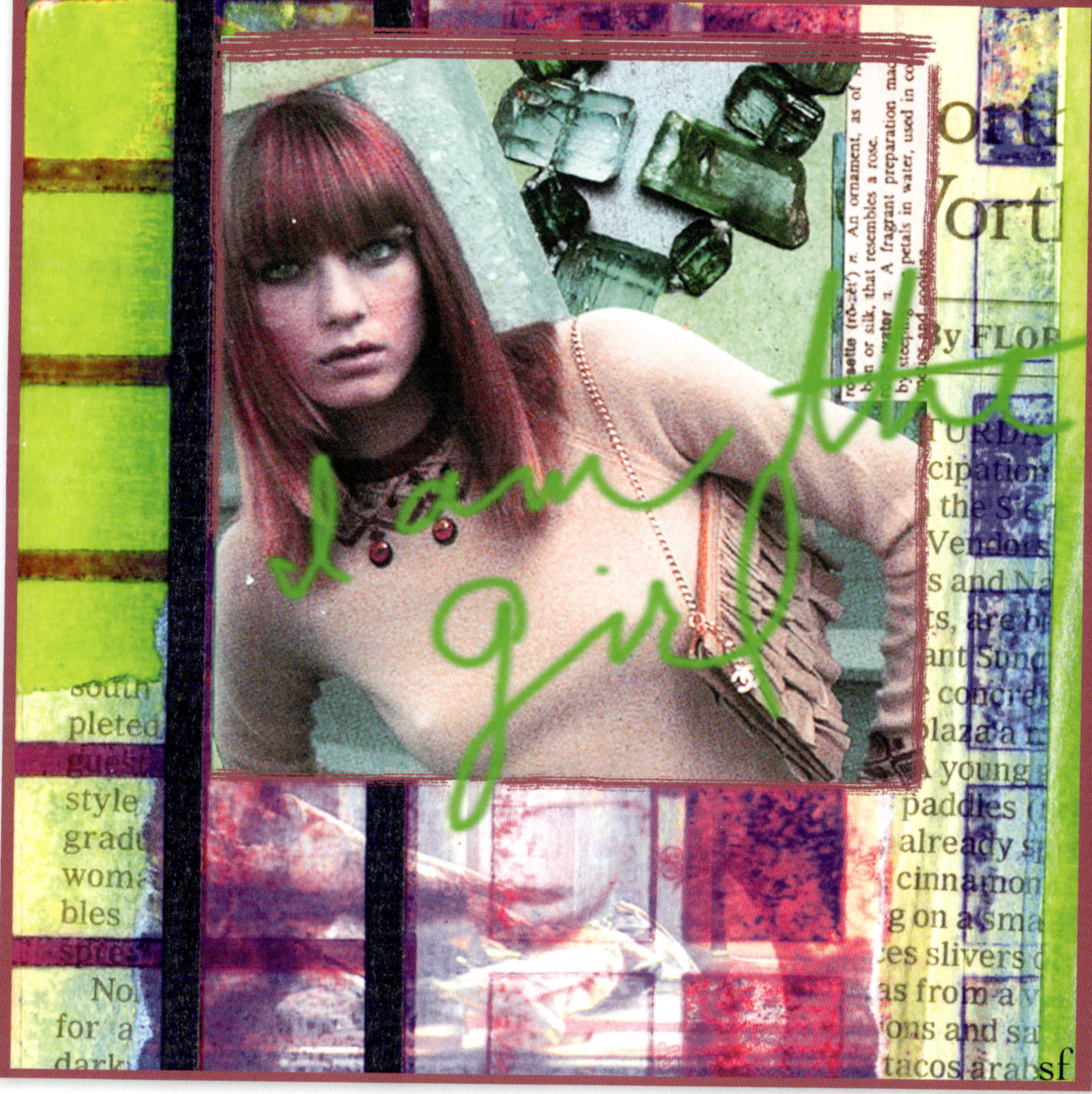

Self-Portrait

This piece is actually a digital deconstruction piece, created from two traditionally constructed collages. I took them apart, recombined the elements digitally, and added graffiti and borders with digital brushes. The ability to combine traditional and mod approaches within an art piece is what excites—and frequently defines—my style.

—Sarah Fishburn

What obstacle has stopped you from achieving an art-related goal?

Obstacles come in all shapes and sizes, but two stood out as particularly common in this group of artists: lack of time and the need to balance art with all the other requirements of life. Internal obstacles were noted as well, including self-doubt, shyness and procrastination. Several artists reported having no obstacles at all. Their secret? Do without goals.

Time. I want to do so many more things than one person could possibly do on their own. I wish I could clone myself at least twice and go in multiple directions at once!

—Pam Carriker

I am extraordinarily challenged by a surfeit of procrastination and also a desperate lack of follow-through. And it would appear, I can't count.

—Sarah Fishburn

The current economy has prompted me to have to return to work. It happens to be a time when I am feeling particularly creatively full of energy, and I have not been able to balance the important things in my life. Obstacles, though, have a nasty habit of feeding ones expression and creativity.

—Karen Cole

The biggest obstacle has been my fear and self-doubts. I have held back from approaching major galleries because I thought my paintings were not ready. It is only recently that I have started to approach a few galleries and submit my work.

—Donna Watson

The fact that I move so s-l-o-w-l-y. Sometimes I feel like I'm running underwater. There are times when I see prolific colleagues and ask myself, "*What* exactly, is my problem?!"

—Lisa Hoffman

File this one under quirky. I don't set goals. None. When I do set a goal, I don't talk about it out loud. I have this feeling that if I set a goal, it's looking to the future, and it prevents me from living in the present.

—Julie Prichard

I believe my own restlessness has stopped me more than once. I keep wanting to move on, dig deeper, go further, which can have both a positive and negative effect.

—Vivian Bonder

I don't have any art-related goals. I paint, draw and make stuff because it's what I love to do. That's it.

—Lynne Hoppe

For me it would have to be location. Living twenty minutes outside a small town on the southwest coast of Norway does make it a little interesting when it comes to exhibiting regularly and meeting local artists.

—Gary Reef

I have struggled to balance career and art. I do art part time, and the more I do it, the more I love it. The more I love it, the more it encroaches upon my work life, to where I spend work vacations in my art studio.

—John Borrero

Have you ever experienced artist's block?

Yes: **81%**

No: **19%**

I am an amateur, and my job and my responsibilities take up most of my time. Nonetheless, I can always find time to draw and paint when I am really motivated. Keeping motivated that way is a struggle for all artists. So I would say my own will is my biggest obstacle, one that I wrestle with and delight in taming.

—Danny Gregory

Lack of time. I have two young children and I am fortunate to be able to stay at home with them. However, this also means that I do not have the full amount of time I used to have to work. I still do what I can. I get to work right away, and all my creative energy comes pouring out.

—Bridgette Guerzon Mills

I don't set goals. I don't think art is something you make goals about. But there never seems to be enough time to do everything I want to do. Sometimes being a responsible adult gets in the way of being less responsible and trying things just for the sake of creative self-expression or exploration.

—Linda Woods

When I was younger, I was a single parent with two children. So working for the man for so many years while juggling college and parenting kept me from being an art major and getting a master's degree. But that goal was then. Now I think it all worked out for the best.

—Judy Wise

There are no obstacles, only the learned skills of balance and boundaries. Balance your creative verve with real-life obligations. Set boundaries of commitments so you don't suffocate your artistic process. Procrastination can be a challenge, but is easily overcome by the discipline of creating regularly. Nothing trumps digging in and doing it.

—Michelle Ward

Time.

—Jill Zaheer

Just as I was about to start my eighth year as a middle school art teacher, the recession hit our school district, and art was on the chopping block. I lost a job that I loved. Now I am a second-grade teacher at a lovely school, and I am still as creative as ever, just in different ways. I still try to bring out the magic in my students.

—Roxanne Evans Stout

Lack of tenacity.

—Patricia Larsen

My own fear. Fear of discovering my desire to be an artist was the height of presumption. And fear that I wouldn't see it as presumption, while others artists in their own right—could.

—Leslie Marsh

Quietly making art in the corner, being shy and proud of it kept me from noticing the creative vastness that was evident all around me. Once I understood that creativity is a spiritual outlet not only for me, the road was clear and lead to a sweet realization that we are all interconnected in art and in life.

—Orly Avineri

In the past, especially when my children were little, I stayed in a job that didn't inspire me because I worried that doing art full time would not bring me the income needed to help raise a family. If only I had known! From the moment I started making art full time, my income doubled and at times trebled.

—Robyn Gordon

That would most definitely be my shyness. I am a very self-conscious person, and not just with my art. Because of this, it's been quite difficult (read "pretty much impossible") for me to approach venues to show my work. Thankfully, I have been forced into submission on several occasions by family and friends.

—Alicia Caudle

What obstacle has stopped you from achieving an art-related goal?

"Obstacle" is not in my vocabulary.

—*Angela Cartwright*

Time. I started my art life at about age sixty. If I had started at about age thirty, where would I be now? No regrets here, just moving on down the road.

—*Don Madden*

My husband's poor health. My husband is my first priority and I fear leaving him alone. He has needs, and I feel it is my responsibility to meet his needs. I am rethinking how to achieve my teaching goals without going too far from home, or leaving home at all.

—*JoAnnA Pierotti*

I would have to say time or the lack of it. Some pieces that I work on take a long time to complete. Research of the subject matter is an integral part of my pieces. Getting the facts correct to correctly symbolize the story is tantamount to the success of an art piece.

—*Judy Wilkenfeld*

My answer seems harsh, but it is not at all—family. For many years it has not stopped me, but made me slow down to spend time with them. Life sometimes throws you a curve ball, and my son's chronic illness called cystic fibrosis did this. I have used what free time I have had for my saving grace—my art.

—*Jen Crossley*

Time, time, time. Art can take all the time and then some. Another lifetime or two would be helpful!

—*Leslie Avon Miller*

Being a musician. It's not easy to juggle two creative outlets that pull you in different directions. Most of the time the two feed off of each other and help each other, but often they can get in each other's way. As Uncle Ben Parker said, "With great power comes great responsibility."

—*Robert Maloney*

Computer connection and disposable income. Maybe not in that order.

—*Nina Bagley*

Do you find yourself influenced by current trends?

Absolutely, I love the newest trends: **6%**

Yes, sometimes they have an impact on me: **62%**

No, they do not affect the direction of my art: **32%**

How do you feel if you don't tap into your creative abilities regularly?

Guilty: **8%**

Cranky: **28%**

Frustrated: **49%**

Doesn't affect me at all: **3%**

N/A – I always tap into my creativity: **12%**

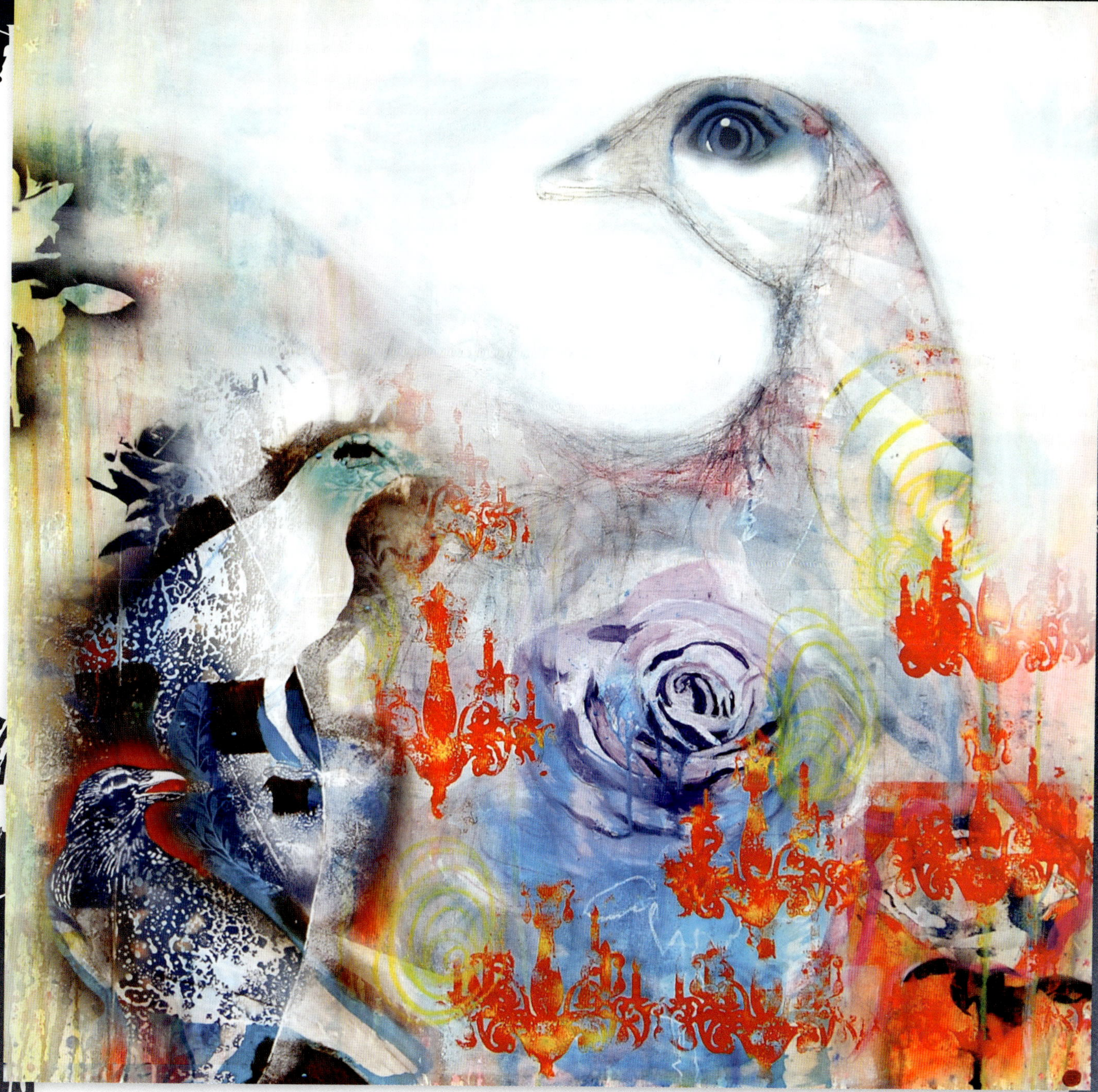

Self-Portrait

The painting is very representative of where I am in my creative journey. I am very much a nomadic drifter when it comes to imagery, medium and techniques, so being a bird is a very good representation of my current mind-set. I am looking back toward the viewer in one last "goodbye" glance, knowing that I must move on, that I must take flight into the unknown of my future. I carry with me my past and present, the images, layers and techniques that have defined me and made me the artist I am today.

—Gary Reef

How do you express anger in your artwork?

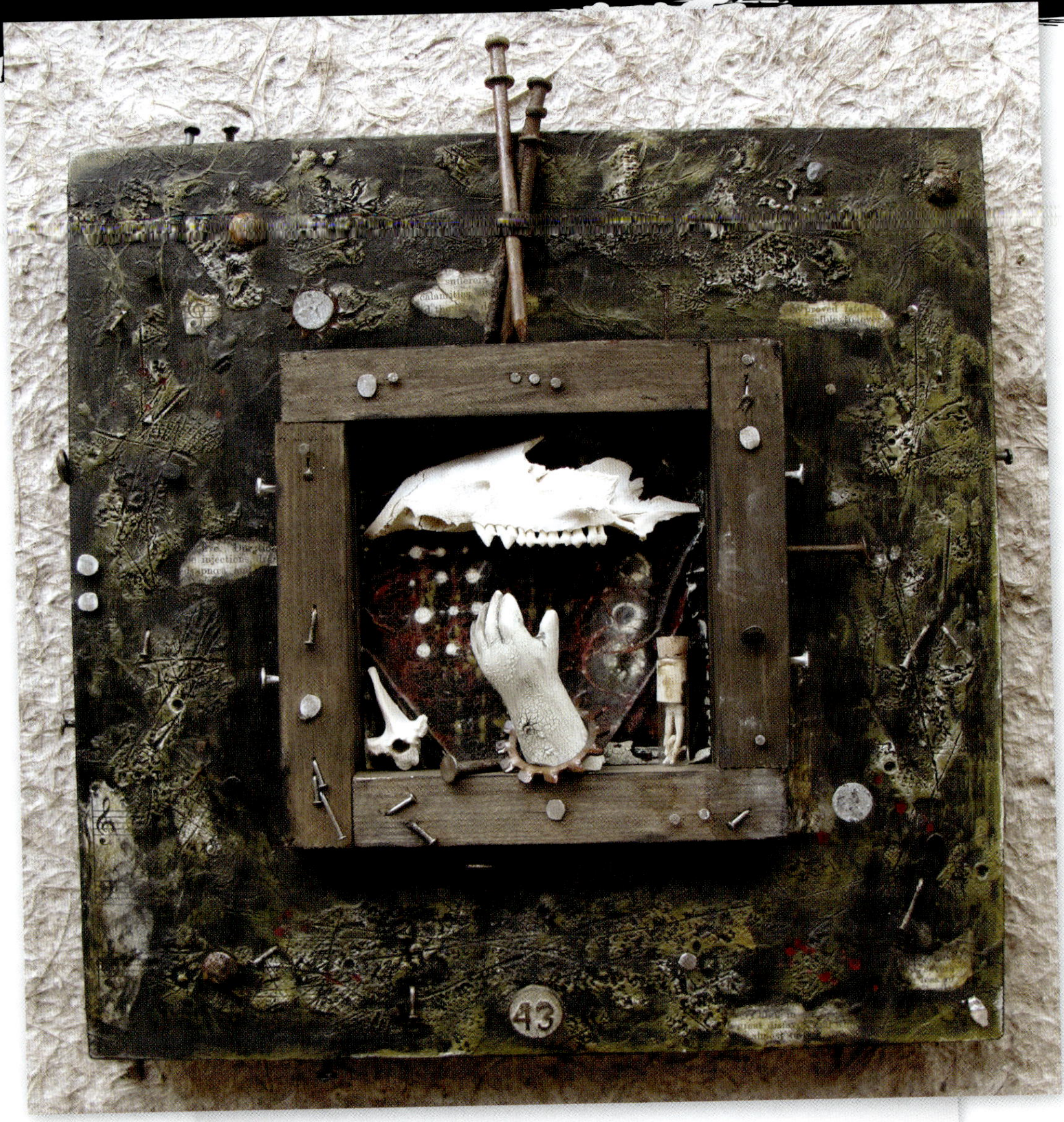

Feigning Death

I had a perfect opportunity to explore how I would express my anger in art at a time I was feeling a bit ferocious. I sawed pieces of wood manually. I pounded nails forcefully into the wood without any regard for where or how they landed. I covered the wooden base with clay, which I stabbed with my awl, gouging it and roughing it up. I painted the surfaces in quick, rough strokes without any planning of an outcome. I added more nails, bending several. The next time I feel overly angry or agitated, I will most definitely be whipping out the handsaw, a hammer and some nails because sawing, severing, pounding and hitting are quite therapeutic indeed.

—Alicia Caudle

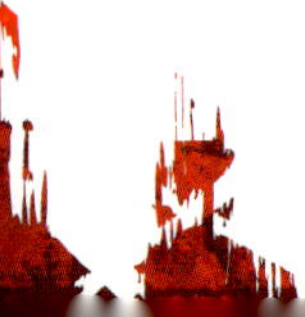

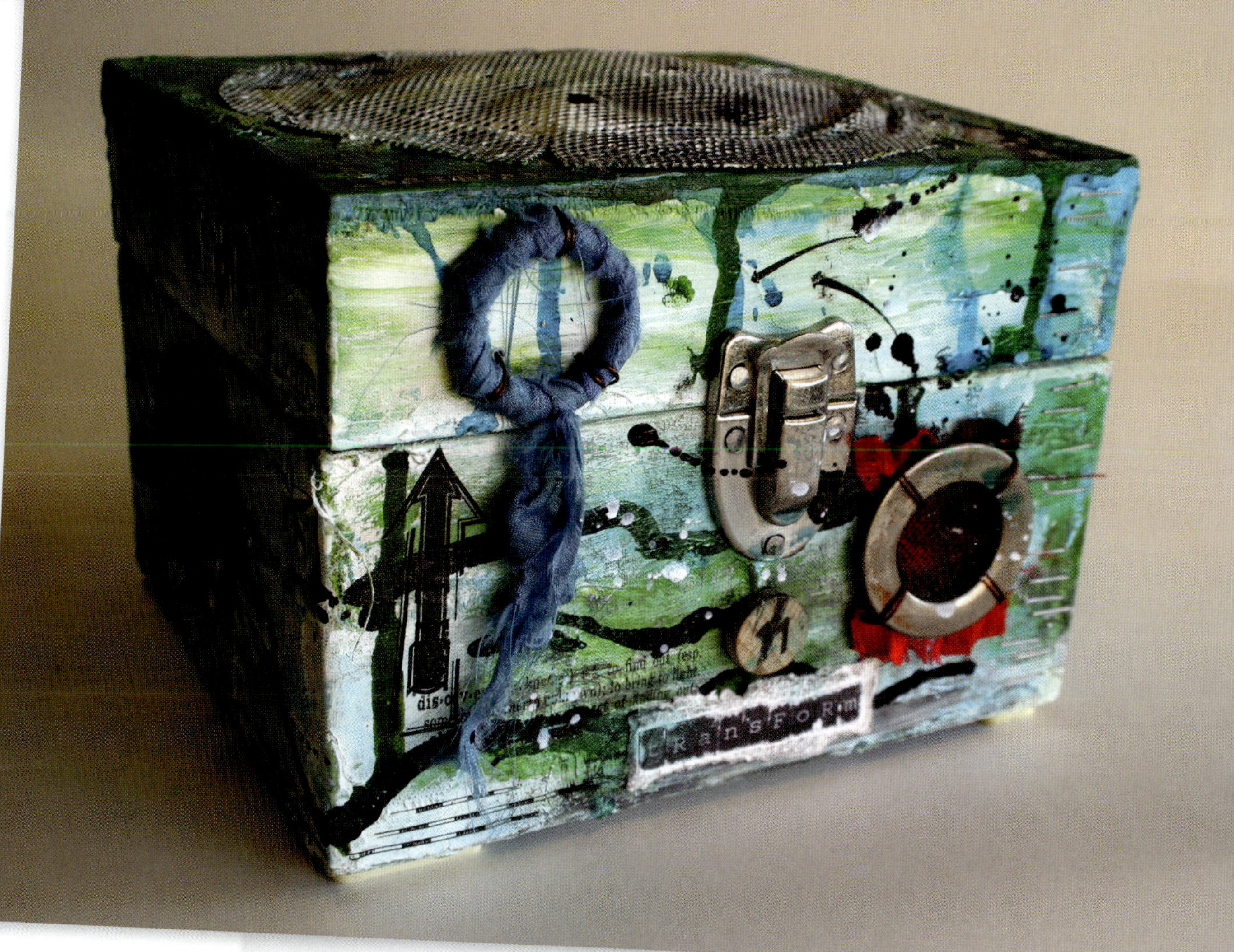

Transformation Box

Even though anger in itself can be a very destructive force, I feel when it is dealt with in a positive and respectful way, anger has the real potential to transform and transmute any blocks, struggles, standstills and stagnant phases. The way I normally express anger in my work is by scratching, layering and truly physically being involved in my work. The idea behind my transformation box is for it to hold small objects and cards—works which are created while having angry emotions and frustrations—and seeing the transformation happen within me while creating.

—Vivian Bonder

How do you express anger in your artwork?

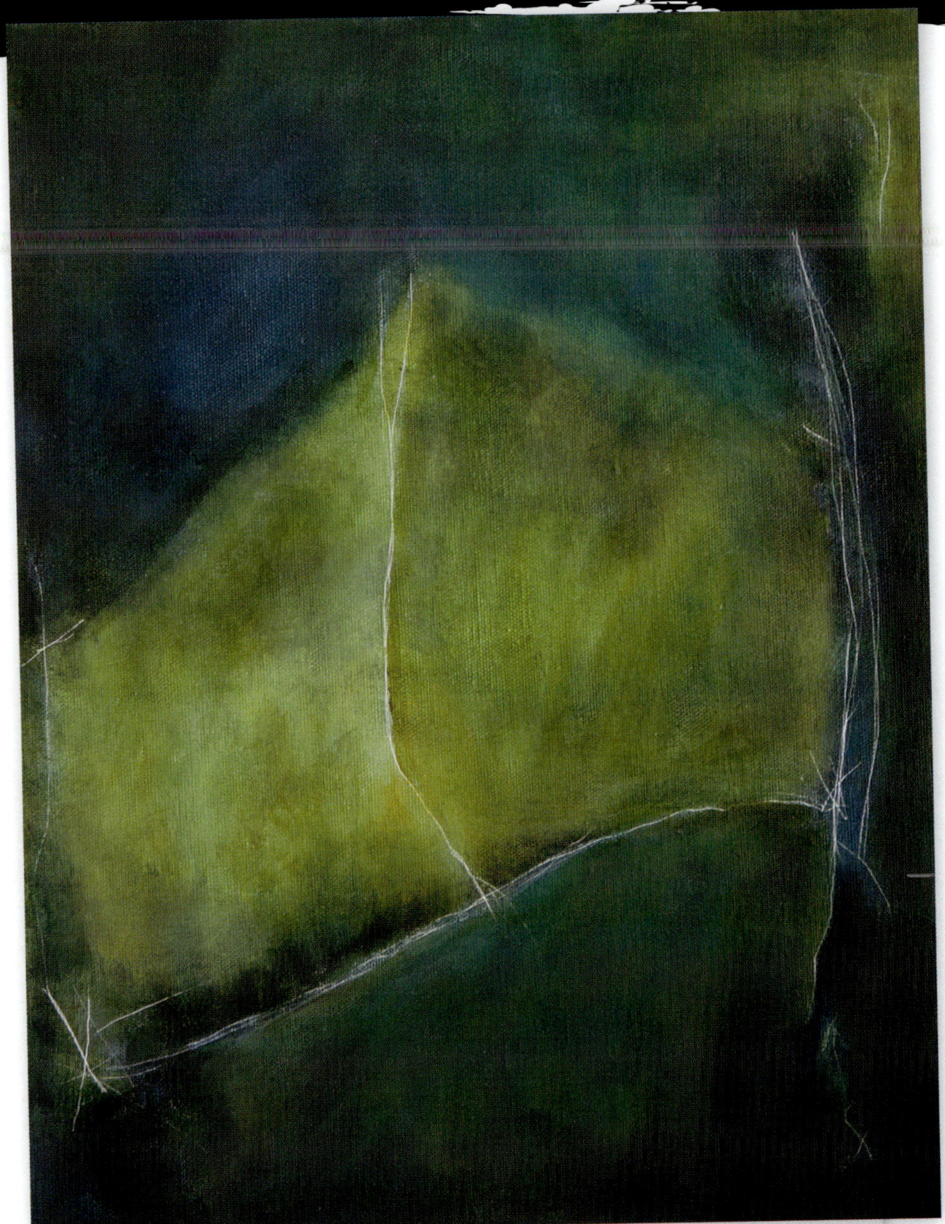

Slope

Anger in my artwork takes many forms. Most notably to me is the process of getting the paint onto the canvas. I forcefully scrub the paint into the canvas and follow by using sharp tools to scratch into the paint and through to the canvas. The definitive gesture is often a cross or an X, which to me means "finished."

—Julie Prichard

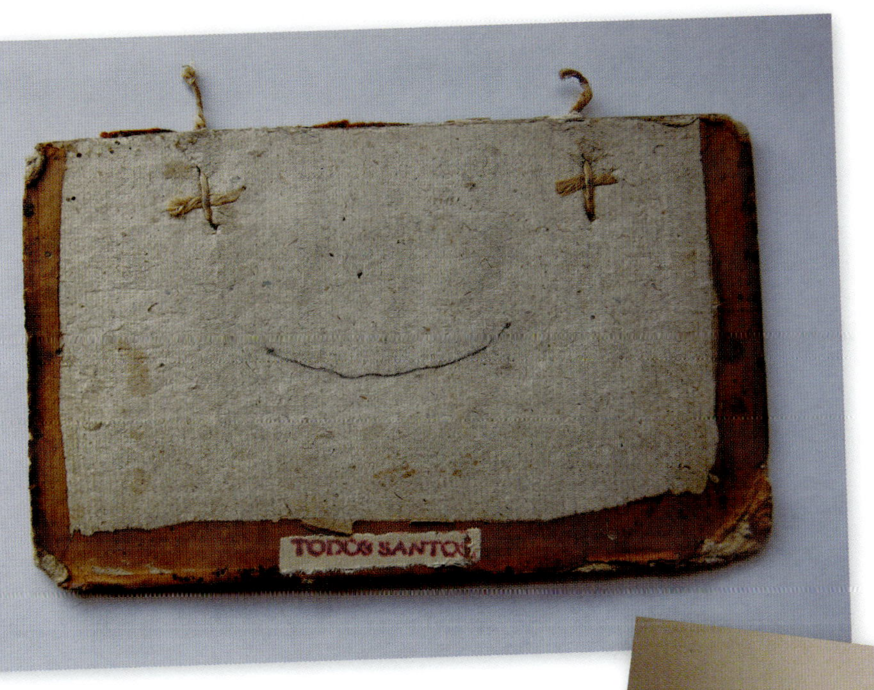

Self-Portrait

Trying not to take myself too seriously, I occupy my day by recognizing objects, colors and surfaces, which are often transformed into making art. Using this as a form of self-expression, I love turning visual statements into stories without using words.

—Patricia Larsen

Self-Portrait

I have always been drawn to creating the female figure and, even more specifically, the mother figure. My life right now is centered around my two young children, so I used the nest in her hair to symbolize motherhood, creativity and fertility. But that is not the only aspect of who I am. My work is another facet. And in my work I see myself as a gatherer. I collect images from the world around me, as well as materials that I come across, and incorporate them in my mixed-media work. I like to think that being a mother and an artist are similar. Both are roles that involve nurturing and creativity, as well as managing controlled chaos!

—Bridgette Guerzon Mills

If you could sell one piece of art to anyone, whom would you want to buy it?

The majority of artists wanted a specific, well-known, public figure to be the buyer. Interestingly, Yoko Ono, Andy Goldsworthy and Tim Burton all were selected twice by different artists. A good number responded that their preference was to have their art purchased by the person who loved it the most. Family members, agencies (schools, hospitals, museums) and former teachers rounded out the remaining choices.

A specific person doesn't come to mind, but ideally someone who connects with my art and is drawn to the different paths I take in the work that I do.

—Robert Maloney

It would sure be nice to hear the head of the Smithsonian on the other end of the phone. *Why*? Are you kidding?

—Angela Cartwright

I am completely happy to sell my work to whomever my work speaks.

—Karen Cole

I'm tremendously honored when one of the artists I admire decides to purchase one of my pieces. So many people have told me that my work calls to mind Tim Burton's work. I find this to be the greatest compliment. It would be amazing for him to one day want to purchase one of my pieces.

—John Borrero

I watched a recorded lecture by artist Wolf Kahn in which he recounted that Bill Clinton bought three of his works as a birthday gift for Hillary. I thought, "Well now, wouldn't it be something to have the president buy my work as a gift for someone dear to him?" So I would choose the president or our first lady. What a thrill!

—Leslie Avon Miller

Damien Hirst. Honestly I don't know exactly why because I don't particularly like his art, but I just think, "Why not?" He is interested in Francis Bacon, and he doesn't talk about art like it's a foreign language.

—Gary Reef

My family. They don't understand creativity and think art is for sissies. My art embarrasses them. On second thought, they don't deserve it. Instead, I'd like Andy Goldsworthy to buy one of my pieces and hide it in one of his environmental art pieces to secretly await discovery in the future.

—Don Madden

I would like the director of a hospital somewhere to buy a larger mixed-media piece for the people in that hospital to be able to sit and enjoy the vibrancy, shine and play of colors within a piece, allowing them to escape their troubles for a little while.

—Vivian Bonder

Yoko Ono. I admire Yoko's passion and her creativity. Since she is her own person, she would buy my art because she truly likes it. I would hope that one day I could make such an important piece of art that she and her friends would gather around and discuss its meaning.

—Julie Prichard

To a professional, well-known artist like Antoni Tapies or Anselm Kiefer. I admire their artwork so much because their work is so personal and emotional and expressive. If they were to acquire one of my paintings it would mean that my work connected with them in a personal way as well.

—Donna Watson

No one in particular, just someone very, very wealthy. I would use some of the proceeds to make thousands of prints and leave them everywhere I go, for anyone to find, so that the wealthy buyer and I can each make an impact on the lives of everyone who is lucky enough to find one.

—Sarah Fishburn

Exercising "artistic privilege" and choosing three: artist and author Danny Gregory, author and window designer extraordinaire Simon Doonan, and, of course, Mark Twain. You have to have a sense of humor to appreciate my work, and I think that they'd just . . . "get it."

—Lisa Hoffman

If I could sell one piece of my art to anyone in the world, it would be to my high school art teacher, Mr. Purucker, and my high school dance teacher, Marilyn Allen. Both of these amazing people believed in me and taught me the beauty of art and movement.

—Roxanne Evans Stout

There really is not any one person whom I can think of who I would want to buy my art in particular. Anytime someone feels compelled to buy a piece of work from me, I feel honored and grateful. It doesn't matter to me if it is someone famous or someone down the street.

—Bridgette Guerzon Mills

While it would be thrilling to have a piece of my work decorating the White House or sitting in the Queen Mum's parlor, I think having my husband come home one day and say, "Look at this incredible piece of art I found! I think it would look awesome in the living room," would be the ultimate thrill.

—Pam Carriker

I'd love to see one of my books go to a collector, as an example of mixed-media art, or a bound vehicle for expression. It would be flattering to think one of my works was on a shelf, deep in the Vatican archives, drawing interpretation. Then again, it would have been interesting to sell something unique to the late master of ironic conceptual art, Piero Manzoni.

—Leslie Marsh

My gut response is Andy Goldsworthy, because his own work has been an enormous inspiration to me, and because I would love the opportunity to stand beside him in a grassy field at the edge of the sea and stack stones or sticks alongside the man. His work takes my breath away.

—Nina Bagley

The highest bidder, so I could finally get me a studio to accommodate my zest for mess making and dancing while finger painting. I would invite many others to do it with me. They will come, as it would be situated in an enchanted rainforest, yet very close to a happening city with a huge art supply store that is next to a huge art bookstore and a cozy coffee/tea house too.

—Orly Avineri

I'd want to sell it to the person who wanted it the most because that's what makes sense to me!

—Lynne Hoppe

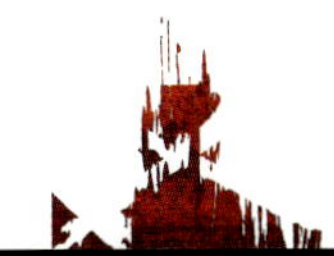

If you could sell one piece of art to anyone, whom would you want to buy it?

Cecil Skotnes. He carved in a way I had never seen before. Cecil Skotnes turned carved wood blocks into an art form. He passed away a few years ago, but if he had ever purchased something that I had made, it would have been a huge boost.

—Robyn Gordon

I would love to sell one of my works to Mrs. Lois Wright who was my sixth-grade teacher. She was always encouraging me. She signed my sixth-grade autograph book with the inscription, "Dear Jill, I expect to see your name in all places of creativity, maybe the Metro Museum of Art one day."

—Jill Zaheer

The very first person who came to mind was Egon Schiele, but he is no longer with us. So, after much thought, I would have to say Tim Burton. If he were to buy one of my pieces, I would be giddy with bliss because artistically I think he rises above and beyond most "common" minds.

—Alicia Caudle

Yoko Ono because her message to the world touches, moves, and inspires me, and I would hope that my work had the same effect on her.

—Patricia Larsen

The artwork I produce, especially those related to the Holocaust in WWII, is so personal and intimate that there would need to be a real connection with the purchaser and the subject matter. I would possibly sell the artwork to a school to educate. To enhance understanding would be my goal. To educate, not to blame, is essential to my artworks.

—Judy Wilkenfeld

I would love to have my art selected as an album cover for my favorite band. Hey, it could happen!

—Michelle Ward

I would want an Italian native in Italy to buy it. I have sold many pieces of my art, but never to Italy. Because of my strong Italian heritage and my beautiful Italian grandmother, somehow I feel I would be leaving a little legacy of her in the land of her origin where part of me came from.

—JoAnnA Pierotti

Sinead O'Connor. She was one of the first women I saw as being outspoken and brave with her words and art. She had a shaved head and wore black boots and sang of her bad childhood, a broken heart, and war, and she didn't seem to care what anyone thought about her. She was my hero!

—Linda Woods

I would want to sell it to the one person who loved it the most.

—Judy Wise

My choice would be my mum. She passed away ten years ago with cancer before I started really getting into my art. I would love for her to see what I'm doing now. I would give anything for her to want to buy a piece of mine. I wouldn't really charge her, but to think that she would think that my work was good enough to buy would be all I could ask for.

—Jen Crossley

Have you ever been jealous of another artist's skills?

Yes: **69%**

No: **31%**

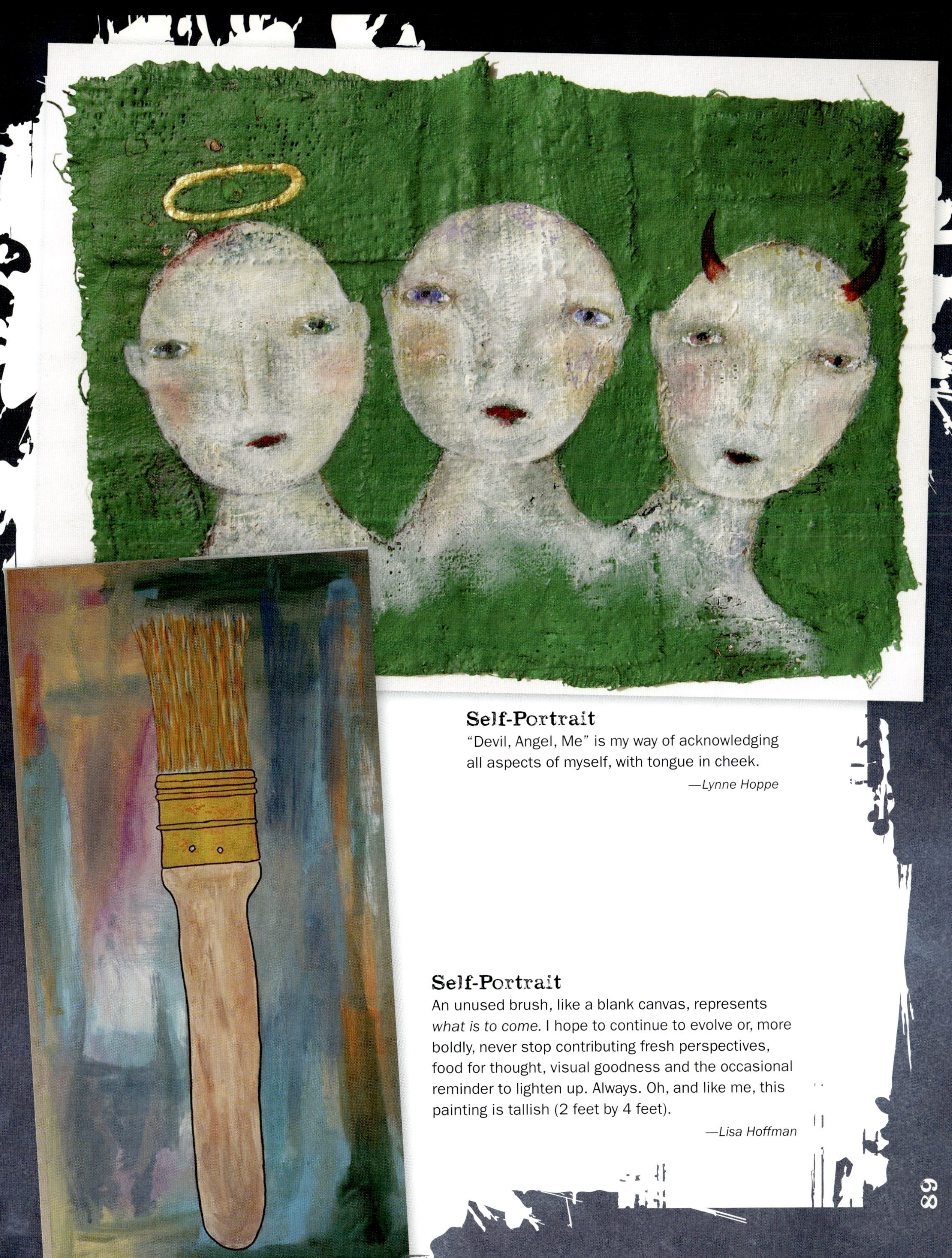

Self-Portrait

"Devil, Angel, Me" is my way of acknowledging all aspects of myself, with tongue in cheek.

—Lynne Hoppe

Self-Portrait

An unused brush, like a blank canvas, represents *what is to come.* I hope to continue to evolve or, more boldly, never stop contributing fresh perspectives, food for thought, visual goodness and the occasional reminder to lighten up. Always. Oh, and like me, this painting is tallish (2 feet by 4 feet).

—Lisa Hoffman

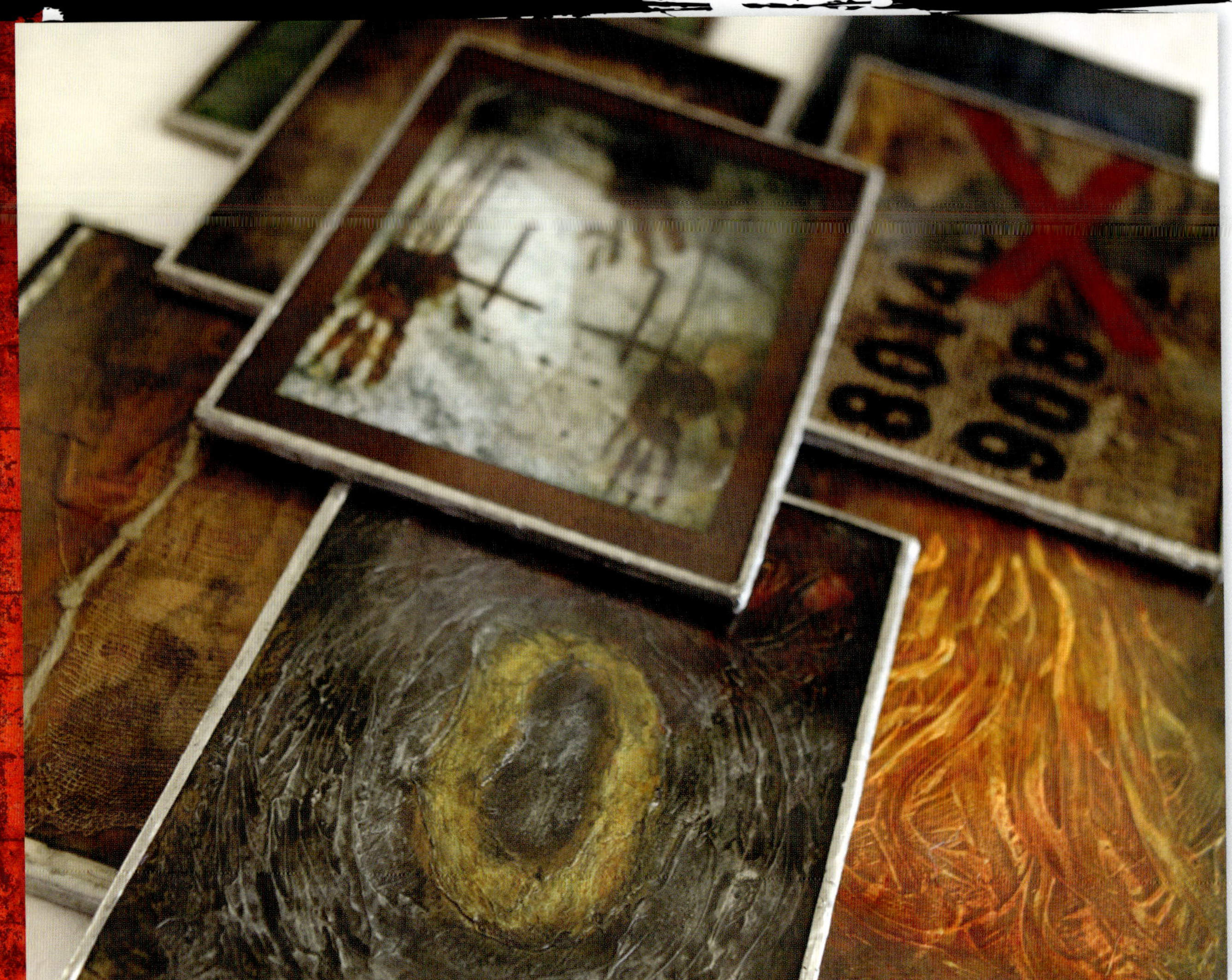

Kol Nidre

Jews who were forced to convert to Christianity at the time of the Inquisition did so under threat of their lives and that of their families. After the said conversion, these Jews were burnt at the stake in any event. Kol Nidrei relates to the prayer or declaration recited by these Jews prior to their excruciating deaths. The piece is made up of eight double-sided mixed-media plates. The subject of vulnerability is echoed throughout this piece. Not only does each of the works under the glass plates refer to the vulnerability of those Jews and heretics living in those times, but the very choice of the materials used expresses the helplessness and most often defenselessness of those tried under the Inquisition.

—*Judy Wilkenfeld*

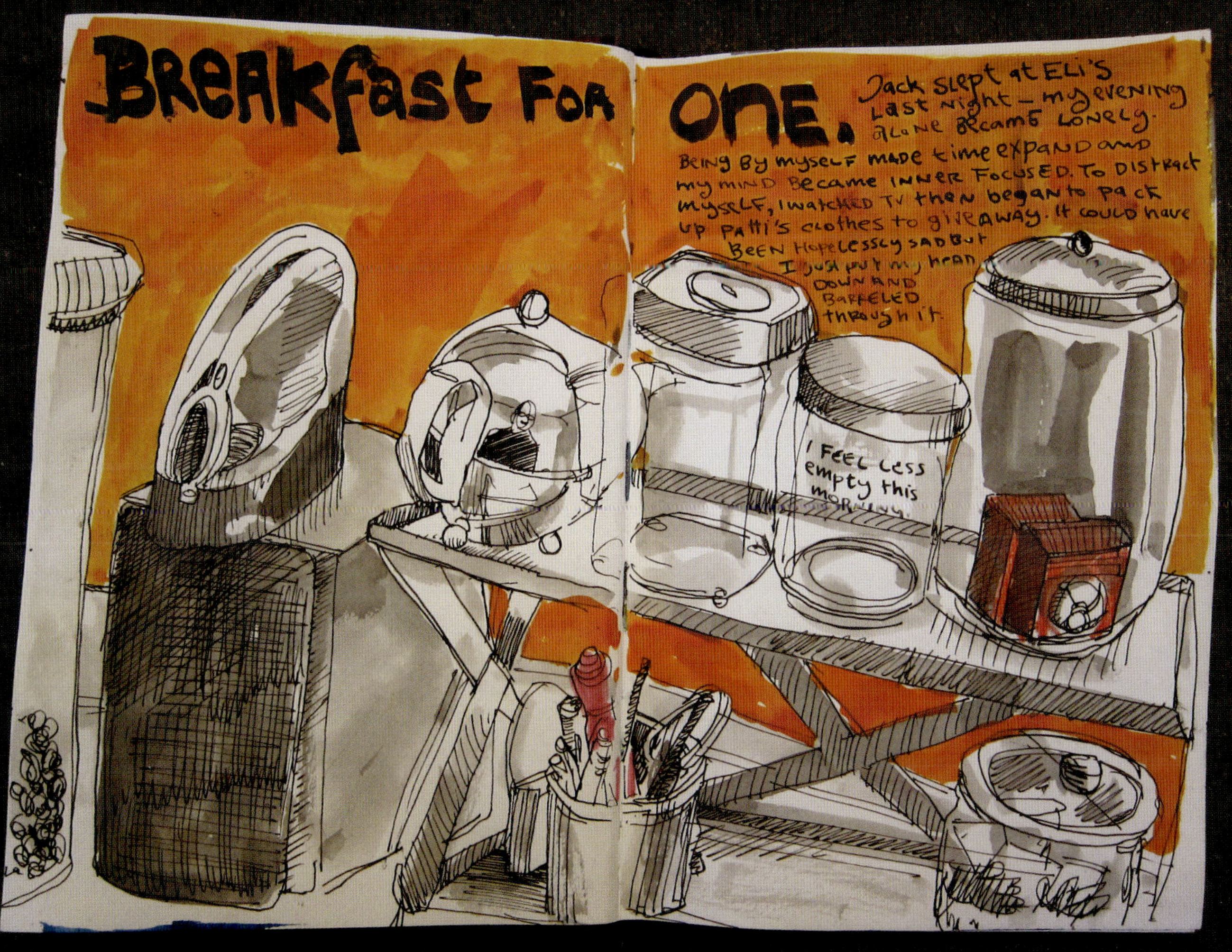

Breakfast for One

I've been documenting my state of mind since my wife was killed. Every part of my day is different, sometimes even in small ways and, without being morose, I feel it's important to contemplate these changes. Even the mundane view I face every morning has new meaning, and drawing allows my subconscious to absorb and integrate that significance.

—Danny Gregory

How do you express vulnerability in your artwork?

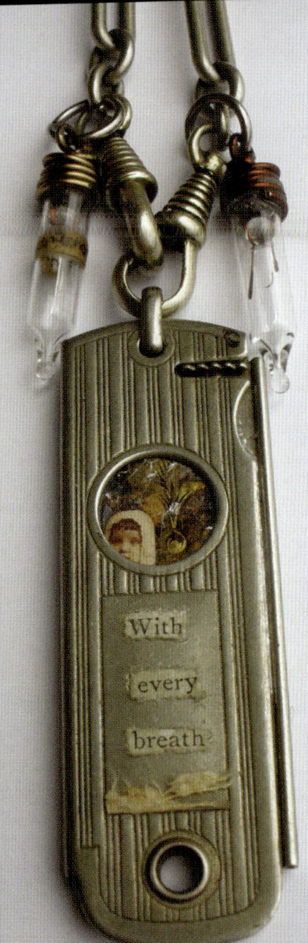

With Every Breath

I like very simple lines in my artwork. I feel less is more sometimes. I find, then, that I tend to question myself. Is it good enough? Is it too simple? Should there be more to this piece than meets the eye? I think you always tend to be vulnerable with your own work. We are our own worst critic.

—Jen Crossley

Do you feel there is too much copying of styles in the mixed-media world?

Yes, artists should be more original: **35%**
Yes, but it does not bother me: **53%**
No, not too much copying at all: **12%**

Just Roll With It

I strive to be less concerned with aesthetics and more concerned with expressing my truth. In time it became my second nature. My vulnerabilities enjoy residing in my art. They are allowed to roam free, say what they want to say, and be what they are. They express me. Odd, but the more fragility I allow in my art, the more strength I gain. If I were to keep my emotional world from being seen in my art, why would I bother making it?

—Orly Avineri

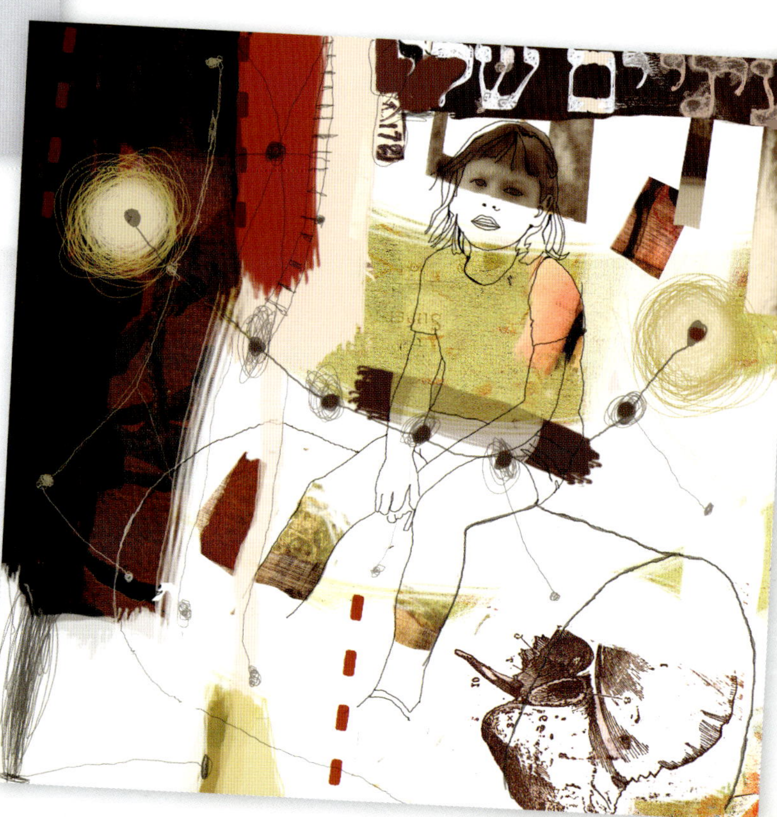

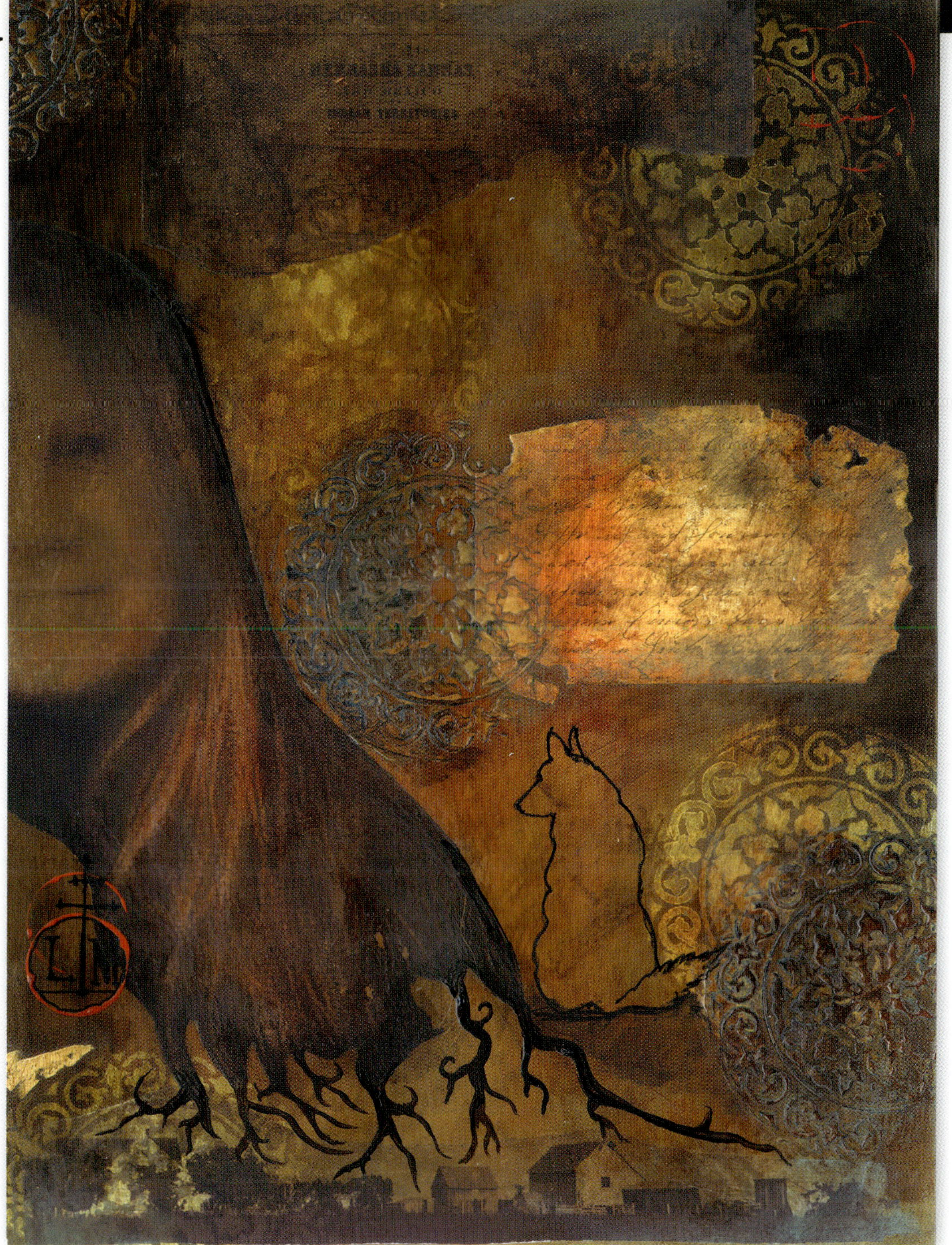

Self-Portrait

I was born in Nebraska, lived in California until I was five, but spent my formative years in New Mexico. Most of my family remains in Nebraska or close to Nebraska. The image of the farm at the bottom of my self-portrait is where my great-grandparents lived, where my grandfather grew up, and where my father was born. The vintage map portion at the top of the piece is of Nebraska, Kansas and New Mexico. I have never seen those three together on a map. The colors are, of course, the colors I always end up with.

—Leslie Marsh

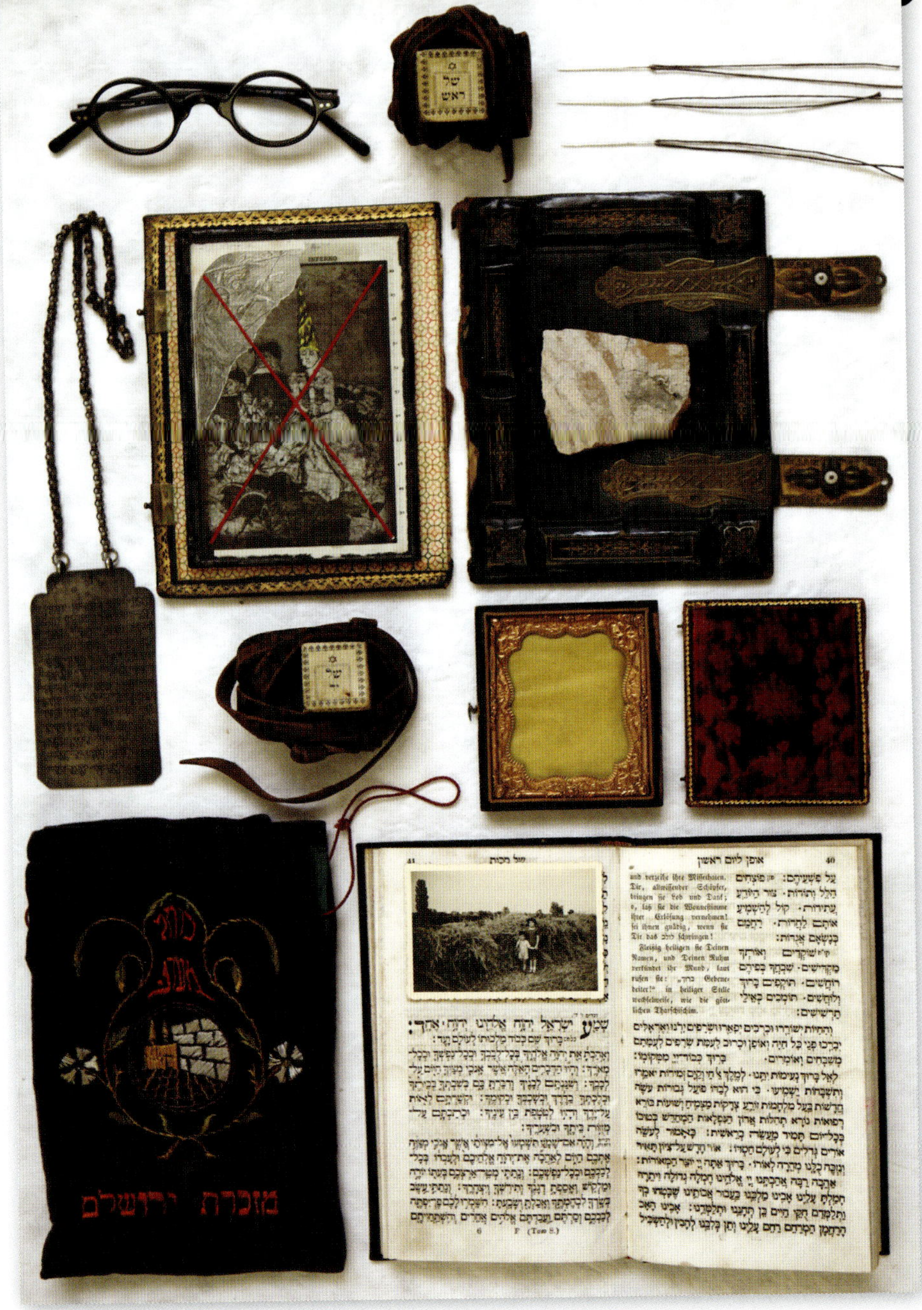

Self-Portrait

The self-portrait relates to my life and work as an artist. It encompasses things past and present, the metaphysical, religious and spiritual elements that make up my art and being. The expression of continuity synchronises with social justice issues, and the vision, whilst sometimes static and ordered, in the end becomes dynamic. The head and the heart work interdependently to assist the vision, strength and hope for future generations. The inspiration behind the piece came from my own work as an artist and as a result of my own genealogical research. Because much of my past commissioned works involved family and/or historical research, I chose those pieces in my home that exemplify expressions of my artwork.

—Judy Wilkenfeld

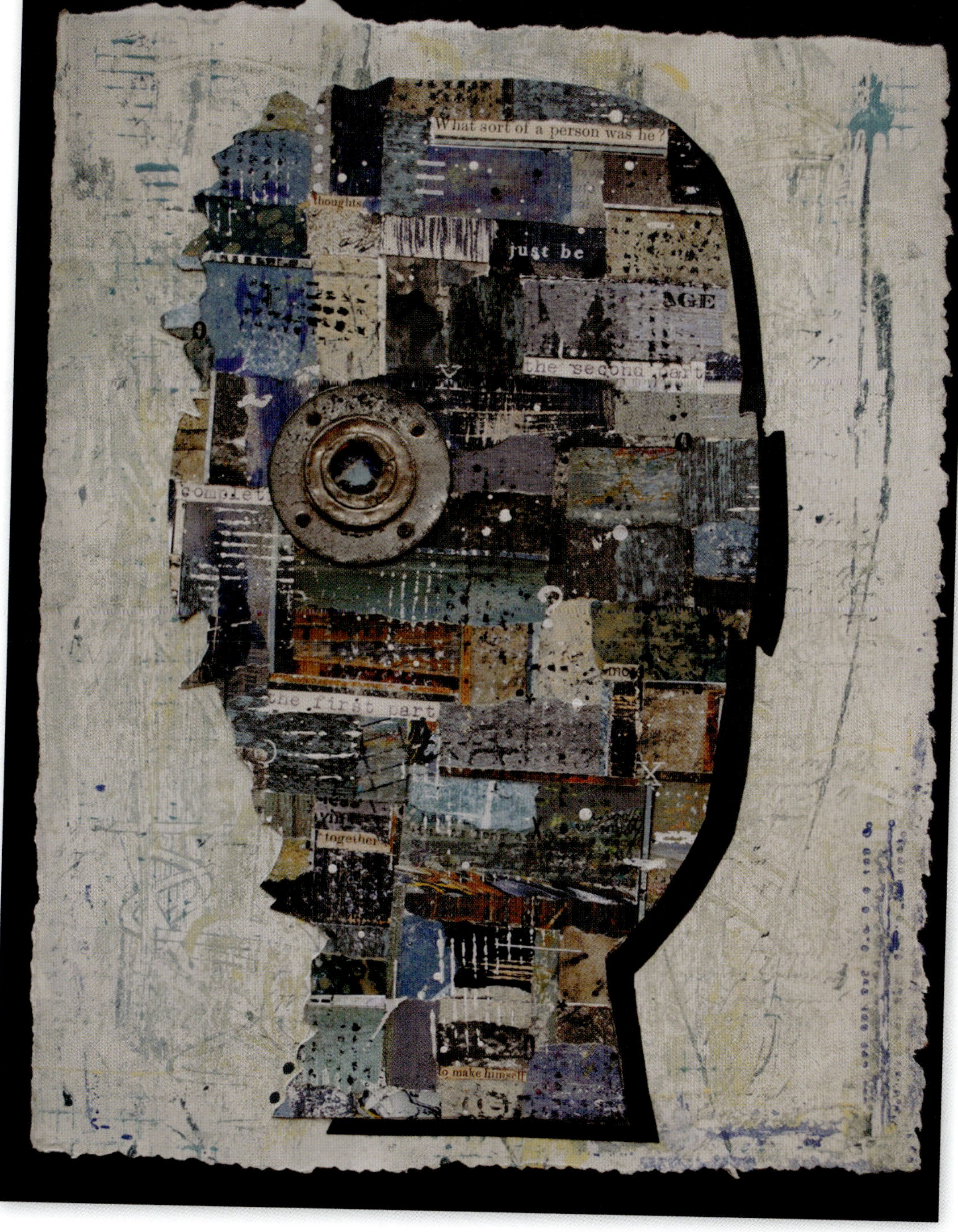

Self-Portrait

My self-portrait reflects the dual nature of my personality. On the one hand, I can be structured, sensible, organized and serious. On the other hand, I can be creative, playful, unrestrained and comical. I combine and integrate both of these aspects in my daily life as an artist and as a psychologist. While the balance between the two sides serves me well in these dual roles, there are definitely times when they battle head-to-head.

—Seth Apter

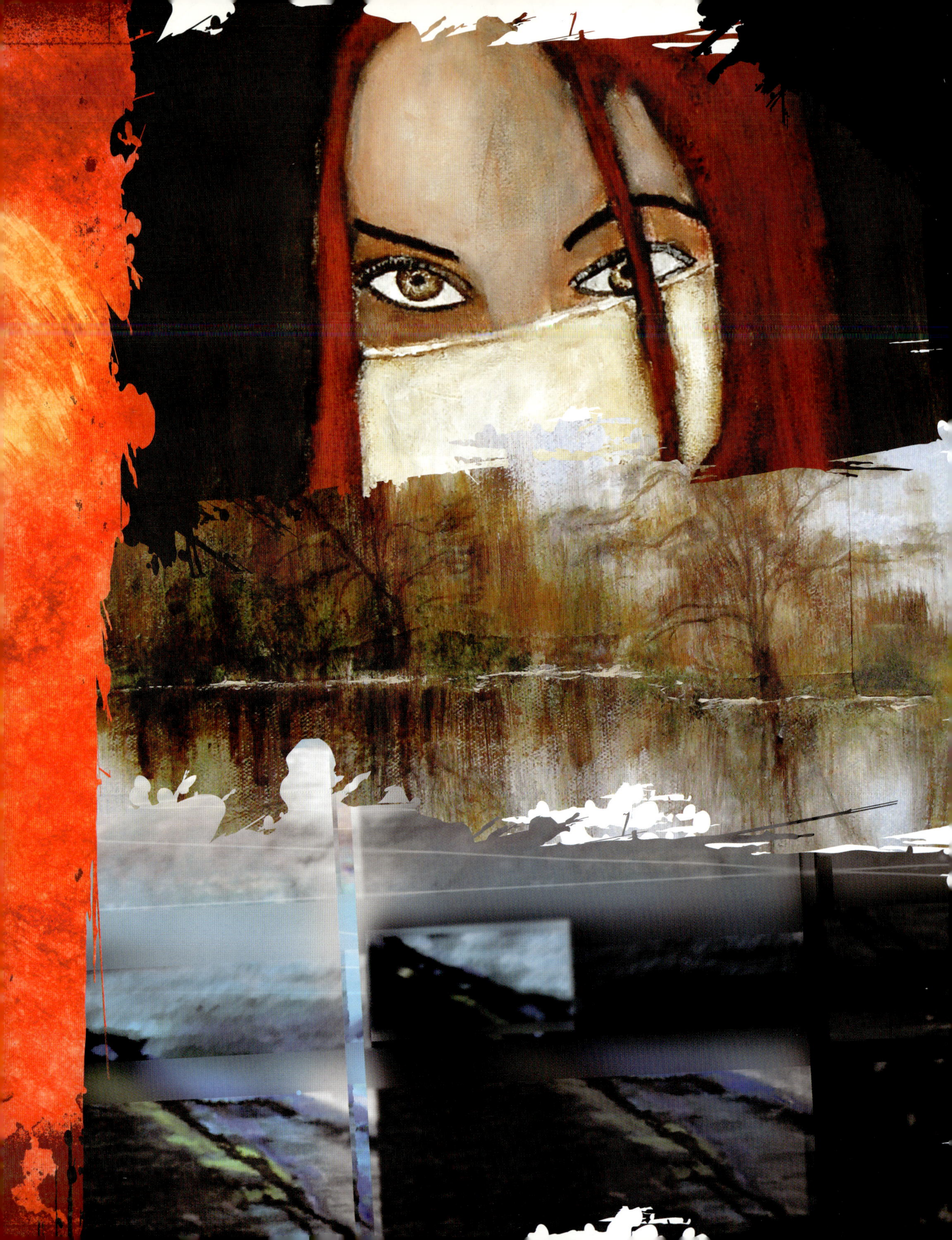

section three

Secrets Revealed

On your journey so far, you have already gotten to know a select group of artists at a much deeper and more meaningful level. They have shared their creative beliefs, artistic dreams, and the emotions that drive their work. Now it is time to dig even deeper. Hidden within all of us are the secrets that we hold; secrets that can sometimes be traumatic, sometimes joyful, but always personal, intimate and powerful. For better or for worse, it is our secrets that often define us. And this is true of the artist as well.

In a manner of speaking, a secret is shared by the artist each time an artwork is created. Understanding the hidden, often untold story behind a piece of art can elevate it to a new level and greatly increase its meaning to and impact on a viewer. Unfortunately, opportunities to be invited inside the soul of the artist are quite rare. That is about to change. On the next step along your journey to the very heart of the artist, secrets are revealed.

In Section Three, you are introduced to a whole new group of artists. Each one has reached deep inside, exposed their vulnerabilities, and offered an intimate portrait of their innermost self. A total of 103 artists are included in Section Three. They share their private secrets and fears. On these pages you will read their responses to a series of thought-provoking questions and see their artwork created after contemplating a number of intimate prompts. The remainder of the survey questions, completed by an even larger group of artists, is also presented.

What is one thing you've never shared with the creative community?

An artwork can only hint at the many layers of often unspoken secrets that reside within every artist. Some secrets are personal, such as depression, domestic violence, illness or self-doubt. Others are more external and include judgment and criticism of others. In all cases one thing is clear: the private, inner world of the artist is fuel for the artistic fire.

Sometimes creating art is a lonely, depressing task! It takes courage, determination, faith, and clarity to face the blank surface upon which we, as artists, place our dreams and visions. I don't think this obstacle is shared amongst ourselves that much, and I know it has happened to me many times.

—Laura Quilligan

A part of my drive to create art is my ongoing battle with depression. The ebb and flow of my creativity seems to follow along with my cycles of depression. The relationship between them is perhaps more symbiotic, as one pulls and pushes the other, and this effectively balances me.

—David Castle

The time we were nearly homeless. Both my husband and I were too ill to work and were barely living on credit cards until they maxed out. Two weeks before we would have been on the street, my husband found work. During that period, the inspiration and warmth of the online art community kept me sane.

—Shayla Perreault Newcomb

Myself! I like to keep a certain amount of anonymity. In general, it is important to me to keep access to the outside world with its environment, aesthetic rules and influence at a comfortably controlled distance.

—Jayne A. Harnett-Hargrove

I am an abortion survivor. My parents really, truly hated me. To have my parents tell me they wanted to abort me and my mother say she wanted to kill herself because I was inside her did nothing for my self-worth. I am still processing this, and art is my voice and has always been my best friend.

—Urbandon

How the death of my father and being orphaned at the age of eleven almost destroyed my desire to become an artist. That my only encouragement was in knowing that my mother and grandmother had been artists, and that I had the inner need and the ability even at that young age.

—Stephen Elliot

Have you ever donated a piece of art for charity?

Yes: **70%**

No: **30%**

Drawing and painting can be difficult because I have a tendency to "forget" the left side of things unless I constantly monitor the canvas. Thank you, brain tumor! There have been times when I have forgotten to paint an entire section of a canvas or have not drawn the whole left side of a face!

—*Laura A. Pace*

I have never told anyone my belief that unless an artist can paint realistic imagery in oils, the person is not really an artist in the truest sense of the word. I imagine this is due to messages that were instilled in me at a very young age, and—yes—I constantly struggle to overcome this concept.

—*Denise Aumick*

I was in an abusive marriage for twenty-eight years, which ended six years ago. Not surprisingly, it was also six years ago that I discovered my love of mixed-media art and began creating. As each year goes by and I feel safer and happier, my artistic life grows and becomes more prolific.

—*Erin Perry*

How do you say you haven't shared your personal tragedies when those are the things that so many times generate your artwork? I have never shared the specifics of the tragedies in my life with the art community, but in so many ways, they have found their way into my work.

—*Art by Canace*

That I have always felt art is impractical. I can't get enough of it, I can't make enough of it, I can't express myself enough in it; yet "art," in the day-to-day goings-on, is so terribly impractical. But in the big picture, art is necessary in the way air, food and God are necessary. Go figure.

—*Patricia Baldwin Seggebruch*

I was suicidal for most of 2007. Expression through crafting and painting helped me to postpone my suicide long enough to overcome those feelings. It takes time, which, sadly, many people don't allow.

—*Chris Miser*

I feel like an art impostor at times, despite the fact that I have a degree in fine art, have dedicated my life to the pursuit of the visual arts, create art on a fairly regular basis and teach others. Public validation for my chosen career path is tough, at best. Self-validation is even tougher.

—*Lisa JonesMoore*

I am very envious of those who have the courage to really put themselves out there in the world. I wish I could develop enough confidence in my abilities to promote myself much more. I want to be among the legion of artists whose talents are well recognized by the art community.

—*Leslie Rosenberg*

I never share that I have bad days. I blog about the good stuff but not about the enormous fear I have of the cancer returning, of the insecurities I have about selling my art. The fear and the doubt aren't things I think about every day, but when these feelings show up, they show up loud and big.

—*Tricia Gillispie Scott*

I have never shared what my secrets are. I prefer that the art speaks for itself. It's supposed to do that, and if it fails, there's no point in masking or interpreting or shielding that.

—*Robert Dresdner*

I am very critical, not only of my own work, but also of others' work. If I come across something I think is not good, I don't say anything and leave. And I have trouble with the fact that some "artists" get overexposed because they shout loud, while, in my opinion, their work isn't good.

—*Marit Barentsen*

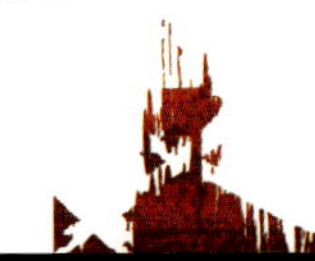

Can you share a secret?

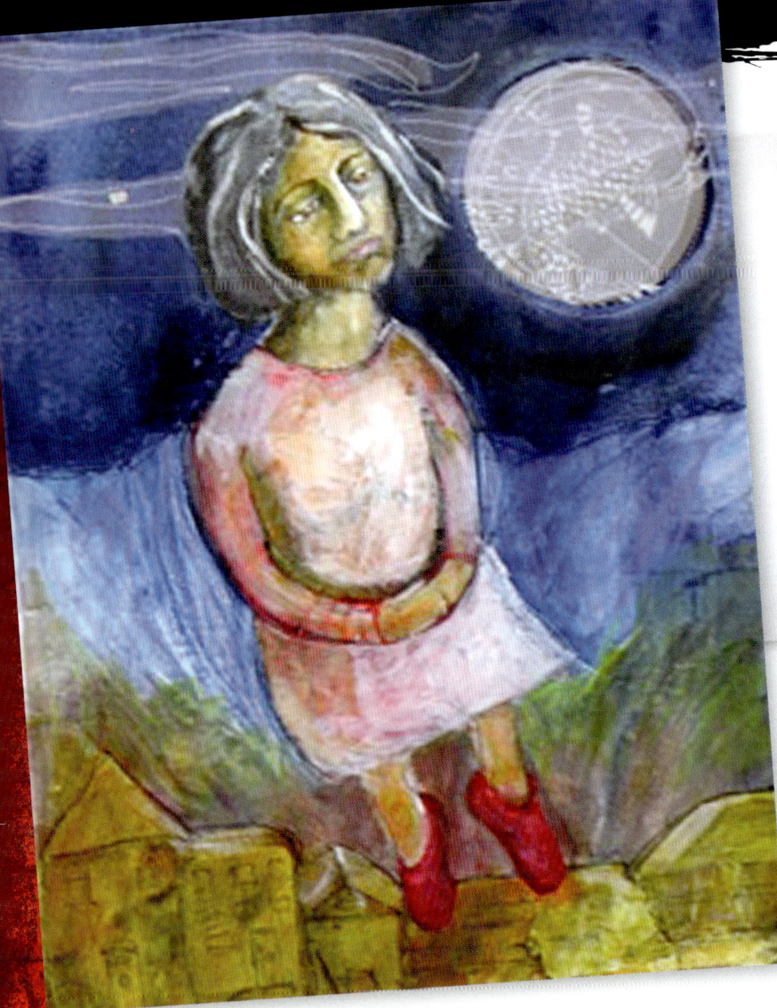

Tethered

I've always felt that I needed to fight to express myself. I was always trying to fly but was eventually convinced that I couldn't go far, and so I took the path most traveled and got married young (and lucky). When my kids were young, there was a constant tug between art and kids. I felt tethered, not free. Now, with my children grown (or nearly), I see my family as a grounding force in my life. This is why there is no obvious rope holding me back in the painting. The rope was always the voice of my critic.

—Diana Trout

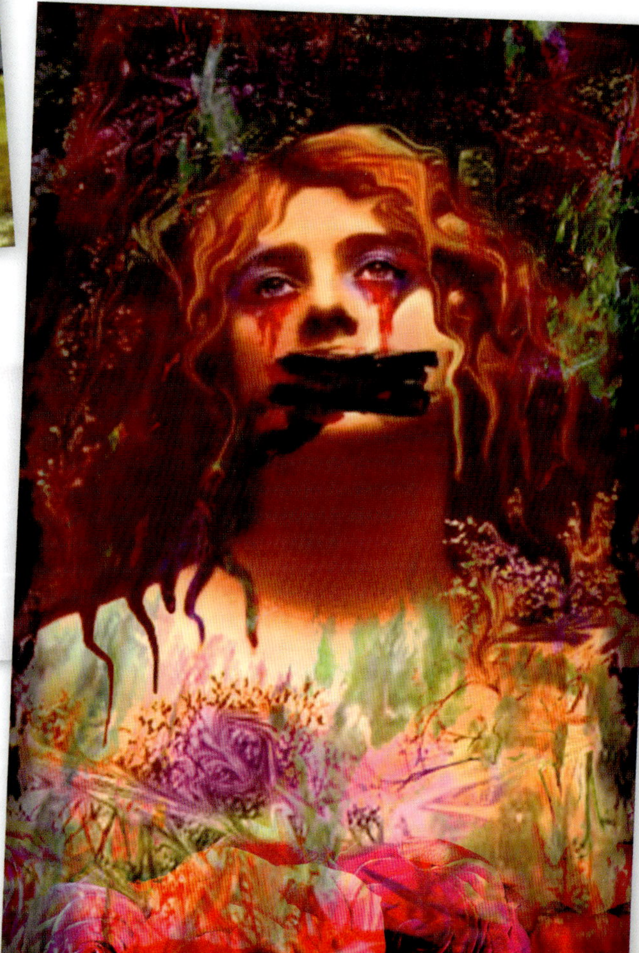

Thirteen Secrets

This piece was created when I had secrets that I could not share with anyone except the canvas. I know my secret will forever be hidden there. She is sworn to secrecy, her mouth painted upon and never to share the secrets with anyone.

—Izabella Pierce

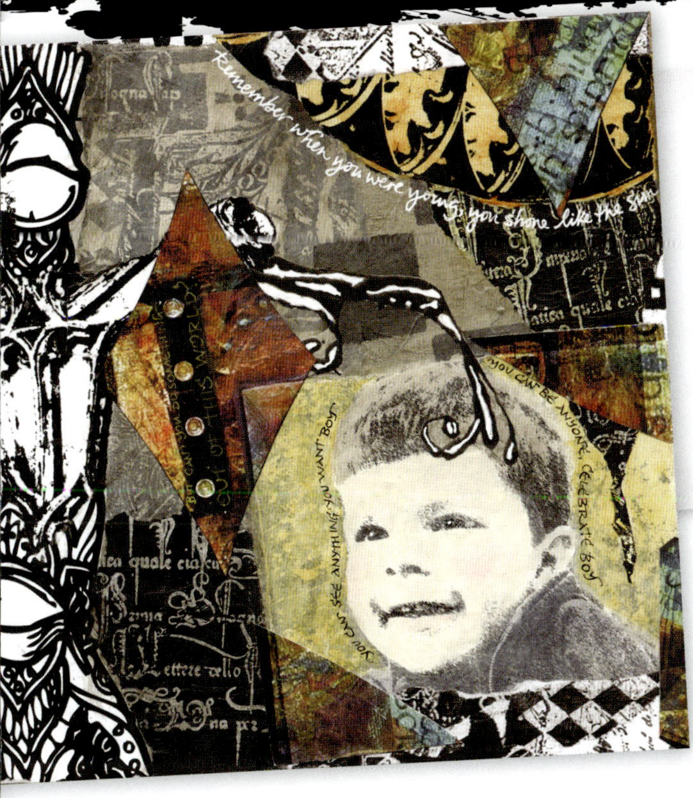

The Invisible Labyrinth

My sweet, four-year-old grandson is autistic. While it isn't exactly a secret, it isn't something I shout out to everyone I meet. Right now he does not speak, so I can only imagine what goes on behind those beautiful eyes of his. My interpretation of his inner world is one of chaos, where there is little resting space. My grandson is, for the most part, a happy boy. I wish him a meaningful, expressive world and look forward to the day when we find our way to each other through "The Invisible Labyrinth."

—Holly Dean

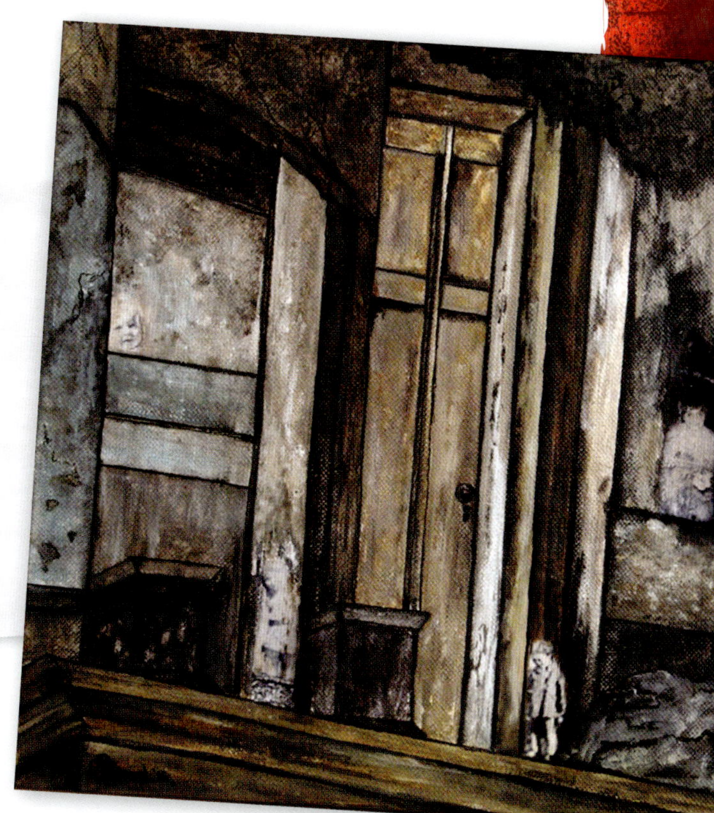

I Am the Secret

The quest to share a secret as expressed in an artwork led me to a strange conclusion—I am the Secret! I am other people's secret . . . not the least of which are the birth mother who put me up for adoption and the sexual predators who violated me as a child. I don't doubt that to this day, decades later, I am still their secret. This painting took on more and more meaning as I worked at it. There were so many different levels, surfaces, and color nuances that perfectly reflected the fact that I am a secret on so many levels and in such a wide variety of shades.

—Sonia Simard

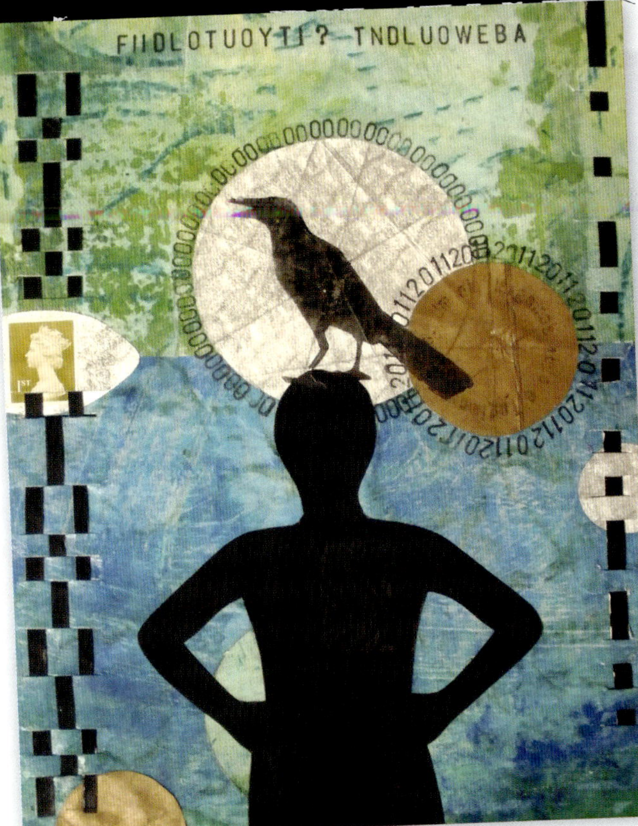

If I Told

While working on this little piece, I thought a lot about the American obsession with knowing everyone else's secrets and with sharing every intimate detail of one's own life with perfect strangers all over the world via the Internet. Has privacy become countercultural? I tried to use images that allude to secrets or mystery. "A little bird told me." A dark, silent figure gives away nothing. A circular message in Portuguese may be a secret. The secret of the words across the top is easily revealed when you look at it the right way.

—Debra Tennison

Heart's Reflection

With this piece I am expressing something that I have learned and would like to believe it is a universal secret—that once you truly love something or someone and, conversely, when you are loved, that love can never be taken away or destroyed, because love is eternal. If you look closely at the figure, she appears to be kissing a mirrored surface or perhaps, hovering over black water illuminated by moonlight. You can see her reflection, but not clearly—so perhaps it is the lips of her lover, perfectly matched to hers. If you look closely at her skin, you can make out two crows sitting in the branches, which might lead you to recall the saying about seeing crows—"one for sorrow, two for joy."

—Susan Tuttle

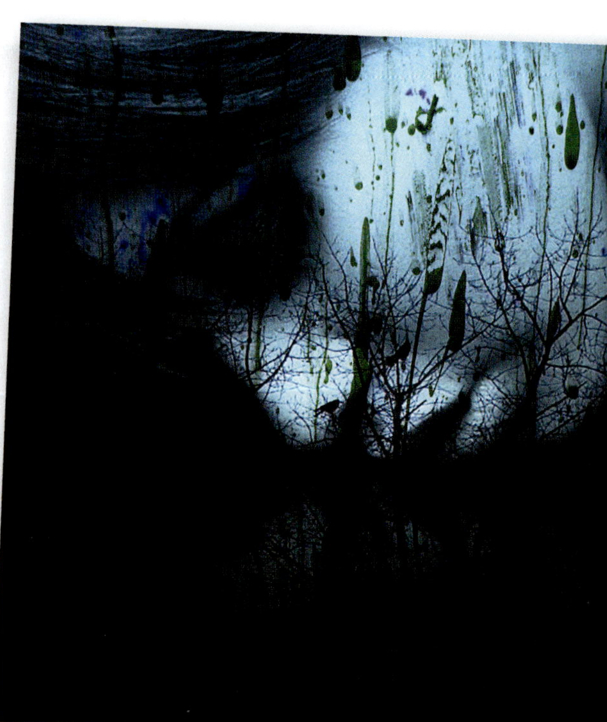

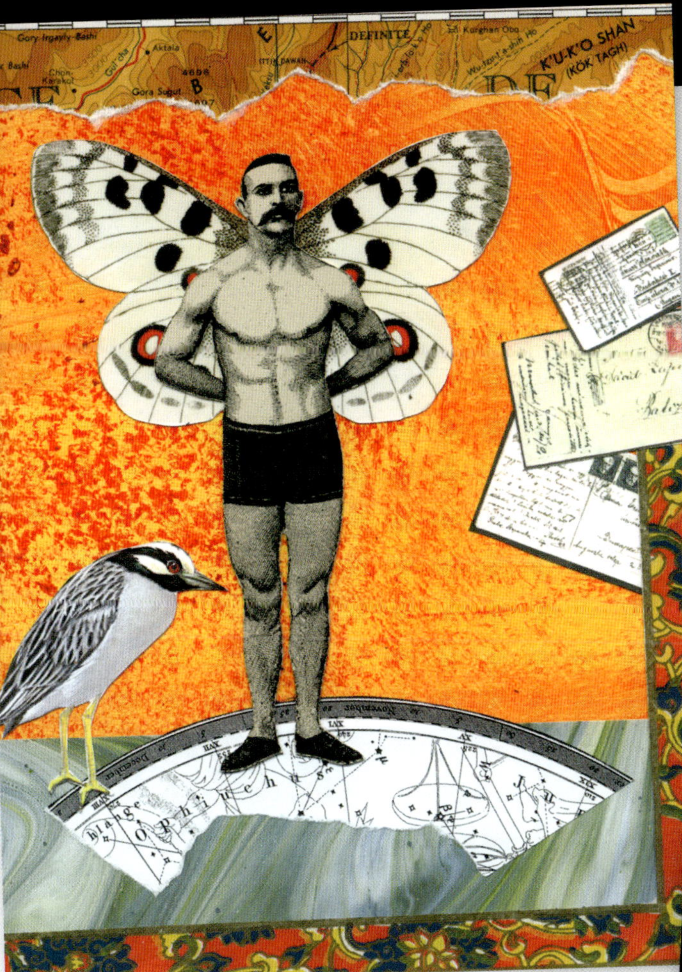

Butterflyman

This piece deals with the secret of a middle-aged man wishing for a body that doesn't show the struggles of time and gravity. Other levels are at play here as well. The butterflyman represents the transformation from the identity of a teacher to a more inclusive whole. New ideas and directions are taking flight—a rebirth, a new script. This is, I suppose, the representation of my secret hopes in my retirement. I feel the piece has the quality of an illuminated manuscript with the colors and different borders—perhaps a first page in my new book of days.

—Terry Garrett

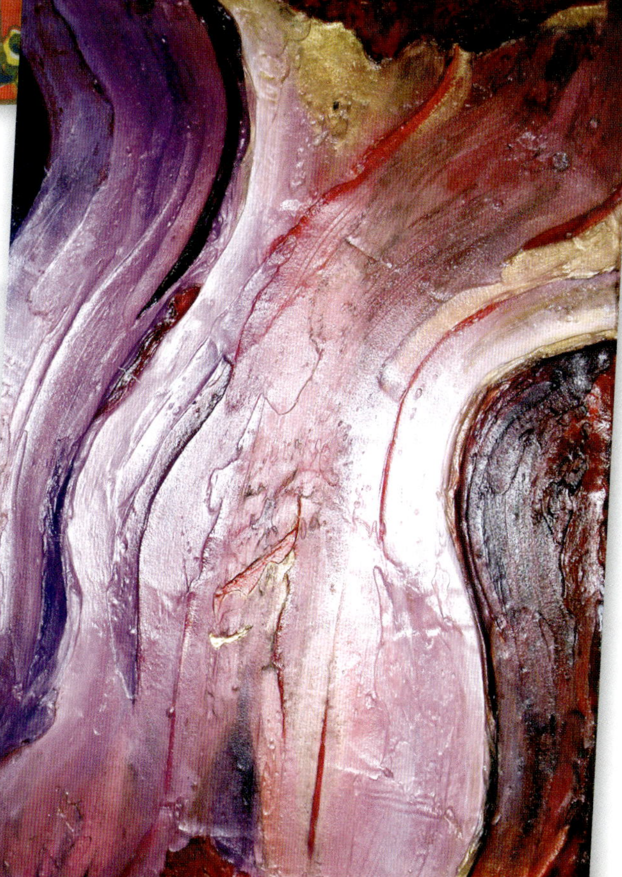

WHO I AM?

This piece holds a very special place within me because I was really struggling with a lot of my sexual past and the different emotions and wounds that I suffered.

—Loryn Spangler-Jones

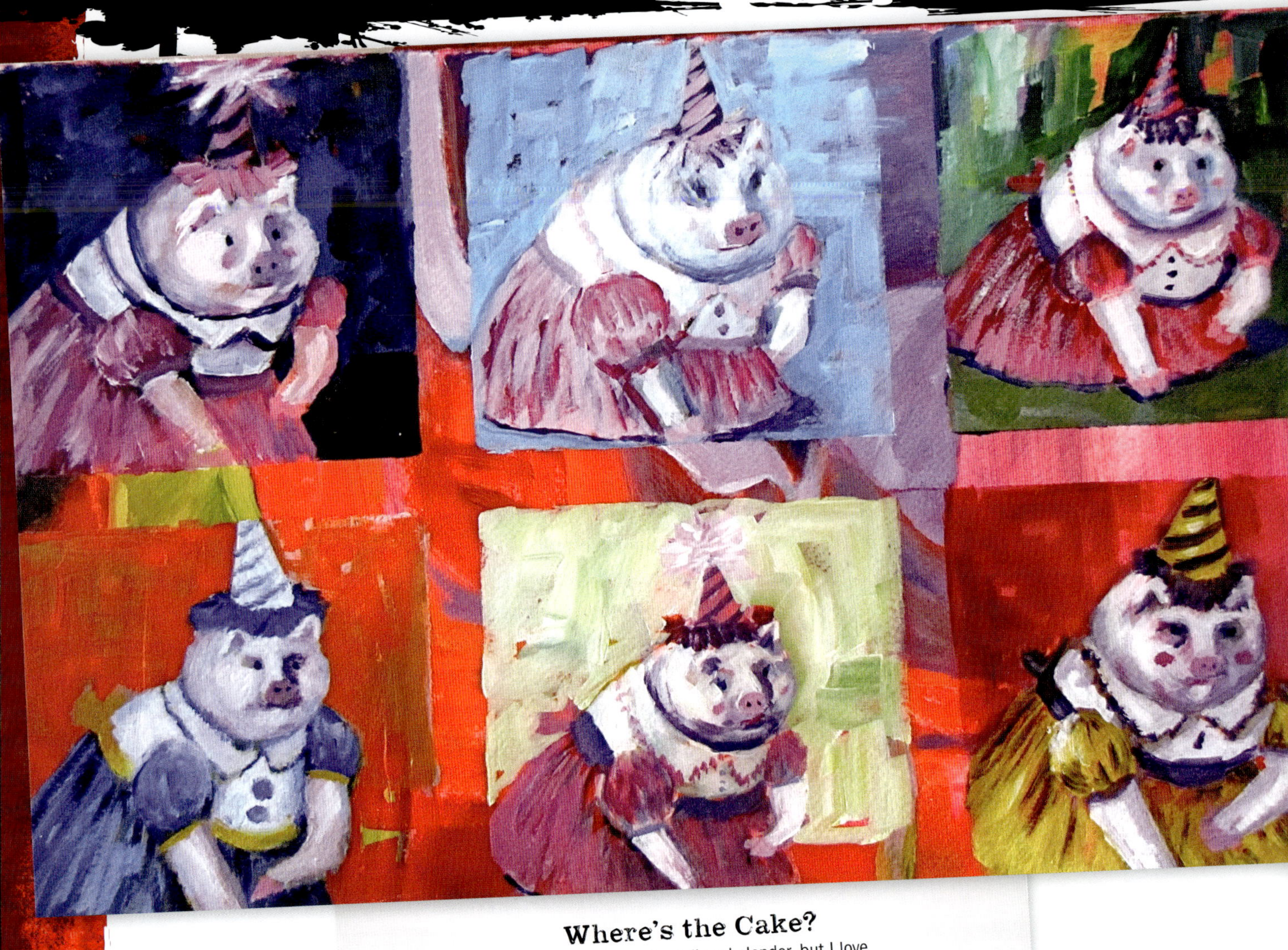

Where's the Cake?

The secret: I'm tall and slender, but I love sweets, and I can sniff out a bakery like a bloodhound. No one knows how much of a problem it is for me. This painting of party pigs is about how important cake is. Some pigs look more patient than others, but sometimes I feel like the one in yellow: where is the cake *now*?

—Terry Rafferty

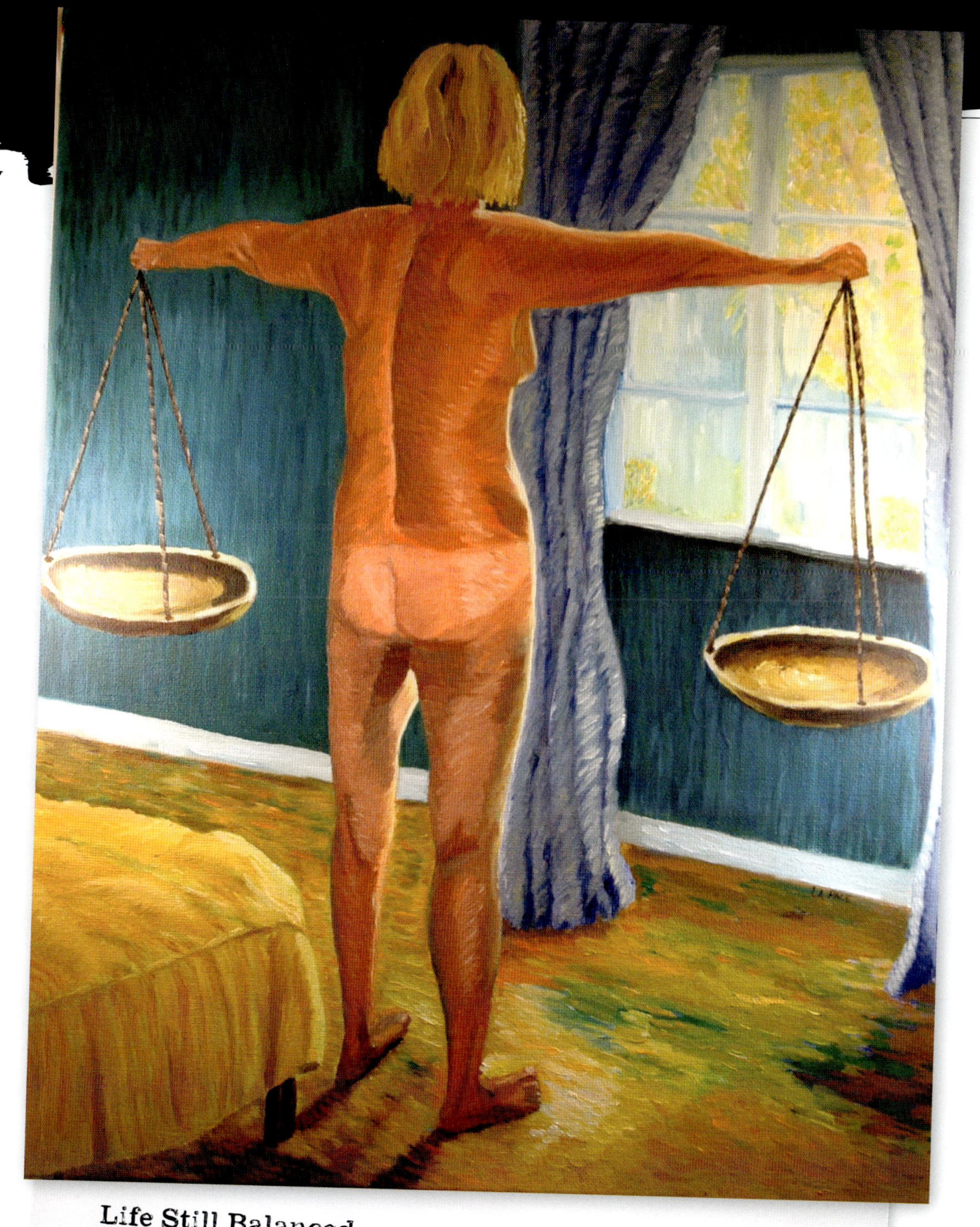

Life Still Balanced

I have lived through one large, destructive brain tumor with consequences far reaching for me. "Life Still Balanced" is how I feel every morning when I wake up: I must rebalance everything. Most people balance many things. Work and family life, art and family, money and anything! I wake up and immediately have to think balance on a more primal level—my body. It just keeps escalating from there. One thing too many on one side or the other, and the whole thing, me, topples. *But*, every morning I get up and rebalance, hopeful of a good, new, perfectly balanced day.

—Laura A. Pace

Do you enjoy working more intuitively or by carefully thinking through your process?

The right brain rules. By far the majority of these artists work intuitively and spontaneously. For many, thinking too specifically about the process actually dampens the creative spirit. That being said, a few artists seek to find a balance between formal preparation and creative abandon. And several noted that certain mediums actually require a great deal of precision for success.

Before I sit down to create, I will have pondered a theme for weeks. I like to carry an idea with me as I walk through my days. I'll consider different mediums and how I may express my ideas. When it comes to actually sitting down and creating, I put my thoughts aside and work intuitively.

—Kathryn Antyr

I use a mixture of these processes. My initial idea will usually come intuitively—while drifting off to sleep, while bathing, in meditation. Then I may carefully plan out how I will construct. Some pieces need a strategy to be structurally sound and, therefore, must have a great deal of processing.

—Karin Bartimole

Many years ago when going through my art education, I did art carefully. After six-plus years of meditating, things changed dramatically. One day when I sat down to create art, to my great surprise, I gently slipped into a magical place, and from that point on, I work intuitively!

—Darlene Wilkinson

If I thought through the process, I'd never create anything. My inner critic would stop me before I ever got started.

—William J. Charlebois

Intuitively. When I just "play" and see what happens, the result is a journey, and it's much more fun. I may have an idea of color or texture that I'd like to see, but much less structured definitely works for me.

—Creative Billie

I very rarely have a plan. For me, it is in the *process* of creating that my enjoyment is found. I learned early on not to get too caught up with what I envision a "finished" piece to be because they very rarely look anything like that at the end of the day.

—Loryn Spangler-Jones

All of my life I have listened to my heart and leapt, sometimes with reckless abandon. I have never lived to regret a single leap. It tends to be the same when it comes to my art. Listening to my inner voice has led to so many serendipitous and magical surprises in my art.

—Susan Tuttle

I usually begin a piece with lots of planning, several small sketches and notes. But when I'm actually creating, plans sometimes go out the window and intuition takes over. Often a mistake or something unexpected turns the piece in a totally new direction.

—Erin Perry

What type of work space fosters the most creativity for you?

Neat and clean with everything in its place: **11%**

Messy with everything already spread out: **18%**

Somewhere in between: **71%**

If you sell your work, do you have trouble with pricing?

No, I have a system that works for me: **8%**

Yes, but overall I am comfortable with my pricing decisions: **42%**

Yes, and as a result I tend to underprice: **48%**

Yes, and as a result I tend to overprice: **2%**

If I work intuitively, my heart and my art sing. If I carefully think through the process, something is lost. It becomes too mechanical and predetermined. I've always said that if the piece creates itself, then I know it's grand.

—Art by Canace

Intuitively is the only way I can work and function. My work is akin to following a map when you can only see a small grid at a time.

—Patti Edmon

I learned from Francis Bacon that chance plays a big part in daily life, so I've always tried to incorporate a loss of control while working. I enjoy the spontaneity of pure creativity and the surprise of things simply coming together like jazz.

—David Brady

I fluctuate from one way of working to the other, searching for balance. Careful thinking can be good to start with. I love being in "the zone," letting the muse take over for a while. The whole process is quite enjoyable to me.

—Holly Dean

I am very intuitive. Listening to what the piece wants to be is part of my artistic practice.

—Lorraine Reynolds

I never think about what I'm doing. If I do, what I produce is always over-thought-out and something I think other people will approve of, not something that is true to me. I usually produce the best work when I'm not thinking about it. It comes straight from within!

—Helen Stead

I am not an organized person, so the creative process is often a chaotic and random event for me. I have a real aversion to following instructions or designing anything in advance. I love the flexibility and freedom that comes with creating.

—Kathryn Dyche Dechairo

I have to say I work both ways, and it just happens. Some of my best work has come from my just getting out of the way. There also have been times where I envisioned a piece in my mind's eye and went right to the studio and made it.

—Terry Garrett

Do you think creative types are moodier than those with less artistic inclinations?

This was a very polarizing question. Many felt strongly that the concept of the moody and tortured artist is just a myth and that moodiness is not at all limited to creative types. In contrast, an equal number felt that artists, themselves included, were indeed a more sensitive and emotional lot. The main reason for this: Artists mine the depths of their souls over and over.

Moody comes in all shapes and sizes, and is not limited to creative types.

—Barbara Kleinhans

To some degree, yes. The very things that create a rich environment for creativity can also cause a person to experience life at its heights and depths. The excitement of seeing the myriad possibilities and being able to inhabit each concept can also lead to feeling overwhelmed.

—Jan Avellana

No . . . anyone can be moody if they put their mind to it!

—Corrine Davis

Artists are often characterized as being unduly sensitive or antagonized by their own demons. It is this dip into an other-world of imagined realm that makes artists true alchemists. Art acts as a palette intermediary, which allows for the exorcism of internal churn into other physical form.

—Stephanie Rigsby

No. What I do think is that creative people allow themselves to open up part of their soul for the sake of their art. You can't immerse yourself in your art and not leak out your soul.

—Dawn Raymond

I tend to think so. I believe that artistic types tend to see the world differently and are more in tune to and affected by the small idiosyncrasies of life in general that most people don't even notice.

—Ingrid Dijkers

Definitely not! Maybe artistic people are just more open about expressing their moods than others. My artistic friends are a lot happier than most other people I know. There is something about the creative process that is absorbing, relaxing, and energizing. I think it's good for my health.

—Kathleen Harrington

How well do you handle the business side of being an artist?

This aspect is usually problematic for me: **52%**
Don't really embrace the business side, but I handle it well: **34%**
I feel equally able to focus on both creativity and business: **12%**
The business side is easy . . . it is the creating that is hard: **2%**

I do think that most artists are on a different emotional level than people who are not artistically inclined. There is an awareness of the world that is perhaps much more unique than that of the majority of people on the planet.

Allison Berringer

I don't think so. I have found that my artistic friends seem to find a balance in their life that many other friends don't. Artists don't seem to escape their frustrations, but rather hone them into an outlet and free themselves of them.

—Kim Palmer

It would appear historically that artists are moody, dark, etc. I am neither, and resent that box we get put in. As if, to be a great artist, it's expected that we are crazy, difficult and wild. Most of the working artists I know are no moodier than anyone else. In fact, they seem a bit more soul-satisfied.

—Diana Trout

Yes, maybe because creative minds build bridges while crossing. At the same time, creativity demands for some bridges to be burned. Creative people constantly walk around with a box full of matches in their pockets, and that's not always pleasant.

—Martin Hoogeboom

Unfortunately, it seems to be the curse that comes with the creative blessing. I work alongside many artists, and we all seem to share the common denominator of anxiety or depression. I wonder if that is the difference in brain function in creative people.

—Teresa Pyskaty-Lamicella

I am not sure if creative types are moodier than those who are less so inclined, but I know that some of the best artwork that I have created has been done when I was under some kind of perceived external pressure or feeling the most angst!

—Robert Stockton

Artists are moodier than your average Joe because they are plumbing the depths of their emotions. They bring to the surface their joy, sadness, anger and views of a world that is not always pretty. Creative types create and explore their own realities—warts and all.

—Urbandon

In general, creative types can portray a kind of moody, brooding personality. It's just an ego-oriented aspect that gets in the way and perpetuates the image of the miserable, self-sacrificing, stereotypical artist. However, I think this stereotype is slowly losing momentum.

—Laura Quilligan

"Moodiness" carries with it a negative connotation. I think, if anything, many artists are intuitive and introspective. No one can function at a high level of output all the time, so sometimes it's necessary to turn inward and spend time alone in order to recharge creatively.

—Lelainia N. Lloyd

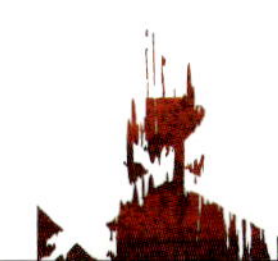

Have you ever lost a friendship over art?

Conflicts with friends and family as a consequence of being an artist are not uncommon. Among this group of artists, friendships have been severed for a variety of reasons, including jealousy, isolation, competing priorities and time limitations. Many artists felt that in a duel between art and friendship, art would be the victor every time.

After graduation I made jewelry using roofing felt. A "friend" asked me how I did it and I showed her. A week later this friend was trying to take sales from me by selling jewelry that looked similar to mine just doors down from the gallery carrying my line. I felt betrayed.

—Karin Bartimole

Yes, making the commitment to my art has distanced me from many former friends. The more I have embraced my artistic dreams and been acknowledged for it, the less I seem to have in common with the people who once occupied my spare time.

—Arabella Grayson

I have never lost a relationship over art, but it has created tension. In one relationship I was told I loved art more than I loved the person I was involved with. It was true. No longer together, I still have art, and it loves me back.

—Patricia Anders

No. As in all arguments, it is usually in reference to something else. You are never fighting about the cap on the toothpaste. So if you did lose a friendship over art, then I imagine there were deeper issues involved or the disagreement is not really about art to start with.

—Charlie Grosso

I actually lost a fiancé over art—not directly, but indirectly. I went away to art school and knew, once I was there, that I was finally fully myself.

—Veronica Funk

No, but the art would win out every time! I won't deny my capabilities because of someone else's behavior or attitudes. That's not fair on me.

—Andrea McNeill

Do you take "being green" into account in your creative field?

Yes, in all that I create: **13%**
Yes, to a certain degree: **63%**
No, but I feel I should: **13%**
No, it is not relevant to my art: **11%**

Believe it or not, yes. But if a friendship can be lost over "something," then it is not a friendship worth keeping.

—Patricia Baldwin Seggebruch

No, but they lost mine. A gallery had put together a big opening for their inaugural show, but I noticed several of my paintings had not been included. They were in the back room, carelessly stacked with nothing in between in one of the big bins. I came to get all of my work the next day.

—Martha Marshall

Not exactly, but I can easily see how this could happen. The times when I have noticed friendships getting in the middle of an experience with art were when the art was being evaluated. This is when jealousy and resentment can interfere with the friendship.

—Erika Cleveland

Yes, I have, and it totally caught me by surprise. I think it's perfectly normal when one of your peers does well and you have that split-second thought of, "Boy, I wish that were me." What's incredibly sad, though, is when we allow that to get between us and rob us both of the shared joy of the moment.

—Lelainia N. Lloyd

Because of art I have very few friends to lose. Art is my life. If you can't accept that concept, then chances are we won't be friends. If I didn't do my art, I wouldn't be who I am; therefore you probably wouldn't be with me. If you can't handle that, I can paint you a door.

—Stephen Elliot

Yes, sadly, more than one. Several due to the fact that people could not understand the time and isolation it takes to create art. One was due to an artist who had gleaned everything she could from me and then dumped me as a friend. One was due to my quitting a group due to health issues and the members having to pick up the slack and work. That was not a bad loss at all.

—Anne M. Huskey-Lockard

I don't believe I've ever lost a friendship over art, but I'm sure that I've lost out on developing some friendships due to art. The majority of my free time is spent pursuing artistic creation rather than socializing.

—Denise Aumick

About ten years ago, I entered a national show and won Juror's Choice. The people in my art group were happy for me, but there was an edge. With one friend, the edge grew, and the friendship ended. I think as artists we all want each other to succeed, but it's difficult sometimes to put our own insecurities aside and truly be happy for another's success.

—Fran Meneley

I can't recall losing a friendship over art, but I must confess that sometimes I'd rather spend time with my art than with my friends. I suppose that's why my closest friends are interested in art.

—Leslie Rosenberg

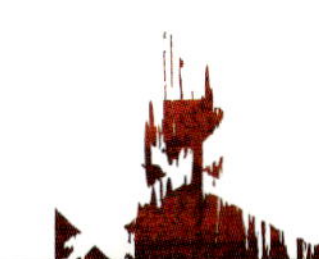

What is one current trend that you wish would go away?

While some artists saw the benefits of trends and felt that there was room for everything, by far the majority had at least one trend that they would like to see disappear. These included specific techniques and supplies, schools of art, the lowering of standards, the commercialization of art and the increase in focus on commerce over art.

The trend I would like to see disappear is the idea that all art making results in art, that nothing we make is unsuccessful. I believe that we need more critical thinking. I would much prefer to hear a thoughtful negative response than endless rounds of "it's great."

—Terry Rafferty

Can't think of one. Each trend is a learning experience at what works and what doesn't. It will go away on its own soon enough! Although . . . art critics (are they a trend?) would not be missed!

—Pat McNally

I wish the trend of using mass-produced supplies would go away! Going back to basics may be more time-consuming, but I think it is ultimately more rewarding. By increasing our dependence on manufacturers, I think we are losing touch with our cultural heritage.

—Lisa Sarsfield

I really wish some of the "conceptual" art would go away. Maybe some people really love that sort of artwork, but for me to enjoy a work of art, I need it to tell a story, reveal something about the world around me, or have beauty, mystery, disgust, humor, great skill or appealing colors.

—Marcia Beckett

I am guilty of it myself, but sticking the word "dream" or "inspire" in a mixed-media piece. Words carry meaning, and when they are over-used, they can lose their power and become meaningless.

—Shona Cole

Birds, only because I get tired of seeing them used so much. Now that I have said that, watch me go make something using birds as a theme!

—Lynn Cohen

One current trend I'd love to see go away is how so many people believe they are artists and attempt to sell their creations. I'm not sure if the Internet has helped to foster the notion that if someone attempts to do anything creative, they are an artist and should try to sell their work.

—Denise Aumick

Do you consider graffiti a legitimate art form?

Yes: **84%**

No: **16%**

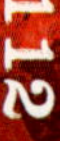

I object to major art shows growing so large that the number of artists is ridiculous. It is obvious that the organizer's focus is on their own bottom line. Visitors to these shows are overwhelmed by too much to look at and, overall, it is a disappointing experience for everyone.

—Holly Dean

Distressing things to make them look old. I love truly rusty, torn, broken, and beat-up objects and images. But I am really tired of seeing new papers and objects being rubbed with brown inks and paint to age them. I think it's all about being authentic with art; if you want old, use old.

—Leslie Rosenberg

I would love to see a quick death to angel wings and dunce caps on anything and everything. As for dunce caps, there are a few places I would put them, and it's not on someone's head. And what the hell is a dunce cap anyway? It is a symbol of ridicule and punishment—lovely.

—Urbandon

Actually, there isn't one! This is not to say that I find all trends worthwhile, but I also know that there is a reason a trend exists and that trends have their own lifespans. I'd much rather let a trend run its natural course—much more exciting that way.

—David Hayes

A current trend that I wish would go away, and I hope this doesn't come across as being an art snob, is the attention that some hobbyists are getting as they are being promoted as artists. It's especially disheartening to see a low level of commitment to creating art but a huge level of commitment to marketing a craft process.

—Veronica Funk

Do you feel a person needs formal training to be considered an artist?

Yes: **2%**

No: **98%**

Using Victorian photographs on everything. Who are these people? Where did they come from and why do I want them in my living room?

—Carrie Faden

Please, may I turn this question around and mention the trend I would like to see grow? It's the Personal Creativity trend: 1. Find your own voice. 2. Make your own marks. It is more hours spent working with our own materials, mind, heart and hands.

—Debra Tennison

Scrapbooking mania. It all looks the same, and there doesn't seem to be a lot of original thought going into the commercial premade stamping craze. I try not to stand in judgment, but do there have to be so many books about it?

—Julie Shackson

Oooooh, I'm going to upset someone here and I *do not* wish to do that. But since I'm being forced, I'd have to say it's cute, tilty-headed girls. I'd feel much better if they just held their heads up straight.

—Kim Hambric

Art that is overly self-aggrandizing. I am bothered by art that serves too much as an extension of the artist's ego and isn't real, or what feels to me like real. What I want to see and what inspires me is anything true and from the heart.

—Erika Cleveland

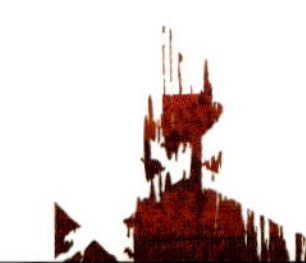

What expresses the innermost you?

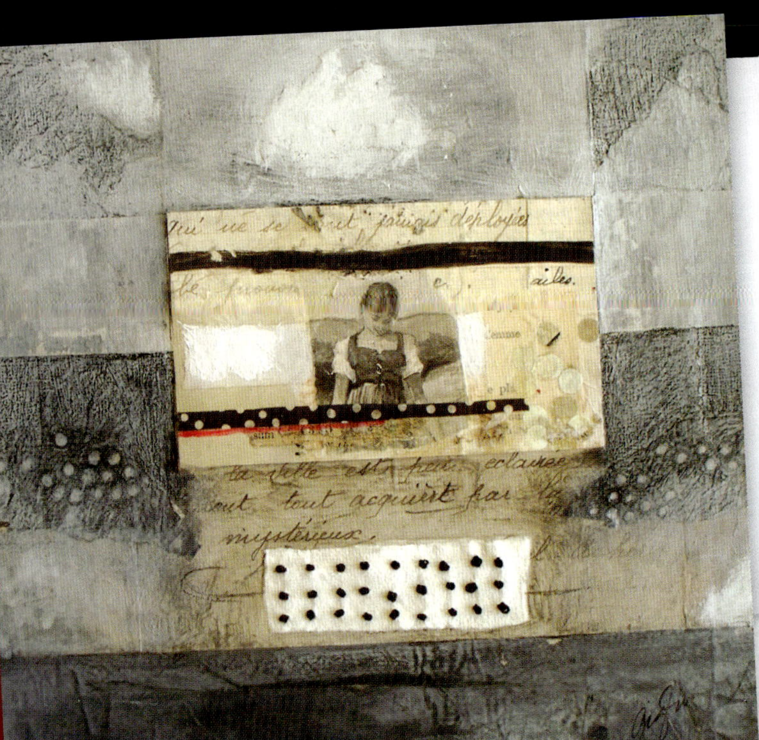

Mysterieux

At the deep well of my being, I feel I am mysterious, unformed and energetic. My painting began much differently and transformed through layers of paint and collage. This mirrors my own transformation as a human being, each year adding layers of lines and age as well as depth and substance. As I sanded back the layers on this painting, I saw a landscape rise into focus behind the main image, which represents me, and I felt that I had found a connection with that innermost part of me where the universal blends with the individual. Just as the center of my being is mysterious, so too, I believe, is the process of the creation of art.

—*Caterina Giglio*

Misfit

At times in my life, I've felt like I just don't fit in: I guess we all feel that way sometimes. I'm married, but we don't have kids, so I don't fit in with the moms or the singles. I live in the South, but I'm not from the South, so I don't fit in with some of the people here. The one place I've always felt like I do fit in is with my art and blogging friends. So my misfit status instantly disappears when I'm with my art buddies. It makes me appreciate them even more.

—*Jane Royal*

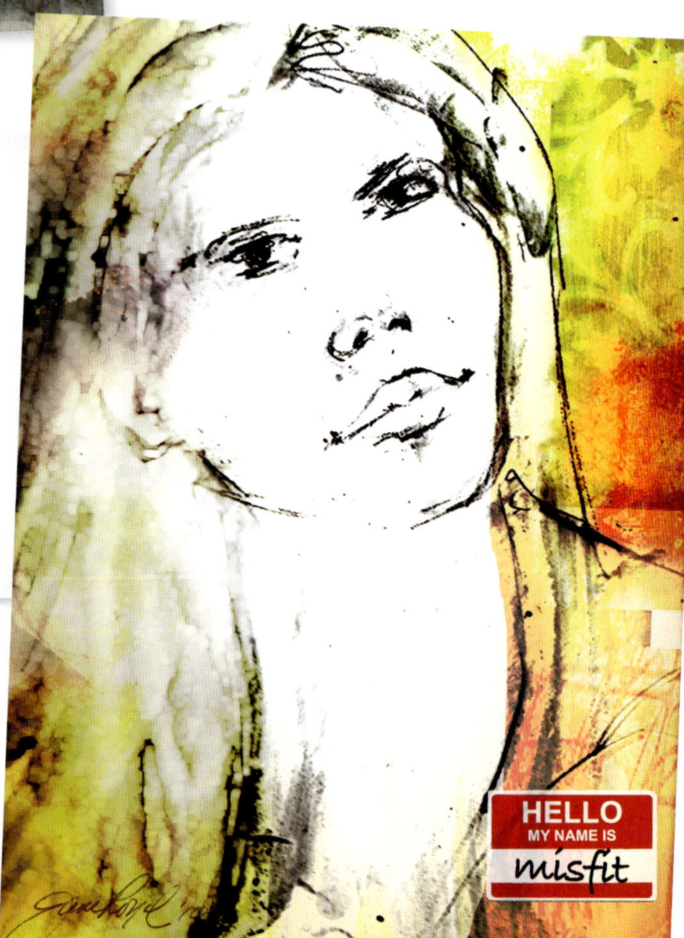

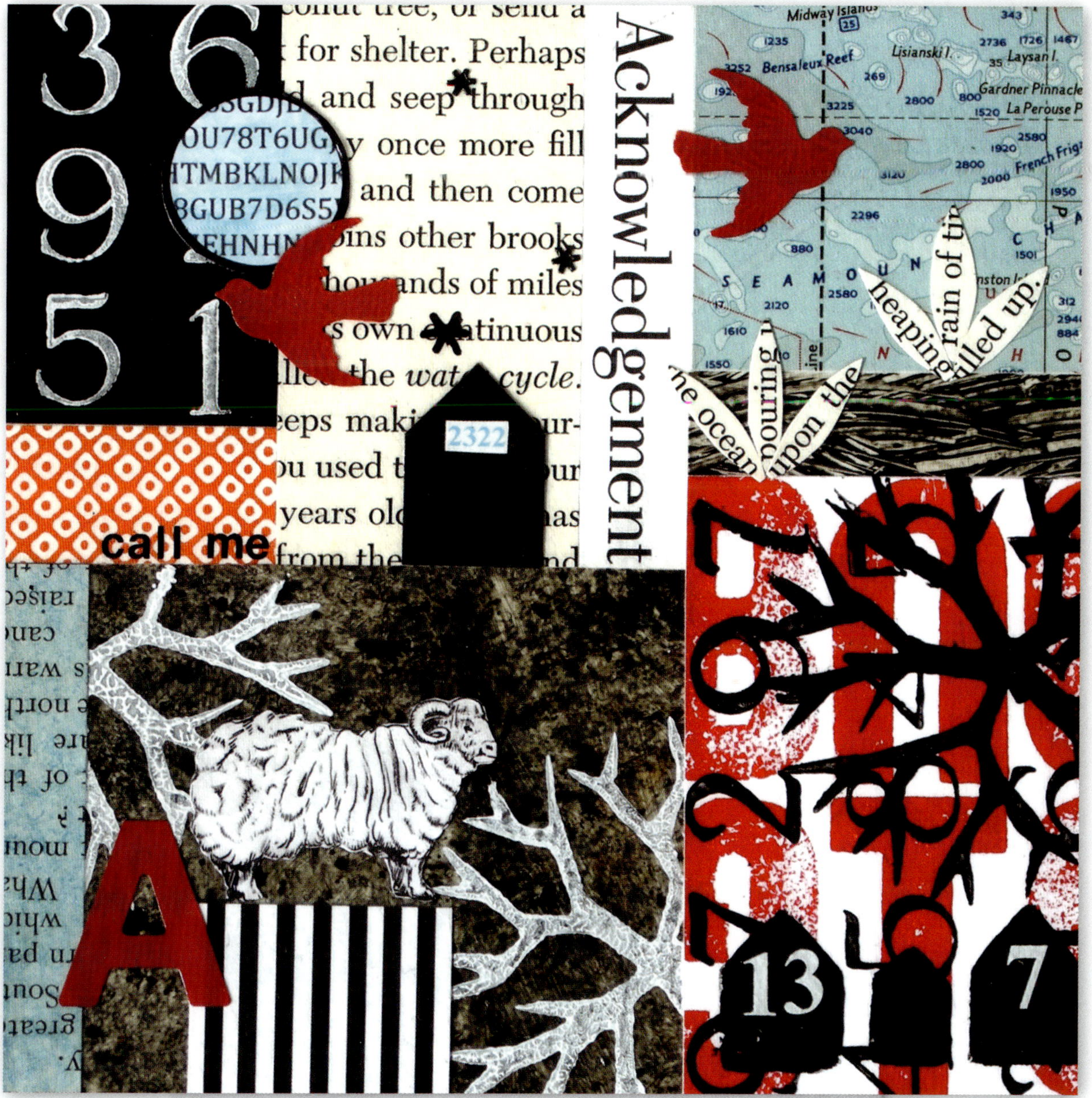

Acknowledgement

To put it briefly: I am a sheep looking for acknowledgment through my artwork.

—*Kim Hambric*

What expresses the innermost you?

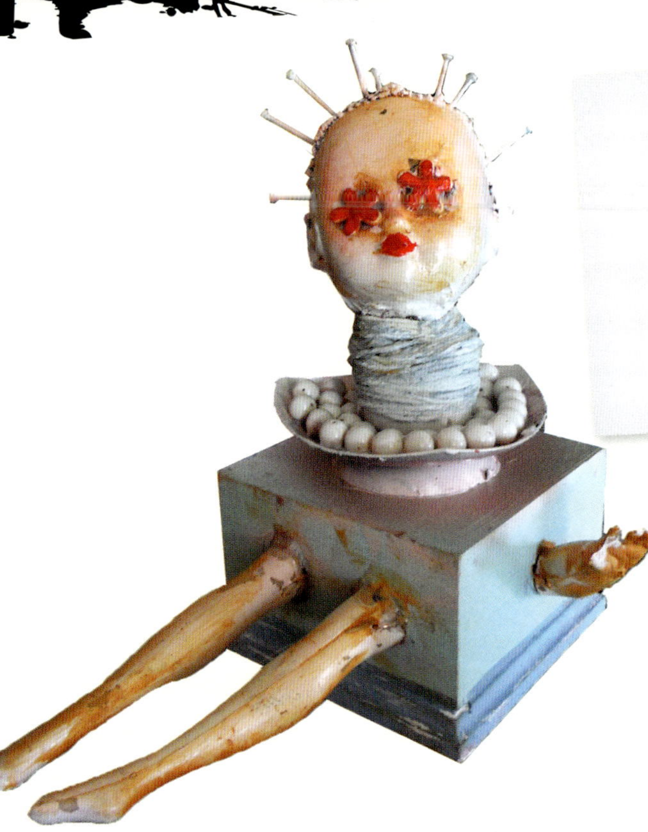

Starry Eyes

The innermost part of me is childlike and infantile. This part of me hides like a small child under the bed, afraid that the Big Bad Wolf will get her soon. The child struggles with establishing an identity and a sense of self separate from those around him. The doll sculpture represents the lost pa of myself, my hurt inner child, my confusion with gender identity and bei a child in an adult body. This prompt helped me voice that which I have been struggling with a long time.

—Thelma van Rensb

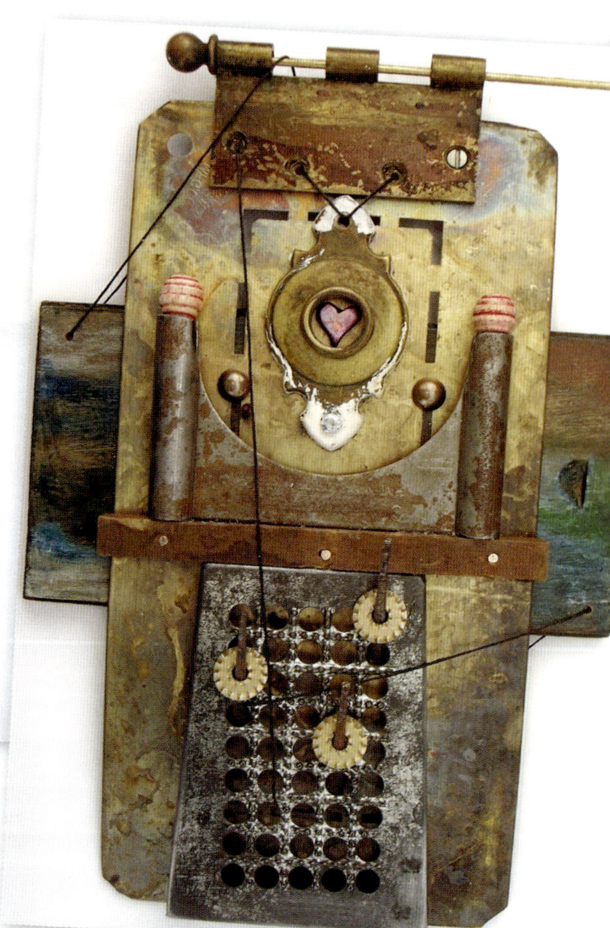

Broken Parts and Pieces

Protected. Hidden. Closed. I have spent much time ducking and covering, running from intimate connections. But somehow, I always had *hope* that things—me—could be different. Is it time that heals or time that enabled me to gain the wisdom to put interpersonal relationships in their proper perspective? Perhaps the knowledge that true intimacy between people doesn't just happen, but brews and steeps in a deep trust that is only gained through steps, has freed me to realize that only but a few relationships will survive these steps.

—Denise Aumick

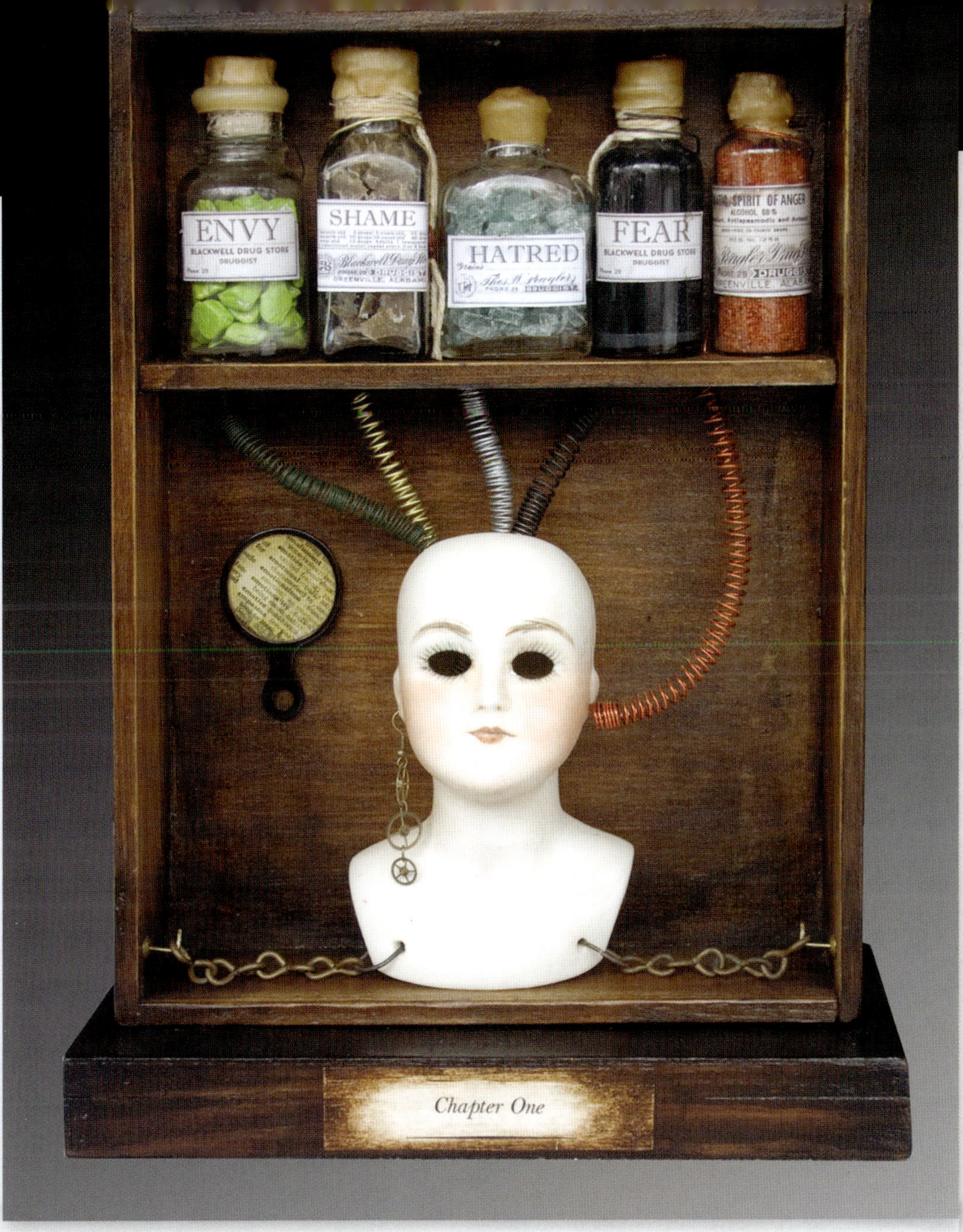

Chapter One

Believing that our innermost selves are comprised of many complex emotions and that the inability to express those emotions is a powerful constraint, I have created this assemblage to convey in a literal sense the bottling of our emotions. All of these are channeled into our heads and should be expressed in one way or another. It's these bottled emotions that keep us chained to a destructive pattern in our lives. It's my belief that these ingrained, innermost behaviors start in the early stages of our lives—our "Chapter One."

—*Art by Canace*

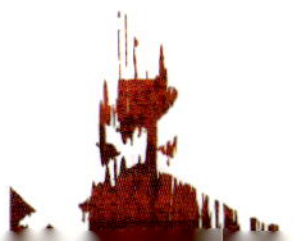

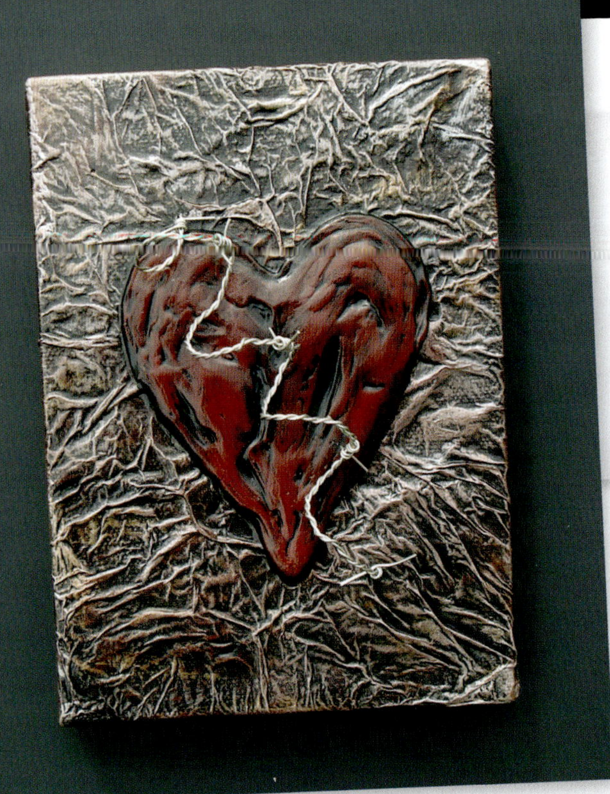

Bound

Over the past several years, I have lost many loved ones. The barbed wire that encircles the heart symbolizes the grief, hurt and pain that are now an integral part of me.

—*Kathryn Dyche Dechairo*

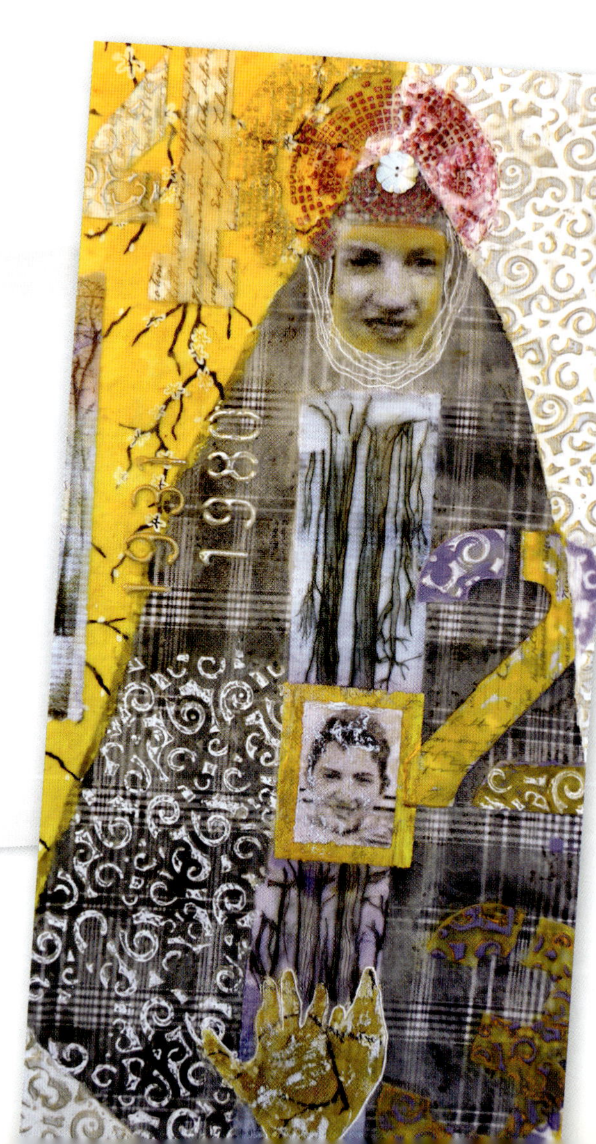

Marilyn

"Marilyn" came to fruition through a lot of artistic introspection that I have been doing recently. I realized that all of my work featured mother figures of some kind! I lost my own mother when I was just twenty-one years old, and very unexpectedly. It hit me that I am searching for my mother through my art. I also realized that this tendency toward "mother" symbolism in my art started around the time when my own daughter and I were having some relationship difficulties as well! I have come to realize, through artwork and journaling, that even though my mom, Marilyn, has been gone from my life for thirty-one years, she still lives inside of me. She was a beautiful, creative and caring person. I find that, more often than not, I try to think of what she would be doing or thinking right now.

—*Lisa Jones Moore*

Rebirth of Light

The pace of life is often fast, and we may live too much in our heads. A recent illness caused me to question how I live and how I use my time. The "Rebirth of Light" reflects my transition from a place of striving for control to one of letting go. The gold symbolizes light, life, hidden treasures and the sacred. Gold is timeless, freeing us from the daily rush to contemplate, relax and enter "the Supreme Moment." This change, or "Rebirth," has filled me with hope and an affirmation for serenity, enchantment and living vibrantly.

—Shayla Perreault Newcomb

Refuge Lake

This piece was painted from a memory of one of the last experiences shared with my mother. We had gone for a drive in the country to see the autumn leaves at a wildlife refuge near her home, the colors of nature showing brilliantly. I have always felt the presence of God when surrounded by nature. That day was perfection; the beauty of nature, the touch of the Great Creator, love shared with another. The mirror surface of the lake became a place to reflect on it all.

—Nelda Ream

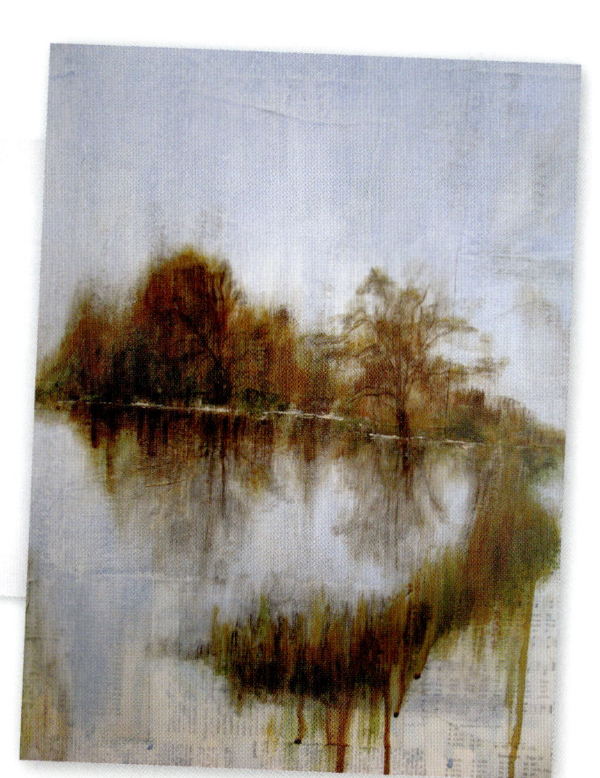

Do you create art to work through inner issues, or is studio time more of a distraction to keep you from facing your problems?

Perhaps it should not be surprising that for most artists, working in the studio is first and foremost simply about the art and their desire to create. That being said, art is therapeutic for many. It appears to serve less as a distraction and more as an opportunity to deal with issues. This seems to occur even when it is not an explicit goal.

I don't see art as a distraction from my problems, nor do I see it as a means to solve problems, at least not directly. I like making art because it helps me to be more mindful, and this makes me happy!

—Rebecca Blackburn

Both. If I am working through an issue in my life, sometimes it's time to go to the studio. Then I step back and look at what I made and what it is telling me. Sometimes studio time is great for a distraction. I like to paint huge sheets of paper so I can get physically into to it—it's such a great release.

—Terry Garrett

I began to do artwork as a way to work through an ongoing depression and discovered that the "zone" of art making is much like meditation, and the process was healing for me. Solving the problems of any given art piece can actually map the way through personal problems.

—Marie Danti

Neither. I deal with life's issues as they come at me so I can get them sorted out, and *then* I can concentrate on my art. If I do it any other way, my mind is not on the job when I am drawing or painting. That leads to shoddy work and wastes time.

—Gillian McMurray

Studio time for me is an exhilarating process. I am not working through inner issues as much as allowing my feelings to come to life in my work. In actuality, I have to remind myself that there is life outside my studio!

—Cathy Minerva

There have been times when I am faced with big, stressful events, and during these times, art is definitely therapy. Art is my friend who I can tell anything and she won't judge me. Someone I can always lean on, cry with, scream at or enjoy a contented, quiet moment.

—Patti Sandham

Do you keep some form of visual journal?

Yes, daily: **18%**
On and off: **66%**
No: **16%**

Neither; I do it for the love of it.

—*Debbie Price-Ewen*

I create art to work through inner issues, to find a voice for my soul. When a theme surfaces, I often do a good bit of researching and journaling, but then free myself up and let the work take me where it will. It is never a means of distraction to avoid facing problems.

—*Liz Hampton-Derivan*

Neither. I create because it is a craving that can't be satisfied any other way. I *need* to create, I just *gotta* do something with my hands, or I'll explode or die or something. Okay, I guess that is an inner issue.

—*Nelda Ream*

I may not always consciously go into the studio to work through my inner issues, but inevitably my inner issues rise to the surface. Perhaps this is the reason that I sometimes struggle to get into the studio to work; I resist the outer work in order to resist the inner work.

—*Jan Avellana*

I never start my work with a preconceived idea of working through a particular inner issue. I have found that often, as I open up through the creative process, I work to deeper life issues. An unexpected side effect is that I often am so deeply focused on my work that I shut aside troubling issues.

—*Pnina Gold*

I never use art to escape specific problems; I like to deal with those head-on and get them out of the way. However, I find that it does help to calm me if I'm stressed or down. Hours can pass without me noticing, and I find it very therapeutic.

—*Jo Archer*

Oh no, the inner issues just seem to pop out, whether I plan them or not.

—*Michael Harford*

I have always loved creating art just for the sake of seeing an idea merge into something visual and/or tangible. I don't use art as a distraction to keep me from facing my problems; instead I use art as an expression of my innermost thoughts and emotions to gain a fresh perspective.

—*Hannah Menkin*

No, I do not create to work through inner issues, and my studio time is not a distraction. I would say that art, and creating it, is a significant part of the balance in my life. I do acknowledge that I can discern aspects of my life experience in my work, and that is fine with me.

—*Sandra Ortiz Taylor*

If I do have any issues to deal with in my life, I always face them head-on. But that is not to say that my issues don't appear in my art. When I look back on what I have produced, I will see patterns that do seem to reflect what I am thinking about in the big picture of my life.

—*Shona Cole*

I create because I have to. I don't know what else to do. I had a damn job for way too many years.

— *Patricia Anders*

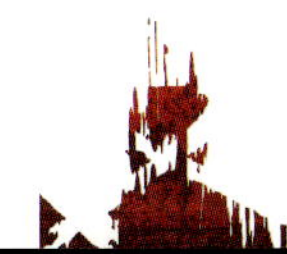

Is creativity built-in, learned or both?

For most of the artists, creativity was seen as an innate, built-in gift that we are all born with. What we learn, in contrast, are techniques that allow our creativity to be expressed. Many artists noted that our inborn creativity is often lost as we age and develop, and that it takes a combination of effort and desire to reignite the creative spark.

Both, definitely. Creativity is there in every individual; it just needs honing, teasing, faith in one's abilities and practice to be able to blossom and grow.

—Kim Palmer

I think it's definitely both. I really believe that the drive to create is a fundamental aspect of being human. I think it gets beaten out of us as children with a rigid adherence to rules about what art is and isn't. It takes mindful practice and a willingness to be brave and manifest it in the world.

—Fran Meneley

I think creativity is an innate human trait, as much a part of every person as our individual psyches. How we express our creativity is as varied as our personalities and influenced by a multitude of factors. What we learn isn't to be creative but how to express our creativity.

—Terry Rafferty

I think creativity is a natural extension of curiosity, so in that sense, I think it is built-in. When a child first picks up a paint-brush they are likely to be fueled by curiosity as opposed to creativity. As we get older, we seek out ways of perfecting our skills, but then we are learning a craft as opposed to learning to be creative.

—Lisa Sarsfield

I believe that creativity is both a product of nature and nurture. In order to develop creativity beyond a certain point, an individual must have a natural sense of wonder about the world and possess a mind that is both curious and inquisitive.

—Robert Stockton

I believe all people have some talent that they are born with. Some people are born with the potential of creativity, and I would say that then comes in degrees. I believe that if one wishes to become an artist, they need to learn how to harness that creativity to its full potential. It's just like exercising.

—Joe Fig

Do you integrate photography into your artwork?

All the time: **14%**
Sometimes: **80%**
Never: **6%**

Do you think it is wrong to alter a book?

Yes, absolutely: **1%**

Yes, depending upon the book: **21%**

No, it gives new life to the book: **78%**

I believe that creativity is built into every single person on earth from birth. We then start the long process of inhibiting that creativity until we get older, wiser and the dam cannot be held back any longer. It is then that we start the process of learning in order to bring that creativity back.

—Carrie Faden

One must have the love of art before one can even dream of creating art. If the desire is there, then the learning can begin, whether internally or taught. However it can also be lost if not practiced or encouraged, or destroyed if discouraged.

—Stephen Elliot

Our very nature is creative. The tiniest action we take and the quietest thought we have is creative at some level. We often have to be taught to recognize our own creativity. It's so inherent that it's like trying to see yourself in the mirror when it is smack up against your face.

—Kathleen Harrington

Both. Many people believe that being creative means they have to be artistic. Really creativity is more about how we do things. Do you follow the rules, or do you consider the possibilities? There are unlimited ways in which we can express ourselves creatively.

—Kathryn Antyr

I think we're all creative. It's just that some of us decide to express it with visual art, others with music, inventing or finding cures for diseases. Just surviving is a hugely creative endeavor.

—Martha Marshall

We come into this world as fully creative individuals, hard-wired to learn from our experiences and to share this learning with others. What we do have to learn is a particular technique when expressing our creativity. And, most times, we all have to unlearn the idea that we are not creative.

—David Hayes

In my opinion, creativity is both built-in and learned. I am a strong believer that there has to be a drive to make art from the soul. That's the basis. And then there are ways to expand your creativity by taking lessons or workshops.

—Marit Barentsen

The creativity is built-in. The techniques to make the vision possible can be learned.

—Corrine Davis

I think we're all born little creators. Isn't every child an artist until they become old enough to doubt it? But I do believe some are born with a creative gift that far surpasses the norm. And perhaps "learning" creativity is really just awakening a latent creativity that all possess?

—Debra Tennison

How has the Internet changed your artistic practice?

The impact of the Internet has been almost universally positive for these artists. It provides inspiration and information, it offers community and support, it increases marketing and sales, and it allows for feedback and exchange. On the other hand, it can be a time waster, cause creative overload and create too many opportunities for plagiarism and the sale of mediocre art.

The Internet is my connection to the rest of the world; it helps me get inspired and helps me market and sell my work. My work became larger, more complex, and more detailed due, in large part, to the feedback and inspiration I found from the safe network of friends online.

—Lorraine Reynolds

The Internet has stopped me from feeling isolated and helped me network with other artists. This has kept me engaged when I was floundering, motivated when I was feeling empty and has kept me abreast of the art world in general.

—Julie Shackson

The Internet has been both a mode for sharing my artistic expression and a wellspring from which to draw artistic inspiration. As an artist living in a small town, the Internet provides virtual experiences that feed my soul just as much as a visit to an actual museum or gallery can.

—Susan Tuttle

Communication. The encouragement I receive from others through my blog is often what keeps me going. I've discovered there are others out there like me—we want to create, yet are somewhat reclusive. The down side is that I spend a bit too much time online.

—Kim Hambric

We all have access to so many people's work now. I try to limit my access to viewing only the work of artists whom I really admire. I feel we can't help but be influenced by the work of others, and the last thing I want to do is come off making copies of other people's work.

—Ingrid Dijkers

I am constantly in awe of the incredible imagination and talent of artists I come across. The one downfall to this is that there is often an information overload, which can have the reverse effect and, rather than inspire, can completely stunt one's creative flow.

—Jo Archer

Over the years I have found myself more guarded and protective of what I share because of those who will copy techniques and ideas.

—Debbie Overton

The Internet has given me a myriad of sources to sell art as well as to see art. In my twenties, unless you had a large following or a gallery willing to back you, starving artist was a literal term. Now with the Internet being the eyes and ears of the world, I have no limitations on selling my work.

—Cathy Minerva

The Internet and my art go hand in hand. After exposure to so many talented artists at the click of a mouse, I have learned, imitated, oohed and ahhed. Without the Internet, I would never have discovered altered art.

—Bleubeard and Elizabeth

It has been a *huge* help. It has helped me understand that what I have been doing most of my life is in fact an art form. It has hooked me up with other like-minded people, and we are able to share information, expand the medium, and take it to the next level.

—Rebeca Trevino

It has given me a sense of community and support. It helps me feel less alone. Some days it really challenges me to step it up, some days it scares me back into myself. Today, being connected to the world seems overwhelming. Tomorrow, it may be a gift.

—Debra Eck

Which of the following do you think will be the most popular online art venue in the future:

Traditional websites: **12%**
Blogs: **32%**
Vlogs (video logs): **7%**
Facebook: **4%**
Twitter: **0%**
Hasn't been invented yet: **45%**

I think the Internet has made art more accessible to many and also allowed us to have more resources to work with. But it also has increased the quantity of mediocre art. I find the Internet to be a great source for research but not in actual practice of making art.

—Charlie Grosso

Artists have a great educator available in the Internet. You can mix with professionals who are generous in teaching techniques and generous in their support. The surprising result for me was going from a more commercial product to a more spiritual expression.

—Shayla Perreault Newcomb

I am a time-traveler. My work is the bubble I live in, and together we travel through time. I am not leaving anything behind, and I do not work for the future, for eternity. Only the present counts, which is exactly why the Internet is an amazing medium to me: I create something, and five minutes later it's on my blog. I leave it there and keep on travelling.

—Martin Hoogeboom

In my opinion, it provides too much distraction! But I can't live without it now. It *does* provide an instant library of images and words that lead to some pretty good ideas for art. The web also provides a sense of belonging for many artists. It is definitely a double-edged sword.

—Lisa JonesMoore

The Internet makes the world smaller and flattens hierarchies. The Internet lets me chat with my art idols as equals. It allows me to share my work with others all over the globe. The Internet has allowed me to be the artist I always dreamed I could be.

—Sarah Whitmire

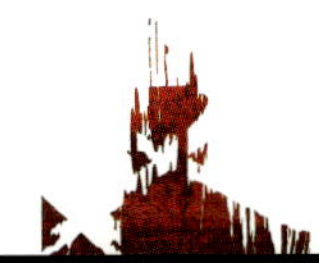

What is your biggest fear?

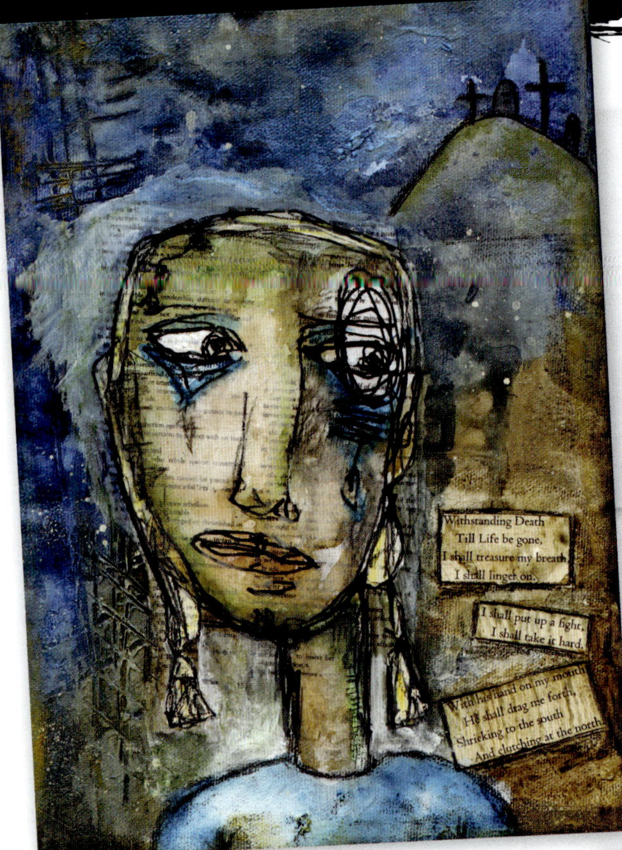

Fear

I have had many serious illnesses in my life. This piece is about the fear of death—which I have had since childhood—and the daily struggle I face, the anxiety over growing old and dying. I believe a large part of the reason I make art is so that in some small way, I may continue on in my pieces after I am gone. The worst thing and biggest fear I have is to die and be forgotten . . . as if I never existed at all.

—Sarah Whitmire

Silenced

"Silenced" reflects my biggest fear of never finding an adequate voice to speak through my artwork about issues that are of deep concern to me. While I was making my piece, the "Don't Ask, Don't Tell" issue was all over the news, and it made me think about how culturally we seem to be devolving into a repressive society of silence and denial where issues we cannot face honestly and empathically are simply covered up. Increasingly the "different" are met with hatred, distrust and disgust. I find that fear and secrecy are connected both in the outer and inner worlds.

—Marie Danti

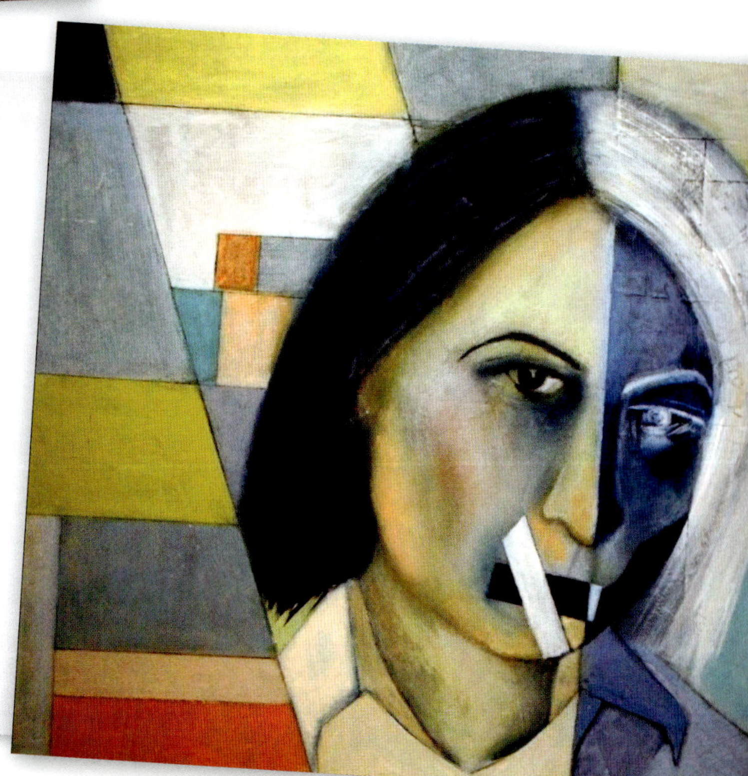

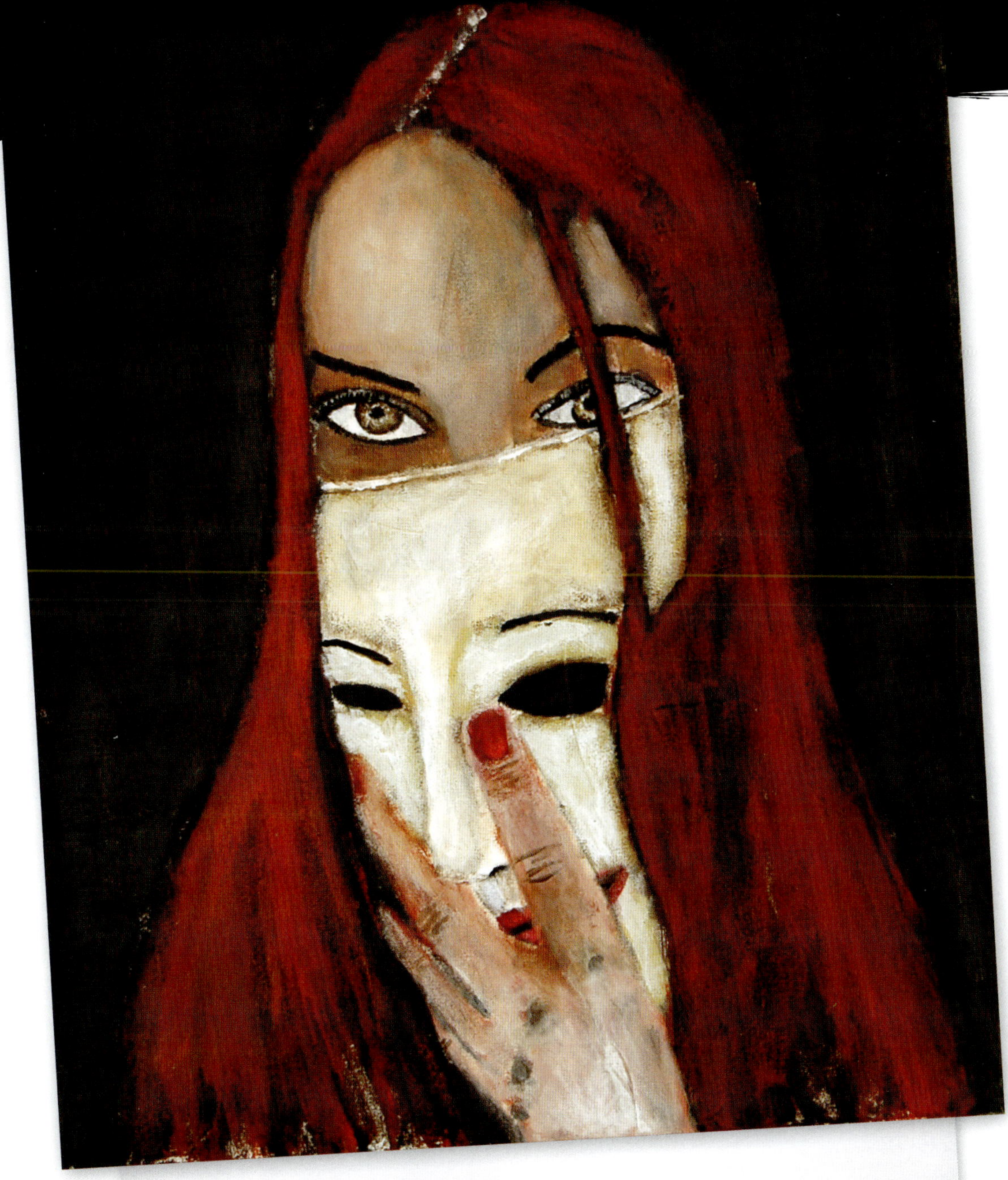

Revealing: Her Self

It's so scary! It's so scary!! How can I show you who I am? Run! Quick! I must hide. I must find my mask, put it on, fast. And turn toward you with a smile upon my face before you have a chance to walk across the room. Because who am I? And who are you? And, what's going to happen if my true self escapes? Oh, so scary. I'm not brave. I make mistakes. I have a fragile ego. I am fearful. I do not like the unknown. Oh, who am I? Where's my mask?

—Miz Katie

What is your biggest fear?

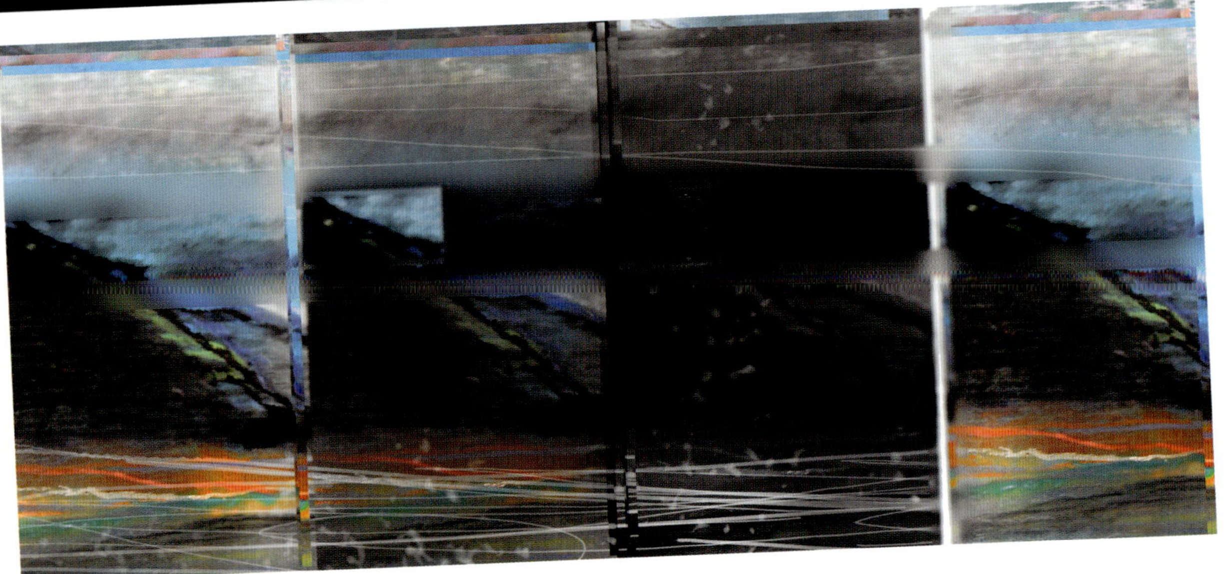

Optic Neurosis

Several years ago I had an attack of optic neuritis that took away most of the sight in my right eye. After some months, I gradually regained my sight, as well as some residual side effects. My biggest fear, which comes back every morning for a fraction of a second before I open my eyes, is that it will happen again.

—Elaine Phipps

Bag Lady

For many years my biggest fear was growing old without enough income to support myself and the possibility of becoming a bag lady. Probably the fact that I went back to school and started a career late in life added to these fears. And prior to that, having had the experience of living on welfare for six years after a divorce and raising two little kids on my own all contributed to this "biggest fear." Fortunately, I now find myself in my seventieth year in good health and having lived frugally and saved/invested, so that even though I continue to work, I can do so without much undue stress.

—Lynn Cohen

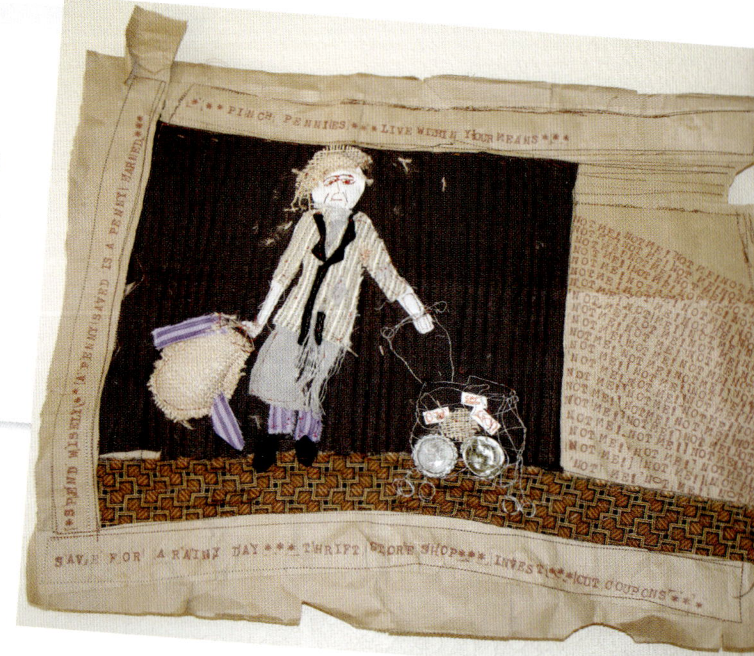

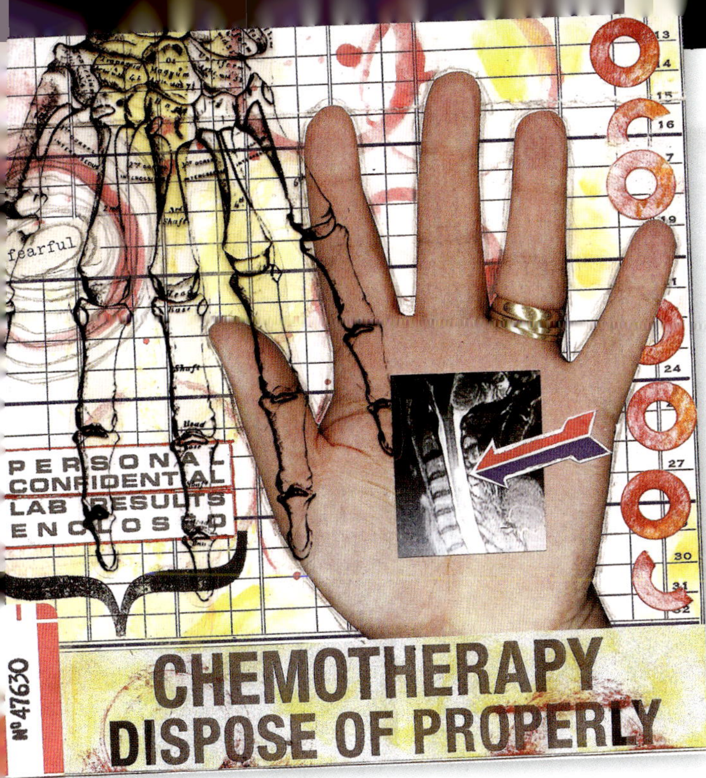

annonMS

This piece is about the chaos that comes from being diagnosed with an incurable disease. On December 18, 2007, I heard the kind of news no one ever wants to get: I had multiple sclerosis, an incurable, life-altering neurological disease. From that moment on, my life was turned upside down. There are times when I feel more like an anonymous file, a diagnosis or a set of symptoms than I do a human being. It scares the living hell out of me, but it is what it is, and while I fear that ultimately the wolf at the door is going to get me, I'm not one to dwell. I've chosen to square my shoulders and set my focus on accomplishing the long list of the things I want to do with my life.

—*Lelainia N. Lloyd*

Fragments Over the Deep Blue

"Fragments Over the Deep Blue" is about sometimes trying to hover above the darkness and not be swallowed by the waves, trying to stay in the light. Decayed roses are symbols for me of close family members who had dementia and have passed on. The semi-live roses on the right represent my mother and aunt suffering with dementia now, while I hold one, wondering whether I will fragment into forgetfulness too at some future point.

—*Delorse Lovelady*

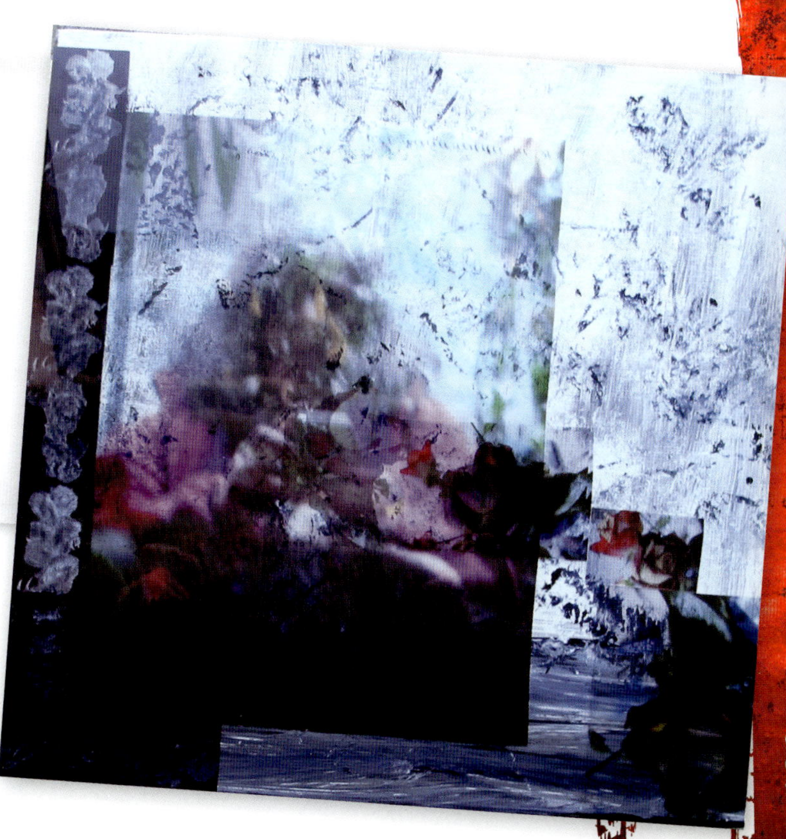

What is your biggest fear?

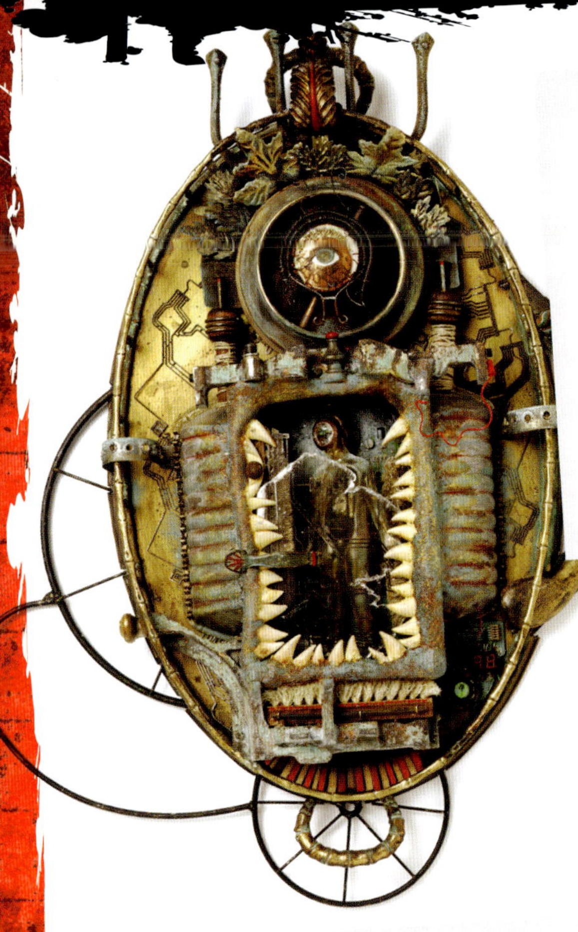

Hollowman

This past year has been a very hard one for my immediate family, both health-wise and economically. I think most Americans would agree that we are going through a rough patch, leaving many of us feeling anything but full in terms of day-to-day happiness. Our daily news broadcasts of war, natural devastations, hunger, sickness and political in-fighting have all taken their toll. With these thoughts in mind as I began, I knew I wanted to use my Dollar Store plastic man. He came complete with colorful internal organs, which I carefully removed. I needed to say in some way that I was feeling hollow inside.

—Judy Anderson

Pieces of Time

How much time do we have on earth? How much time are we given? We are not unlike holiday-makers who arrive at a destination, stay for a stretch of time, and inevitably one day have to leave . . . and perhaps return home? There is a tinge of sadness when I think of what might have been, had I been more of a doer and not so much of a wonderer. When middle age crept up upon me like a thief in the night, I realized that there are so many things still undone, but now time is no longer on my side. Will there be enough time for me to create memories with and for the ones I love?

—Luthien Thye

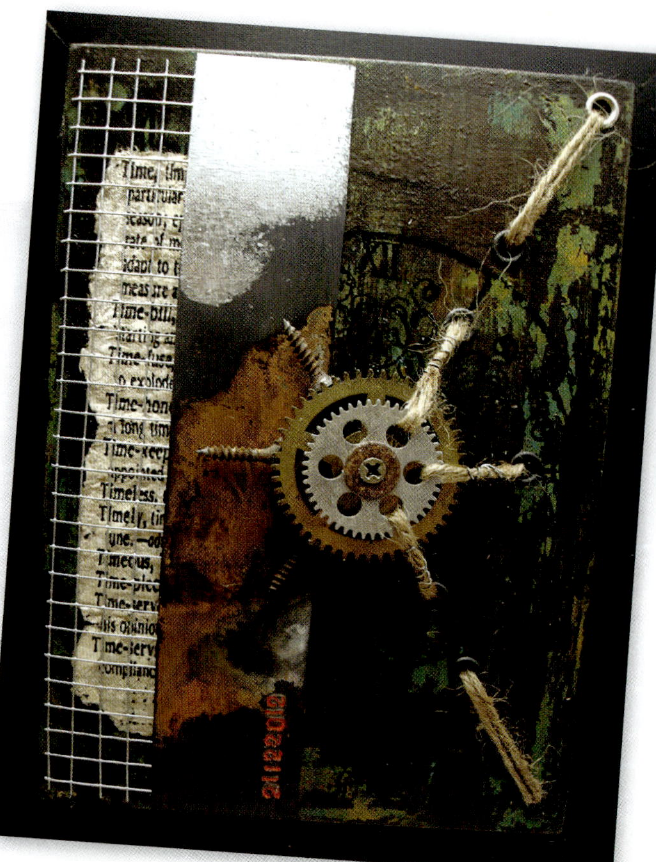

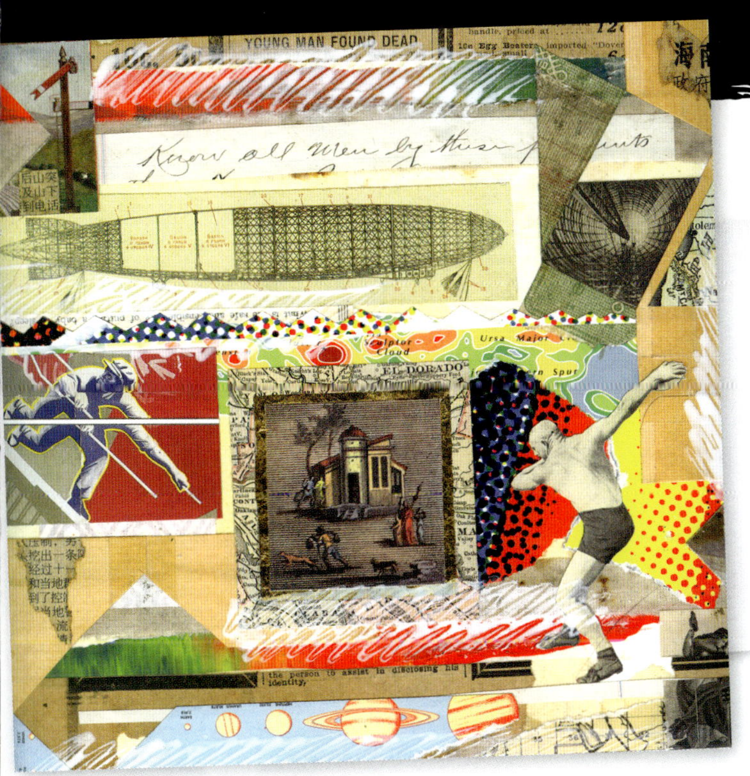

Last Days

"Last Days" represents my version of the "fear of the unknown." This Last Days (as in End Times) is not necessarily the version as depicted in the Book of Revelation, but simply the idea that life is, at best, quite uncertain! What little control we appear to have over our own, individual destiny is of fairly small account, and completely overshadowed by the fact that any of us can have our life irrevocably altered in an instant, by the unexpected, the unforseen, or the unimaginable!

—Robert Stockton

Passage

The fear of stillness and silence, life deconstructed; marching into the ages . . . because life is open-ended but finite . . . jagged signs and symbols present themselves along the path, but we never truly know what they foretell or when the journey ends . . . the circle of life . . . the passage of time and the very short window of our existence within which to achieve our goals . . . to see our children leave the nest . . . to flourish . . . to find their own destinies . . . the number 21 . . . a rite of passage . . . though tempered as noted on Roman sundials . . . "without the sun I am silent."

—Lisa Jurist

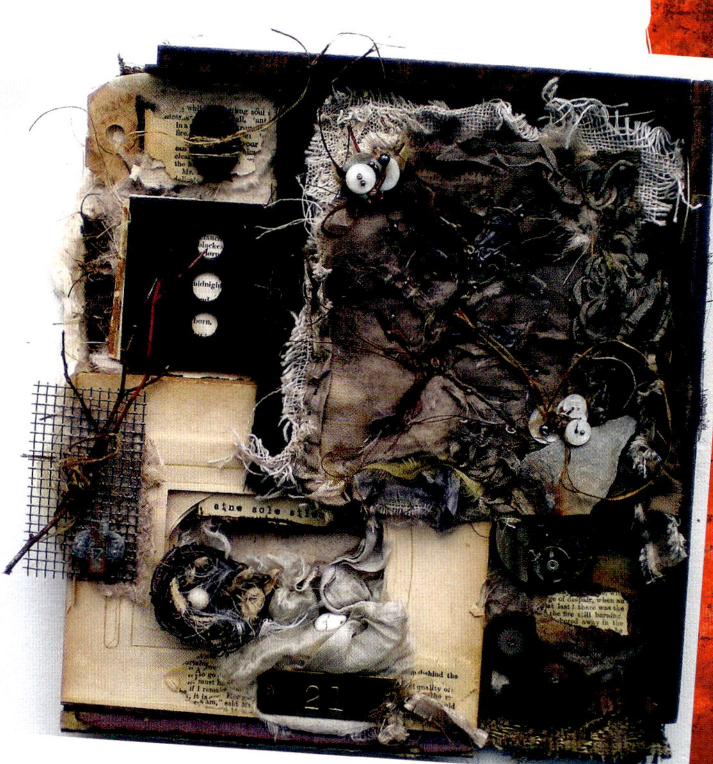

Have you ever received artwork from others and reworked it as your own?

Many of these artists were strongly opposed to the idea of repurposing artwork from another artist, believing it to be disrespectful and outright plagiarism. There were a good number, however, who have done this very thing, most often using unrecognizable pieces as components for their own work. For these artists, the idea of plagiarism was not in any way their intent.

Yes. It was nominal work with some bad memories attached; I reworked the pieces, made them glow, and then used them as a blog giveaway prize. The winner was delighted, I was happy with the result, and it was out of my studio! But that being said, there are very few pieces I would do that to.

—Anne M. Huskey-Lockard

I have never taken another artist's original work and reworked it to make it my own though I have used portions of copies or prints of other artist's work in my own artwork on an occasional basis. This reminds me, however, of the best-known example of appropriated art: Rauschenberg's "Erased de Kooning Drawing" of 1953.

—Robert Stockton

I once received a black-and-white drawing from an artist friend and used it as a base for my collage. As an artist and instructor, I have used line drawings of famous artists as studies to practice and teach my students about artists' techniques. We all learn from others and copy from others.

—Hannah Menkin

Nope, but I sure think about it sometimes. Not that I want to change someone else's work to claim it as my own, but rather I want to share in the essence of it and add my own experience of it. This impulse is a challenge and a message to me to find an avenue for collaboration.

—Kathleen Harrington

No, but I can't say I wouldn't do that. I suppose it would depend on the situation and what the artwork was. A painting? No. Batches of painted paper? I think I would find a way to work it into my art.

—Dawn Raymond

I have never reworked anything that has come my way, and I believe I never will. Because I consider art an extension of the artist's personality, emotions and soul, I feel that fiddling with their construction would be fiddling with their innermost spirit, and, this is unacceptable to me.

—Allison Berringer

My most favorite art-related activity other than making art is:

Reading art books and magazines: **23%**
Organizing the studio: **5%**
Taking a workshop: **20%**
Visiting galleries/museums: **22%**
Surfing the blogs: **30%**

Have you ever been involved in an artistic collaborative project?

Yes, I have collaborated before: **66%**

No, but I would like to: **28%**

No, and I have no interest in doing so: **6%**

No! It would be like tweaking a writer's novel by changing the ending or adding a character. I would not even consider it. Creating artwork is a very personal experience, and to change it in any way after the artist has completed it would be to make the artist's statement invalid. No matter what you did to it, the artwork would never really be your own anyway.

—Judy Anderson

Oops. Yes. I gessoed over a canvas I received in a swap. It made a wonderful structure, by the way!

—Lise Hofmann

Nope. I have given away art received from others that wasn't quite my style to those who would appreciate it. But I don't feel right about reworking another's artwork unless they specifically ask me for my help.

—Sarah Whitmire

Yes, when I was doing mixed-media work. I would take old collage pieces of others that no longer inspired me and use them in my own work as torn pieces of background. I would paint or collage over them so they weren't recognizable.

—Laura A. Pace

No. But I was very tempted to recently when I received a large print with flat colors that lacked the vibrancy on the original painting. I really admire the artist and decided to leave it be.

—Stacey Merrill

I have never reworked art received from others . . . yet. But artwork bought at thrift shops is fair game.

—Nelda Ream

Sacrilege! Never! To take someone else's work that they have shed blood, sweat and tears over and form it into something else that *you* think is better is too much to bear.

—Gillian McMurray

No, I could never do that. Each person's art is a reflection of themselves. To try to rework another's art would not only be an insult to that person but to myself as well.

—Karen Anne Brady

As a surface designer/fabric painter, I have cut up, or overdyed pieces of fabric for collage work from friends. And over the years, I have done some sort of "upcycling" of others' art.

—Laura Quilligan

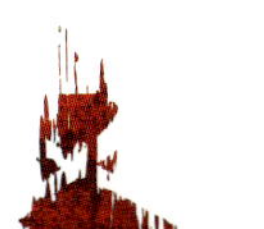

What do you think your preferred art medium says about your personality?

The personality of an artist is not only reflected in their artwork but can be seen loud and clear in their choice of artistic medium as well. For some, watercolors equal controlled chaos and mixed media equals curiosity. This connection even holds true for those artists whose preferred medium changes all the time, where this reflects restlessness and unpredictability.

Ninety-nine percent of what I use is recycled, and I think that aspect best reflects my personality. I am aware that every day I leave a negative imprint on this earth just by being here. One way I am able to help reduce that impact is by reusing things that others have disposed of.

—Lisa Sarsfield

Childlike with a fragmented identity.

—Thelma van Rensburg

That I am invested in reframing/restating the past, my past, in detailed (abrasions and all), honest and beautiful ways.

—Arabella Grayson

My pieces are often dark, expressing my grief over the loss of loved ones. Multiple layers are reminiscent of everything about me—my feelings, my emotions, my thoughts, my dreams and my experiences. I use a color palette that is subtle and blends together, very much like my personality.

—Kathryn Dyche Dechairo

Maybe that I'm still a little boy who loves to build huts and sandcastles and also loves to play with pieces of paper.

—Eric Adama

I work in a lot of different mediums: painting, sculpture, photography, print making. Maybe it just means that I like to challenge myself. Once something gets routine or too easy, I move on to something else.

—Joe Fig

I have been photographing my surroundings for twenty-five years and continue to have a fascination with doors and windows. I believe now that there is a connection between being on the outside and wondering "what's in there" and the creative work that I do.

—Patti Edmon

Watercolor could be described as controlled chaos, which is a way I would describe myself. I often feel that I'm just enough in control of my creative thoughts and emotions to keep the chaos from bubbling to the surface and out into the world.

—David Castle

Very little. I could read into it and imagine that painting in oil has some deep root in some strange need to translate life, to remake it, to express it or to rescue or reduce it somehow. But whatever anyone could say would only be limiting and couldn't be as worthwhile as simply seeing my work and responding to it.

—*Robert Dresdner*

That I have finally come into my own. I am no longer searching for me; I am found.

—*Laura A. Pace*

I love collage. I love the act of cutting and pasting. I love putting the pieces together and telling a story through images. I wrote once about feeling like a collage myself, scarred as I am with surgeries and skin grafts, stitched into someone vibrant and whole.

—*Tricia Gillispie Scott*

I love digital art because it is so easy to change something I don't like. The fact that nothing I did was good enough to please my father while growing up explains why I like the ability to easily change something I don't think is perfect.

—*William J. Charlebois*

There is no question why I love mixed media! I have a personality that is curious about everything. I am a puzzle-solver, the resident sayer of "What if?" I see connections in objects that others would never put together. Mixed media is me, and I am it.

—*Anne M. Huskey-Lockard*

I do not really have a favorite medium, which in itself says it all about my personality: unpredictable and restless. I would love to feel perfectly at home in the contemplative silence of painting, but my restless mind does not allow my focus to linger.

—*Martin Hoogeboom*

My preferred media change all the time. But I think what is consistent is that I love to have full control of something from start to finish. I love the mystery of finding out what something becomes. I like what I make to be something that is an improvement over nothingness or chaos.

—*Chris Miser*

My work has many layers, some seen and others not. By peeling them away, more is revealed. Looking beyond the surface is always more revealing, honest and, in the end, more interesting, and I think my choice of mediums reflects that.

—*David Brady*

Have you ever sent a piece of mail art?

Yes: **77%**

No: **23%**

What is your secret dream as an artist?

Artists are dreamers at heart. Some dreams are grand, such as becoming famous or being in the collection of a major museum. Some dreams are modest, such as finding one's true niche or continuing to grow as an artist. But perhaps the most popular dream of all is simply to be recognized, respected, validated and understood as an artist.

To produce work that people can relate to, that can offer a new perspective and make them think about their lives in a new way. For me, that would be the best thing in the world.

—Helen Stead

Recognition; to be heard.

—Debra Eck

I have great respect for those who discover work they are passionate about and then pursue it for a lifetime, becoming masters of their craft. I, on the other hand, have a history of dabbling in this or that. Maybe I'm too lazy or too easily distracted, or maybe it's just that I have yet to find the craft that will inspire in me the required passion.

—Debra Tennison

Not to channel Miss America, but I hope to make a difference. I went through a long period of being artistically blocked and came out of it. So a big part of my mission as a teacher and artist is to take art from the precious and bring it to the everyday. I'd also like to make a big pile of money—oh, and be world-famous.

—Diana Trout

I would love to develop a truly original technique which I would then like to master.

—Sonia Simard

Some people have the ability to forget life, to forget the past: I do not possess that talent. If you're able to forget the past, you're able to face the future. I find myself standing with my back against the future, overlooking a landscape of the past. My secret dream is to be able to face the future in both life and work.

—Martin Hoogeboom

That local museums would actually show local art! Most major museums have the space, volunteers and connections to provide exhibitions showcasing emerging artists and tie them in with local charities. There is always a gap between the museum and the artist at the lower level.

—David Brady

To be a famous unknown! By that I mean that people would like my work and want it in their homes, but they would never really know me or who I am so that I could maintain my privacy and time to create.

—Karen Anne Brady

Because much of my art relates to growing up as a white child in the Apartheid years in South Africa, my hope is that one day my art is in a museum illustrating one artist's perspective and tangible experiences of a time of extreme injustice, conflict, and ultimate peace. I want to tell my story for all those hundreds of us who left South Africa at a terrible time.

—*Lesley Price*

My secret dream as an artist is for my work to be in someone's art collection four hundred years from now. That would be the biggest compliment to me—that someone was moved by one of my paintings from generation to generation.

—*Juana Almaguer*

I have no secret dream. I'm living my dream as a full-time artist; I am living the art-full life.

—*Patricia Anders*

I think I must be too pragmatic to allow myself a dream. Just hanging on for the ride has been enough to fill my imagination for this lifetime.

—*Jayne A. Harnett-Hargrove*

My secret dream as an artist is to continue to grow and learn as much as possible in my lifetime from what the creative process has to teach me.

—*Marie Danti*

That the story I'm telling with my art is understood.

—*Eric Adama*

My dream is to have my artwork respected, celebrated and collected. I would love the opportunity to have my works in a respected Art Museum and to ultimately have a following where my name, style and art would be recognized as a valued and respected contemporary artist.

—*Teresa Pyskaty-Lamicella*

My dream is just to always make art, be an artist, and express myself through my mixed-media art. I've always been a shy person, and art has allowed me to express myself to the world.

— *Liz Hampton-Derivan*

How many different collections do you have?

None at all: **15%**
One and only one: **2%**
Two to five: **38%**
Six to ten: **20%**
Eleven to twenty: **7%**
I lost count after twenty: **18%**

Over 100 Artists

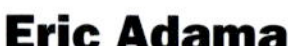

Eric Adama
www.ericadamajournal.blogspot.com

Juana Almaguer
www.galleryjuana.com

Patricia Anders
www.patriciaanders.com

Judy Anderson
http://gallery.me.com/judyrick2

Kathryn Antyr
www.collagediva.com

Jo Archer
www.jo-crowroad.blogspot.com

Art by Canace
www.canace.net

Denise Aumick
www.wildthreadstudio.blogspot.com

Jan Avellana
www.hazelnutcottage.typepad.com

Marit Barentsen
www.maritspaperworld.com

Karin Bartimole
www.aviewbeyondwords.blogspot.com

Marcia Beckett
www.vividlayers.blogspot.com

Allison Berringer
www.musingsofnosilla.blogspot.com

Rebecca Blackburn
www.discardedbeauty.wordpress.com

Bleubeard and Elizabeth
www.alteredbooklover.blogspot.com

David Brady
www.bradyart.com

Karen Anne Brady
www.irelandbrady.blogspot.com

David Castle
www.DavidCastleArt.com

William J. Charlebois
www.wjcsdigitalworld.blogspot.com

Erika Cleveland
www.eachdayisapresent.blogspot.com

Lynn Cohen
www.artquiltsbylynn.blogspot.com

Shona Cole
www.shonastudio.blogspot.com

Creative Billie
www.billiescraftroom.co.uk

Marie Danti
www.cinnamonstudio.blogspot.com

Corrine Davis
www.corrinesart.blogspot.com

Ingrid Dijkers
www.IngridDijkers.com

Holly Dean
www.hollydean.blogspot.com

Kathryn Dyche Dechairo
www.dychedesigns.blogspot.com

Robert Dresdner
(No website)

Debra Eck
www.debraeck.com

Patti Edmon
www.pattiedmon.blogspot.com

Stephen Elliot
www.youtube.com/user/steel7jack

Carrie Faden
www.thebohemiancouch.com

Joe Fig
www.cristintierney.com

Veronica Funk
www.veronicafunk.com

Terry Garrett
www.flickr.com/photos/56871929@N00/with/4120186730

Caterina Giglio
www.caterinagiglio.blogspot.com

Pnina Gold
www.pearlandroses.wordpress.com

Arabella Grayson
www.redroom.com/member/arabella-grayson

Charlie Grosso
www.charliegrosso.com

Kim Hambric
www.kimhambricart.blogspot.com

Liz Hampton-Derivan
www.lizhampton.com

Michael Harford
www.coffeemessiah.blogspot.com

Kathleen Harrington
www.birthingyourcreativefire.blogspot.com

Jayne A. Harnett-Hargrove
www.harnetthargrove.blogspot.com

David Hayes
www.clearerreflections.blogspot.com

Lise Hofmann
www.lisehofmann.com

Martin Hoogeboom
www.martinhoogeboom.com

Anne M. Huskey-Lockard
www.tinyurl.com/2wbpckf

Lisa JonesMoore
www.jonesmoore.blogspot.com

Lisa Jurist
www.mudhoundprimitives.blogspot.com

Miz Katie
www.mizkatie.com

Barbara Kleinhans
www.barbarakleinhans.com

Lelainia N. Lloyd
www.tatterededge.blogspot.com

Delorse Lovelady
www.heartfireart.blogspot.com

Martha Marshall
www.marthamarshall.net

Gillian McMurray
www.gillianmcmurray.blogspot.com

Pat McNally
www.artfullyooglebloops.blogspot.com

Andrea McNeill
www.found-art.blogspot.com

Fran Meneley
www.franmeneley.typepad.com

Hannah Menkin
(No website)

Stacey Merrill
www.artsnark.blogspot.com

Cathy Minerva
www.earthgaia.com

Chris Miser
www.parabolicmuse.blogspot.com

Shayla Perreault Newcomb
www.shaylapn.blogspot.com

Debbie Overton
www.debbieoverton.com

Laura A. Pace
www.foundmemoriesart.blogspot.com

Kim Palmer
www.merlin-merlinsmusings.blogspot.com

Erin Perry
www.alteredbythesea.com

Elaine Phipps
www.elainephipps.com

Izabella Pierce
www.izabella.typepad.com

Lesley Price
www.lesleyannprice.yolasite.com

Debbie Price-Ewen
www.debrinaaltered.blogspot.com

Teresa Pyskaty-Lamicella
www.whirlingdervishart.com

Laura Quilligan
www.improvcloth.blogspot.com

Terry Rafferty
http://terryrafferty.com

Dawn Raymond
www.catharticcreativity.blogspot.com

Nelda Ream
www.neldaream.com

Lorraine Reynolds
www.glimmeringprize.com

Stephanie Rigsby
www.colorchrome.blogspot.com

Leslie Rosenberg
www.leslierosenbergart.blogspot.com

Jane Royal
www.paintedheartstudio.blogspot.com

Patti Sandham
www.jazzgoil.blogspot.com

Lisa Sarsfield
www.lisasarsfield.blogspot.com

Tricia Gillispie Scott
www.triciagillispiescott.com

Patricia Baldwin Seggebruch
www.pbsartist.com

Julie Shackson
www.julieshackson.com

Sonia Simard
www.ateliercuriostudio.blogspot.com

Loryn Spangler-Jones
www.loryns-blog.livejournal.com

Judith Stadler
www.judithstadler.blogspot.com

Helen Stead
www.helena-rose.com

Robert Stockton
www.absolutearts.com/scrapbox

Sandra Ortiz Taylor
www.sandraortiztaylorart.com

Debra Tennison
www.n2theblue.blogspot.com

Luthien Thye
www.alteredalchemy.com

Rebeca Trevino
www.rebecatrevino.blogspot.com

Diana Trout
www.DianaTrout.com

Susan Tuttle
www.ilkasattic.blogspot.com

Urbandon
www.urbandon.blogspot.com

Thelma van Rensburg
www.art.co.za/thelmavanrensburg

Sarah Whitmire
www.caspiana.com

Darlene Wilkinson
www.artticulation.blogspot.com

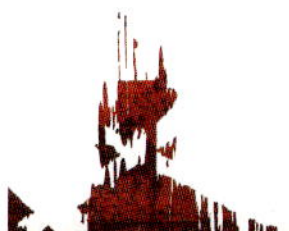

Index

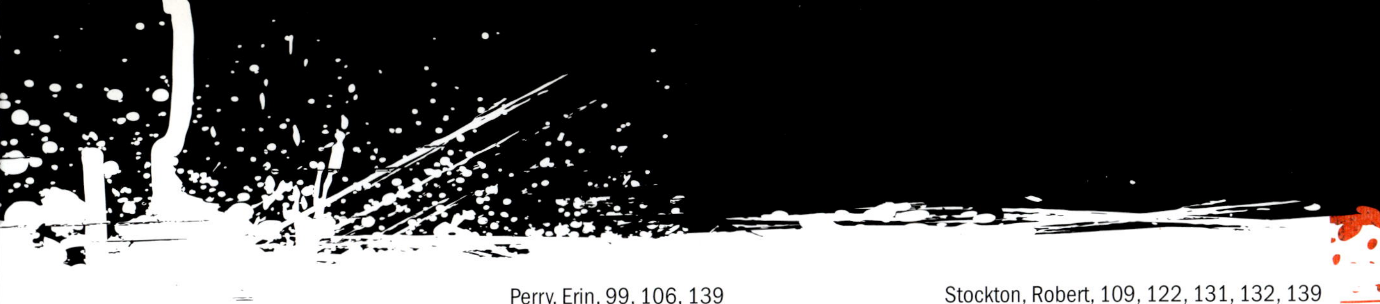

Dedication

This book is dedicated to my mother. It was she who gave me my sense of purpose and the desire and motivation to follow through with what I believe in, no matter how rough the road might become. I miss her deeply and hope that somehow, somewhere she knows that her dream for me of writing a book has now come true.

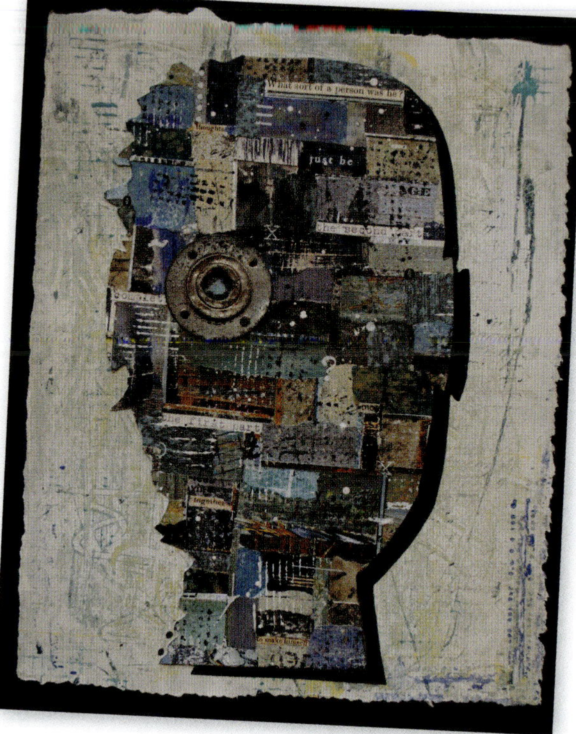

Acknowledgments

First and foremost, *The Pulse of Mixed Media* would not exist if not for the artists. I thank each and every artist in this book for their honesty, vulnerability and creativity. This book would also not exist if not for the creative gifts from all the participants in and visitors to The Pulse, my online collaborative project that formed the basis for this book. My heartfelt thanks go to the extra-special Tonia Davenport from North Light, who not only initially approached me with the idea of making this book, but who also became the best editor I could have ever asked for. A big thank you also to Corrie Schaffeld who designed the cover and to Geoff Raker who designed the interior pages. And finally, thanks to my very special family for their never-ending love and support.

Editor: Tonia Davenport

Cover Designer: Corrie Schaffeld

Interior Designer: Geoff Raker

Production Coordinator: Greg Nock

 Published by North Light Books, an imprint of F+W Media, Inc., 10151 Carver Road, Blue Ash, Ohio 45242. (800) 289-0963. First edition.

16 15 14 13 12 5 4 3 2 1

Distributed in Canada by Fraser Direct
100 Armstrong Avenue
Georgetown, ON, Canada L7G 5S4
Tel: (905) 877-4411

Distributed in the U.K. and Europe by
F&W Media International, LTD
Brunel House, Forde Close, Newton Abbot, TQ12 4PU, UK
Tel: (+44) 1626 323200, Fax: (+44) 1626 323319
E-mail: enquiries@fwmedia.com

Distributed in Australia by Capricorn Link
P.O. Box 704, S. Windsor, NSW 2756 Australia
Tel: (02) 4577-3555

Seth Apter, Revealed . . .

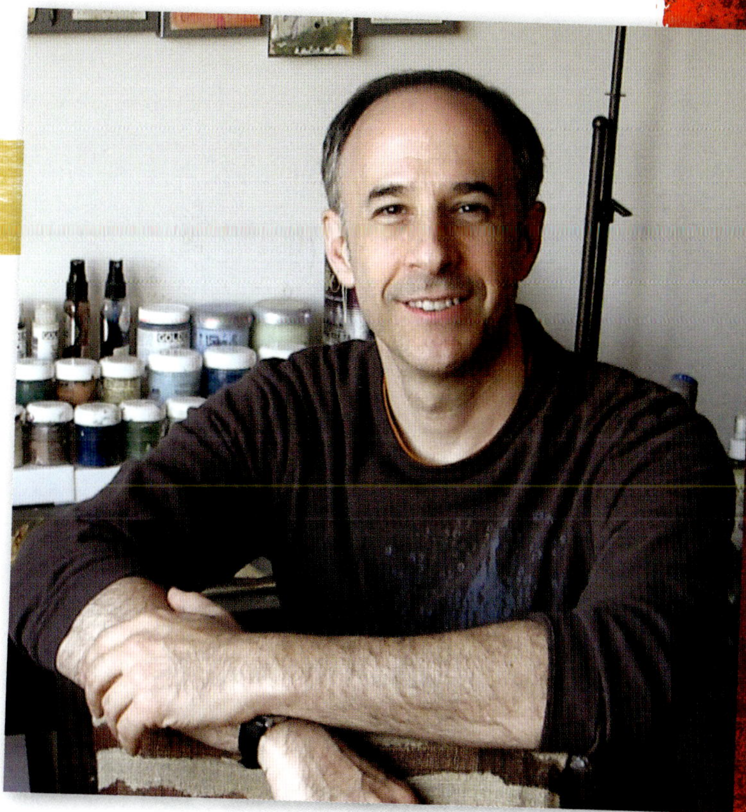

The Pulse of Mixed Media represents the integration of two distinct yet overlapping sides of Seth Apter. It combines his passion for art with his experience in psychology. As a mixed-media artist, his work has been published in many books, national magazines and independent zines, and has been exhibited in multiple galleries. He is the host and organizer of a number of international collaborative art projects as well. As a Ph.D. in psychology, Seth has studied human behavior, published numerous scientific articles and provided therapy services to a wide range of people. He splits his time between creating art in his studio and seeing clients in his private practice office—life experiences that join together to form the foundation for this book. Seth lives in New York City and finds inspiration every time he walks out of his door into the streets of the city.

Visit Seth online at
www.thealteredpage.blogspot.com

Liz –
Thank you for being a
part of my adventure and
always remember to keep
your finger on the pulse.
Best always –
Seth

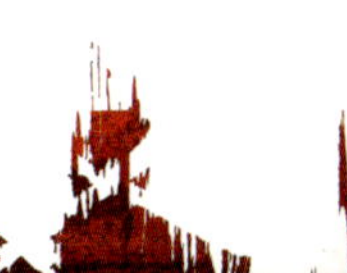